LEOPARDS

IN THE

TEMPLE

Leopards break into the temple and drink to the dregs what is in the sacrificial pitchers; this is repeated over and over again; finally it can be calculated in advance, and it becomes part of the ceremony.

—FRANZ KAFKA, *Parables and Paradoxes*

LEOPARDS IN THE TEMPLE

The Transformation
of American Fiction
1945–1970

MORRIS DICKSTEIN

Harvard University Press
Cambridge, Massachusetts
London, England
2002

For Lore again,
with love and gratitude,
and for Jeremy and Rachel

CONTENTS

PREFACE

The distant origin of this book, I would guess, was in the passion for fiction that I developed as a teenage boy in suburban Queens in the 1950s. Baseball was my first love, no doubt about it. But thanks to the local public library, which supplied me with a smattering of classics and the latest bestsellers, I became as enamored of novels as kids later did of rock music, movies, or favorite TV shows. I read them mostly for the story—to be lifted out of myself, to rub shoulders with other people in other worlds, to find out what would happen next—but also, I think, to savor the pleasure of the created thing, the well-made artifact. As I got lost in *The Scarlet Letter* or *A Tale of Two Cities* on the long subway ride to school each day, I remember feeling the thrill of something exotic—from the intriguing story and remote setting, but also the finely spun web of language. I recall, too, my sense of amazement at watching Dickens pull all the threads together into a seamless fabric, a perfect piece of craftsmanship, something I felt again many years later as I finished Thomas Pynchon's *V.*

I read a few great books almost by chance, but I was omnivorous and undiscriminating. I'm sure Herman Wouk's *Marjorie Morningstar* satisfied me almost as much as *Wuthering Heights* and *Old Man Goriot,* and it told a story that hit much closer to home. But it was not until I read Bernard Malamud's *The Assistant* and *The Magic Barrel* in the late 1950s that I understood how art could deepen your view of your own world. In my case this was the world of lower-middle-class Jewish families, of New York neighborhoods with their half-assimilated immigrants and roughly Americanized children, of small shopkeepers with huge economic anxieties and young people caught between their own half-understood needs and the religious and moral surveillance that hemmed them in. I had always taken novels personally, given myself up to them and lived inside them, feeling disappointed when they ended, yet they had never reached me in this deep, problematic way. The world of literature was one thing; the world of the Jews I grew up with—my father's days and nights in the store, my mother's operatic anxieties, the synagogue and Hebrew classes where I'd been anointed as the next savior—was quite another. But in Malamud and

Grace Paley, even in Wouk and Leon Uris, these distant worlds came together to show me that fiction could offer more than an escape, could reflect back parts of my daily life I thought I knew intimately. As I grew dis-
enchanted with the religious texts I had grown up on, secular literature
became a kind of scripture for me, a continuous commentary on living in
the world.

In this book I try to come to terms with the writers who emerged during the most impressionable period of my reading life, not the bestselling
authors who pleased me then, whose work would be of mostly sociological interest today, but the writers who have enriched our culture for the
last half century, even as fiction itself has declined in importance. Though
they were compared invidiously to Hemingway, Faulkner, and Fitzgerald
when they first appeared, the best writers who began publishing after the
war, like the leading painters, playwrights, and musicians, eventually became some of the longest running acts of the twentieth century. This goes
not only for those still writing in the new millennium, including Saul Bellow, Norman Mailer, Gore Vidal, Philip Roth, and John Updike, but for
others who died sooner or whose work foundered, among them Flannery
O'Connor, Ralph Ellison, James Baldwin, Jack Kerouac, James Jones, J. D.
Salinger, Vladimir Nabokov, and Bernard Malamud. I grew up with these
writers, inhabited their mental space for most of my life. Their very voices
rang in my ear as I followed the unfolding drama of their careers from book
to book. My aim in this group portrait is to show how they transformed
American writing, how they interacted with their own times, but also why
the work of these latecomers, who arrived at the tail-end of the modernist
comet, proved so imposing and long-lasting.

Some of this influence and staying power was simply due to their own
gifts, which still astonish me as I teach and reread their work. But part of it
came about because they were outsiders, which was how I saw myself when
I first read them. Instead of old-stock Protestants from New England or the
Midwest, many of the newcomers were urban Jews or blacks only a generation or two from the shtetl or the plantation; one was a serious Catholic in
the Protestant South; others were gays half-emerging from the closet or
Harvard men who came from humble backgrounds. They didn't always
mind their manners or try to fit in; they brought their histories with them.
They were like Kafka's ravenous leopards, invading and disrupting the
sheltered precincts of our literary culture. They brought sex out into the
open in an unprecedented way. Because of the war, they also were witnesses
to extremity, violence, and inhumanity, the story of the twentieth century.
This was a moment when outsiders were becoming insiders, when Ameri-

can literature, like the society it reflected, was becoming decentered, or multicentered, feeding on new energies from the periphery, as it had done many times before.

The seemingly tranquil postwar period was a turning point that saw many far-reaching developments we still feel today, from unparalleled prosperity and technological wonders to major new international commitments. With the help of new media like television, Americans turned inward, to each other, and outward to the world in ways they never had before. The essential continuity of postwar life has helped keep the writers current in a way that their Depression counterparts only occasionally are. In an effort to understand these writers, I also try to make sense of the society around them, which drew me into historical as well as literary issues. I hope I've done some justice to both. Even more than the 1960s, this is a period too often reduced to stereotypes, and its culture has been seen by some literary scholars and art historians as little more than a reflex of the Cold War, repressive, patriotic, and militantly small-minded. My aim in this book is to draw a more complicated picture, to do justice to the variety of voices that make this era richer, more contradictory, and more self-critical than we have previously imagined.

č

Much of this book was first written for the new *Cambridge History of American Literature,* edited by Sacvan Bercovitch. I am grateful to Jeff Kehoe and Harvard University Press for believing that it should be expanded into a separate book and to Cambridge University Press for allowing me to use this material here. Above all I'm thankful to Sacvan Bercovitch for his patient encouragement and valuable comments on my manuscript, and to my fellow contributors, John Burt, Cyrus R. K. Patell, and Wendy Steiner, whose fine work on other facets of postwar fiction, including Southern writing, multicultural fiction, postmodernism, and post-1970s feminism, enabled me to concentrate on the earlier writers who most engaged me. I profited from the insight of numerous critics of postwar fiction, including John W. Aldridge, Robert Bone, Leo Braudy, Malcolm Cowley, Chester E. Eisinger, Josephine Hendin, Irving Howe, Tim Hunt, Stanley Edgar Hyman, Peter G. Jones, Frederick Karl, Alfred Kazin, Thomas Hill Schaub, Mark Shechner, Ted Solotaroff, and Gore Vidal, and from historical studies of postwar American life by Willliam H. Chafe, John Patrick Diggins, Godfrey Hodgson, Kenneth T. Jackson, William E. Leuchtenburg, William L. O'Neill, James T. Patterson, and Daniel Snowman. Most of these debts are recorded in the bibliography. Stanley

Burnshaw, Eugene Goodheart, Larry and Suzanne Graver, Alfred Kazin, Richard Locke, and Anne Roiphe were generous with their friendship and their keen interest in this project. I learned much from graduate students in my courses on postwar fiction, among them Peter Mascuch and Bill Mullen. Stephen Motika deserves thanks for the index. As usual, Lore Dickstein's enthusiastic support made all the difference.

New York, January 2001

LEOPARDS

IN THE

TEMPLE

❧

INTRODUCTION:
CULTURE, COUNTERCULTURE,
AND POSTWAR AMERICA

S ome periods of history take on a legendary character, which usually means that we have substituted a few stereotypes for the complexity of what actually happened. Many still think of the 1920s as one long party, a hedonistic romp for the fun-loving young, though F. Scott Fitzgerald, who helped establish that image, later worked hard to revise it. The thirties have come down to us in black and white images of apple vendors and dust storms, all social misery and middle-class anguish, though the books and films of the era tell a more complicated story. Newsreel views of the 1960s, which rarely venture beyond protest demonstrations, campus conflicts, stoned hippies, and Beatlemania, have invaded the memories of those who were there, who now recall those film images better than what they themselves saw. The postwar period, especially the 1950s, has been simplified into everything the sixties generation rebelled against: a beaming president presiding over a stagnant government, small-town morality, racial segregation, political and sexual repression, Cold War mobilization, nuclear standoff, suburban togetherness, the domestic confinement of women, and the reign of the nuclear family.

Like most stereotypes, this picture of the 1950s has a certain truth to it. Because both sides see the postwar years through the prism of the 1960s, conservatives and liberals can agree on many details while judging them differently. The titles of their books tell the story. To radical journalists and historians the 1950s were *The Nightmare Decade* (Fred Cook) or *The Dark Ages* (Marty Jezer), the period of *The Great Fear* (David Caute), when so many were *Naming Names* (Victor Navasky). To writers less enchanted with the 1960s, the preceding years were *The Proud Decades* (John Patrick Diggins), the moment of the *American High* (William L. O'Neill), *When the Going Was Good* (Jeffrey Hart). By the 1970s, in sharp reaction to the recent turbulence, a tranquil, pastoral image of the fifties took hold in popular culture, a fun image of carefree adolescence in the days before the fall. Thus George Lucas's nostalgic film *American Graffiti* gave birth to the sitcom *Happy Days* and the hit musical *Grease,* which had little in common with the troubled images of adolescence projected during the period. More recently, serious novelists have been busy idealizing their formative years, as

Philip Roth does in *American Pastoral* and Gore Vidal does in *The Golden Age*. There is more than a trace of irony in most of these titles, but they show remarkable unanimity in portraying the period after 1945 as insular and innocent, the antithesis of the radical decade.

By the mid-1980s, however, a different viewpoint began to be heard, though it has yet to make much headway against the popular image. In a study of postwar intellectuals, *The Liberal Mind in a Conservative Age* (1985), the historian Richard Pells rightly argued that the social critics of the 1950s, including William H. Whyte, David Riesman, and C. Wright Mills, by focusing on conformity, psychological manipulation, and the malaise of the middle class, had prepared the ground for the more radical criticism that followed. Pells suggested that there was a good deal of continuity between the two periods. Another historian, Lary May, edited a valuable collection of essays, *Recasting America* (1989), which explored many of the tensions and contradictions of the postwar years and drew attention to developments in the arts and intellectual life that hardly fit the somnolent image of the period. William H. Chafe has repeatedly emphasized the "paradox of change," the momentous social transformations—in the life of the middle class, for example, or in the position of blacks and women— that were taking place behind the conservative façade. On the other hand, some scholars in American Studies and art history who approach the arts as expressions of social ideology have tried to demonstrate that nearly every cultural phenomenon of those years, from genre films and literary criticism to abstract art, was somehow a reflex of the Cold War, a "hegemonic" expression of the "national security state" and the containment policy toward international Communism. What passed for culture became a way of indoctrinating Americans and aborting independent thought. Such arguments, which rarely appealed to factual evidence, have given rise to a school of Cold War scholarship that takes little account of other influential factors in postwar social life, from the baby boom and economic expansion to the education boom and shifting roles of women, blacks, and ethnic minorities. Based on a presumed ideological bent that can hardly be verified, such arguments depend on tenuous links between politics and culture that are sometimes suggestive but too often arbitrary or reductive.

My aim in this book is to give a more varied, less familiar picture of the postwar years by taking a fresh look at some striking changes in the arts, especially in fiction, and at the strong radical undercurrents that led directly to the culture wars of the 1960s. World War II had brought a powerful but artificial unity to Americans, first by ending the Depression, which had highlighted class divisions; then by giving Americans a cause to fight for, a life-and-death struggle fraught with patriotic and personal feeling; and finally by deflecting internal conflict among social groups for the duration of the war. But the war also shook Americans loose from their local moorings, from religious roots and isolated lives in small towns, from urban ghettos and other homogeneous communities. Young men who had never strayed fifty miles from home were shipped off to distant training bases and overseas missions; others migrated to take up jobs in defense industries. City boys and country boys, the children of immigrants and the children of sharecroppers were thrown together for the first time, like an accelerated version of the melting pot or a poster for the Popular Front. At the same time, new communication links like Edward R. Murrow's live news broadcasts from besieged London were beginning to make the world a smaller place. There was no return to isolationism after the war, as there had been after the First World War. Instead, the physical destruction of much of Europe, the unconditional surrender and occupation of Japan, and the breakup of the old colonial system left the United States in a powerful economic and political position, which would soon be cemented by strategic alliances such as NATO.

A more cosmopolitan America was coming into being, a good deal more open to social differences yet resistant to political dissent and social criticism. Outsider groups such as blacks, women, and Jews, even working-class and rural Americans, having seen something of the world, were not about to return to the kitchen, the ghetto, or the menial jobs to which they had been confined. As industry turned to consumer goods, to new housing and technology, the growing economy opened the gates to a social mobility only dreamed of during the lean years of the Depression. The GI Bill of Rights, designed in part to keep returning servicemen from flooding the job market, created educational opportunities that would equip veterans for a role in the expanding economy. This enabled them to start families, just as new highways and expanding suburbs allowed them to raise those families outside the city. Their earnings, like the aid we sent to Europe under the Marshall Plan, fueled the economy by heating up demand for goods and services. This in turn stimulated a burgeoning consumer society as more and more Americans, moving up into the middle class, reaped the benefits of improved technology, better housing, shorter working hours, more leisure time, and increasingly comfortable lives. The fruits of this prosperity were not spread equally. African Americans still faced formidable barriers as to where they could live and work, but even for them the war opened many doors that could never be shut again. It was not long before the good life became the sovereign right of every American, at least in theory—and that theory would cast a long shadow.

The arrival of these outsiders in the mainstream of American society had a close parallel in the arts. Just as the needs of the economy opened professions previously closed to Jews, the needs of a newly cosmopolitan culture, born in the shadow of unspeakable wartime carnage, opened up literature and academic life to Jewish writers. Specialists in alienation, virtuosos of moral anguish, witnesses to the pains and gains of assimilation, they had a timely story to tell. Race had always been close to the heart of American life but the war against Germany, Italy, and Japan brought this issue home more than anything since the Civil War and Reconstruction. Black writers too had a tale to tell, as Richard Wright had recently shown in *Native Son* and *Black Boy*. Thus began the stream of outsider figures who would do more than anything else to define the character of postwar writing: Ralph Ellison's Invisible Man, a vibrant voice from the underground rehearsing his own idiosyncratic version of black history; Flannery O'Connor's eccentric Misfit, some kind of messenger of God who expresses his frustrations through serial murder, or her Displaced Person, a European refugee literally crushed by the no-nothing society he does not begin to understand; Norman Mailer's White Negro, the hipster as moral adventurer and sociopath; the new kind of American saint of Jack Kerouac and the wayward, misunderstood adolescents of J. D. Salinger; the ordinary grunts oppressed by their officers in so many war novels; the anguished old Jews and magical schlemiel figures in Bernard Malamud's stories; the loopy intellectuals who fill Saul Bellow's fiction with their long memories and sardonic cultural speculations; the refined old-world decadents of Nabokov, with their classy style and kinky or comical longings; Philip Roth's protagonists, who make grand opera of their sexual needs, exposing the stigmata they received in the gender wars. These characters, all in some way projections of their distinguished authors, are like Kafka's leopards in the temple, implosions of the irrational, children of the Freudian century, sharp-clawed primitives who would somehow be integrated into the once-decorous rites of American literature, who would *become* American literature.

Like the efflorescence of social criticism in the 1950s, the emergence of these writers points to the essential continuity of the postwar decades and reveals the roots of the counterculture of the 1960s. Along with many filmmakers, playwrights, musicians, and painters, these novelists dramatize the unease of the middle class at its moment of triumph, the air of anxiety and discontent that hangs over this period. From our dim memories of the early years of television, the dying days of the Hollywood studio system, and the popular songs of the Hit Parade, we still think of the 1950s as a time of sunny, even mindless optimism, only slightly dimmed by preparations for World War III. This is an example of selective cultural memory.

In fact, from Cole Porter and Busby Berkeley to Frank Capra, there was a good deal more optimism on show during the grim days of the Depression than in the supposedly buoyant years of economic expansion after the war. In the arts, perhaps the best known evidence of the dark side of postwar culture is film noir, the vogue of cheaply made crime movies so unlike the gangster films popular before the war. The earlier movies were really success stories; they were built around crudely charismatic men who were legendary for their amoral energy, management style, and genius for power, acquisition, and display. Though their fall was built into their rise, the death of the gangster was a glorious coda to his overreaching life rather than a moral lesson. Censors understood this early by cracking down on what they rightly saw as an idealization of the antisocial. But after the war, crime movies become a tissue of paranoia, betrayal, and fatality from which no true heroism emerges, certainly not among the forces of the law, who usually come off as faceless organization men, and hardly ever among the criminals themselves, who kill and are killed without being romanticized.

Everywhere in postwar culture we can see the marks of anxious division, even self-alienation. Some of the bleaker film genres of the 1950s, such as horror and science fiction, obviously reflected the anxieties of the Cold War and the atomic age, including the fear of menacing aliens, radioactive mutations, and nuclear annihilation. In movies like *The War of the Worlds* (1953), audiences identified with apocalyptic scenes of the destruction of New York or Los Angeles by a seemingly invulnerable force. But the dark elements that surfaced in film noir, in domestic melodramas, and in revisionist westerns are harder to explain. The John Wayne of Ford's classic prewar western, *Stagecoach* (1939), was a typical thirties character, an outlaw yet a gentleman, socially marginal like other admirable figures in the film yet unambiguously heroic. The film shows up the hypocrisy of respectable citizens like the thieving banker, while dramatizing the redemption of the those they've rejected, such as the alcoholic doctor and the good-hearted whore, whom Wayne courts and wins as if she were the finest lady. But the John Wayne of many postwar westerns from *Red River* to *The Searchers* is a more complex figure; he can be stubborn and unreasonable, obsessed with betrayal and hell-bent on revenge. This is even more true of the embittered characters played by Jimmy Stewart in gritty fifties westerns by Anthony Mann. In one of the harshest of these films, *The Naked Spur,* Stewart plays a bounty-hunter who stalks and captures a sinister killer but for mercenary reasons. He had gone off to fight the Civil War— as the so-called "greatest generation" would later fight World War II—but returned to find his woman gone and his land sold from under him. Like the Wayne of *The Searchers,* he is a morally ambiguous figure, wounded, guarded, and hard to fathom, who must earn his bit of heroism by learning to be human again—to trust, relent, and forgive.

The Freudian wave that washed over American culture in the forties and fifties brought not only introspection but an undercurrent of hysteria into otherwise conventional genre films. These include Raoul Walsh's Oedipal gangster movie *White Heat,* in which Jimmy Cagney plays the gangster as mama's boy, who suffers from migraines and needs her to remind him to keep up a tough front; Nicholas Ray's anti-McCarthy western, *Johnny Guitar,* with Mercedes McCambridge consumed by her erotically tinged hatred of Joan Crawford; and Douglas Sirk's vertiginous melodrama, *Written on the Wind,* in which Dorothy Malone plays a wayward heiress who sleeps with every man she can find because she can't sleep with Rock Hudson, and dances herself into an erotic frenzy in her room while her father drops dead on the stairs below. Meanwhile, her playboy brother (Robert Stack) destroys himself slowly with alcohol and self-hatred. The love of a good woman (Lauren Bacall) and a faithful friend (Hudson) almost saves him, until, beset by jealousy and sexual anxiety, he "accidentally" shoots himself. If social suffering, poverty, and exploitation topped the agenda of the arts in the 1930s, neurosis, anxiety, and alienation played the same role in the forties and fifties when economic fears were largely put to rest.

On the other hand, some films noirs were driven less by paranoia than by romantic fatalism, a sense of doomed love, as in *Double Indemnity* (1944) and *The Postman Always Rings Twice* (1946), based on lurid novels by the hard-boiled writer James M. Cain, and in Nicholas Ray's *They Live By Night* (1949) and Joseph H. Lewis's *Gun Crazy* (1949), stories of fugitive couples pursued by the law. Unlike most postwar stories, film noir is often grounded in pulp material from the 1930s, which gives it a hard edge of cynicism and romantic abandon along with a look of fatality. Noir was not so much genre as a style and outlook that showed up in many kinds of Hollywood films; it was the great naysayer in the postwar banquet of American self-celebration. Playing on the lower half of double bills, most genre films did not have to meet the ideological test of featured productions; they flew below the radar of significant Hollywood filmmaking, creating their own kind of counterculture within the heart of the entertainment industry and offering an implicit critique of the Pollyannish, upbeat elements of the mainstream culture. This can be seen in photography as well. For every heartwarming cultural marker, such as Edward Steichen's celebrated 1955 *Family of Man* exhibition, there was a bleak rebuttal like Robert Frank's seminal collection of photographs, *The Americans* (1959), with its unpoetic view of the heartland as a grungy scene of everyday vacancy and blank happenstance.

This thread of anxiety, paranoia, and inner conflict was a decisive element in many postwar works, but as a film noir shows, it was far from the whole story. There was also a wild emotional vitality, a primitivism inherited from modernism, that fed paradoxically off the economic expansion and the new social mobility. We see this expansive energy in the avant garde among bohemian painters, jazzmen, young rockers, and Beat poets but also at the heart of American popular culture. Television was the bête noire of intellectuals critical of mass culture, but they had been just as dismissive of American movies during the glory days of Hollywood before the war. TV united the American public into a single audience even more than movies or radio had done, but it also privatized leisure time by relocating it in the home and focusing on family fare. At the same time, early television spread the spirit of vaudeville to a mass audience with wild farceurs like Milton Berle, Jimmy Durante, and Jerry Lewis; satiric geniuses like Ernie Kovacs, Imogene Coca, and Sid Caesar; veteran radio comedians like Jack Benny, Edgar Bergen, and Fred Allen; and even borscht-belt entertainers such as George Burns. Highbrow critics saw only fragile kitchen-sink realism in live TV drama and little more than mind-numbing repetition in early sitcoms like *I Love Lucy* and *The Honeymooners,* which have been rerun ever since as classics of marital mayhem and anarchic social comedy. Their zany irreverence, like the later mockery of Joseph Heller in *Catch-22,* played well against postwar pieties. Critics missed the crucial point that repetition and variation, not novelty, were staples of the popular arts. With its vast appetite for material, early television, like all popular media, relied on ingenious formula and the gusto of physical performance rather than the sort of originality that sustained high art. If the content of early TV was constrained by family values and conventional gender roles, there was a raw, ebullient energy that complemented the buzz and dynamism of American society. As TV became pervasive, it would also reshape the political landscape more than any other force, starting with the Army-McCarthy hearings and the Kennedy-Nixon debates. Like other postwar institutions that were at once conservative and revolutionary, television too was part of the "paradox of change" during the Cold War years.

Part of the legend of the postwar era is that it was small-minded and repressive. This accords with our memories of the limited political options available during the 1950s, but this was not entirely the result of the Cold War. McCarthyism and militant anti-Communism were less a reaction to the Soviet threat abroad or disloyalty and espionage at home than a political wedge used by Republicans to fracture the New Deal coalition, in the same way that they would recapture power by demonizing liberalism in the 1980s. To be accused of being soft on Communism could be fatal to a political cause or to one's chances of working again in fields like the movie industry. The Cold War descended on the 1950s like a damp, gray fog, blanketing and muffling the landscape with its polarizing view of an embattled America. There were some curious features to that landscape, from the duck-and-cover drills that prepared school children for the coming nuclear war to the underground shelters where they would presumably find refuge when it actually broke out. In this torpid political climate, the range of open debate was more restricted than at any time in the century, especially after the outbreak of the Korean War in June 1950. McCarthyism and the blacklist mentality enforced these limits, ruining the lives of many who stepped out of line or stood accused of harboring radical views twenty years earlier. Above all, it was not a good time to be black in America, to be poor, which made you almost invisible, or to be a woman, many of whom joined the great migration to the suburbs, where, as Betty Friedan argued, married women were being pressed back into roles they thought they had escaped during the Depression and the war. It was not a great time to be a liberal because you could easily be labeled a Communist, a pinko, or a fellow traveler. It was not a great time to be young and horny, since a pair of twenty-year-olds who wanted to be together had to get married (though it *was* a good time to raise the children who would soon follow).

But scholars who put too much emphasis on McCarthyism and repression, or who fail to see how much the condition of women and blacks was quietly changing, come up with a skewed picture of the period. Thus the historian Elaine Tyler May argues that there was a domestic equivalent to the containment policy pursued by the United States against the Soviet Union. This was certainly true in politics where, as I have said, patriotism and anti-Communism became ways of discrediting liberalism and breaking up the electoral majority once enjoyed by the New Deal. But May extends the notion of containment to social life as well. "Postwar Americans fortified the boundaries within which they lived," she says. "They wanted secure jobs, secure homes, and secure marriages in a secure country . . . Containment was the key to security." But this is merely a verbal melding of two forms of security, two kinds of containment. After describing the containment of nuclear weapons and of domestic Communists, May turns to people's personal lives. "In the domestic version of containment," she writes, "the 'sphere of influence' was the home. Within its walls, potentially dangerous social forces of the new age might be tamed, where they could contribute to the secure and fulfilling life to which postwar men and women aspired . . . More than merely a metaphor for the cold war on the homefront, containment aptly describes the way in which public policy, personal behavior, and even political values were focused on the home."

But "containment" *is* a metaphor, a questionable analogy between personal and international security, the home and the world. Moreover, it suggests that the prevailing social force of the postwar years was constriction, policing, and intimidation, a sort of emotional McCarthyism. Yet for all its constraints, this was a period of unparalleled economic growth and social mobility, when the lives of many American changed more than they had in the previous two centuries. What containment really means is that revolutionary hopes for egalitarian social change, which flared up during the economic crisis of the 1930s, died down during the prosperity that followed the war. This is another way of looking at the period through the eyes of the 1960s or through the critical lens of academic disciplines that flowed from the sixties. It scarcely acknowledges what May herself calls the "potentially dangerous social forces of the new age."

Certainly there were efforts to confine women to traditional roles, but this was undercut by much of what was actually happening. Despite the fabled retreat of Rosie the Riveter to home and hearth, the number of women who worked outside the home, especially married women, doubled between 1940 and 1960, though this mainly meant in low-level, pink-collar jobs rather than in the professions. The increase was especially marked among married women and mothers with younger children. Despite the domestic stereotypes of the fifties, the economic role of women was quietly changing as more Americans joined the middle class. Two incomes helped foot the bill for the new social mobility. Similarly, the civil rights movement of the late fifties and early sixties did not come from nowhere, but developed out of continuous civil rights agitation that began with the return of black soldiers from war, continued with the desegregation of the armed forces in 1948 and the Supreme Court's unanimous decision to desegregate the schools in 1954, and was driven home by direct action, nonviolent demonstrations, and congressional legislation in the aftermath of John F. Kennedy's assassination. The cradle of the civil rights movement was the postwar years, not the 1960s, when it began to splinter. As William H. Chafe writes in *The Unfinished Journey*, "there existed remarkable continuity within the black protest movement between 1945 and 1960." This progress was unquestionably advanced by the literary work of Wright, Ellison, and James Baldwin in the same period, which, along with the writings of social scientists like Gunnar Myrdal and Kenneth Clark, introduced many Americans to the inner experience of racism and discrimination. If this was containment, it failed miserably.

Another radical turn of the forties and fifties was the explosive emergence of youth culture. This too was partly an offshoot of economic
growth, which placed a great deal of disposable income and free time in the
hands of the young and built up a new market that would grow ever larger
in the years that followed. If the official values of postwar America were
complacent or repressive, young people became part of a culture that spoke
to their alienation yet bristled with spontaneity, energy, and instinctive vitality. Not incidentally, these were the very qualities cherished by the avant
garde, from bop musicians and abstract painters to Method actors and Beat
poets. Like the social critics of the period, they emphasized individuality
and self-expression in a society that too often rewarded time-serving and
conformity. At the heart of the new counterculture of the 1950s, the balance between civilization and its discontents was shifting, as theorists like
Herbert Marcuse, Norman O. Brown, and Paul Goodman would soon try
to show.

In fiction this took the form of picaresque novels of flight and adventure
loosely based on Mark Twain's *Adventures of Huckleberry Finn,* including
Salinger's *Catcher in the Rye,* Ellison's *Invisible Man,* Bellow's *Adventures of
Augie March,* and Kerouac's *On the Road.* In each of these books the first-
person voice, with its vernacular ebb and flow, conveys the dreams and
frustrations of the youthful protagonist. All were written in nervous, syn-
copated, jazz-like riffs veering unpredictably between the colloquial
and the literary. The mixed background of these writers—black, Jewish,
French-Canadian—contributed to this creative crossing of styles, which
had a huge influence on the writers of the next decade, including Philip
Roth and Thomas Pynchon. "At the simplest level, it had to do with language," Pynchon later said in *Slow Learner* about the sources of his work,
citing "Kerouac and the Beat writers, the diction of Saul Bellow in *The Adventures of Augie March,* [and] emerging voices like those of Herbert Gold
and Philip Roth" as important breakthroughs. But if the sixties writers
resonated to the linguistic freedom of their predecessors, especially their
fresh, innovative rhythms, they were also invigorated by their loose-limbed
forms, which reflected the quest of their protagonists. All these young
heroes, like Huck Finn himself, are searching for freedom, eager to escape the conventional and oppressive social roles that others have foisted on
them. Ellison's hero is initially eager to please but gradually realizes that
he is being manipulated at every turn: "Everyone seemed to have some plan
for me, and beneath that some more secret plan." Again and again, Holden
Caulfield finds phoniness and inauthenticity in the adult world around
him. As Huck and Jim fled the bonds of slavery, the tyranny of respectability, and the hypocrisy and corruption of the towns along the Mississippi, so

their successors recoiled from the 1950s regime of family and responsibility. They look to create themselves, to escape the blessings of civilization, just as Huck Finn at the end will "light out for the Territory." In a world that tailors maturity into a strait-jacket, they are determined to avoid growing up.

The first of these books, *The Catcher in the Rye,* helped kick off the youth culture that soon burst onto the screen in movies like *The Wild One, Blackboard Jungle,* and *Rebel Without a Cause* and took over popular music with subversive performances by early rockers like Elvis Presley, Chuck Berry, and Little Richard. Under the guise of a sociological study of juvenile delinquency and youthful alienation, filmmakers explored a new emotional terrain in the smoldering, inarticulate masculinity of actors like Marlon Brando, James Dean, and Montgomery Clift. The malaise of the young, which we still trace back to the generation gap of the 1960s, really began with these damaged figures whose sensitivity and estrangement may reflect the suppressed traumas of the war years. They bring together a cool, insolent rebelliousness, an almost masochistic sense of victimization, and a new kind of high-voltage sexuality. Elvis modeled himself on the surly, misunderstood figures of Brando and Dean but found his music in the rhythm and blues of the black ghetto. He tapped into the emotional plangency and sexual directness of the blues. His pelvic gyrations, censored on national television, elated teenage girls and shocked contemporary guardians of morality. He took even more from black culture than Mailer and the Beats, cutting a path for the rockers of the 1960s. Rock brought a driving physical energy into popular music. In *Blackboard Jungle,* the opening performance of "Rock Around the Clock" by Bill Haley and the Comets, instead of conveying youthful savagery or anarchy (as the plot dictates), became the clarion-call of a new generation.

Despite the limitations of the Hollywood Code, grown-up expressions of this sexual energy could be felt in other American movies, especially film noir. Here is one extended example. Joseph H. Lewis's vertiginously romantic *Gun Crazy* takes up the Bonnie-and-Clyde legend of the outlaw couple, first developed in the 1930s in Edward Anderson's novel *Thieves Like Us* and Fritz Lang's film *You Only Live Once.* In *Gun Crazy* the romance begins with a mutual fascination with guns. Where Lang, in classic thirties style, portrays the fugitives as hunted innocents, victims of a harsh, destructive society, Lewis gives his lovers a Freudian charge of sexual intensity, making their gunplay stand in for their sex play, the animal magnetism that draws them and keeps them together. The film has a wild, kinky sexual energy, a driving, obsessive rhythm that only B-movies and pulp novels were then free to pursue.

Where many films noirs present women as inscrutable, treacherous se-
ducers, scarcely more than a projection of male longings and fears, *Gun
Crazy* gives us Laurie, a carnival performer whose restless craving for excitement makes a man (and an unwilling killer) of Bart, her shy, tormented
lover. They're "like a couple of animals," says her sleazy, jealous employer,
whom she has jilted. Laurie literally seduces Bart into becoming a stick-up
man. We stereotype the postwar period as the heyday of domesticity, when
young vets and their wives settled down to raise families. This is true
enough, but here we get another view. Domesticity is represented by the
dull, meager lives of Bart's sister as she struggles to raise her small children, and Bart's boyhood friends, who have become law-abiding pillars of
the small town where they grew up.

Laurie turns Bart's life upside down, but he remains more boyish than
hard-boiled. He feels increasingly troubled as their crime spree continues,
especially after one caper turns into a killing. His fears and his moral scruples are built into his raw, gawky, neurotic masculinity. But the lovers cannot separate, hard as they try; whenever they go straight, their world turns
flat and dead, since ordinary life cannot compete with the thrill of risk and
crime. As the law catches up with them, they lose everything and flee back
to the quiet town he came from. In the morning mist of the nearby mountains, with the air so thin she can barely breathe, trapped among peaks that
remind us of the ones they tried to scale, they achieve their love-in-death in
the natural world where he first learned to shoot. There he finally kills her
(and dies) to keep her from harming his old friends.

It is hard to know what social significance to give a film as masterfully
idiosyncratic as this one. Like other films noirs, *Gun Crazy* is shadowy,
doom-laden, and fatalistic; it illustrates the dark side of the period's official
optimism. But it also conveys a huge charge of excitement that anticipates
the new counterculture of the 1950s. Though *Gun Crazy* never crudely
equates guns and sex, it shows how a popular Freudianism, with emphasis
on the irrational, the instinctual, and the unconscious, altered the spirit
and content of earlier film genres. The film makes ordinary life seem
flavorless while it idealizes the animal vitality that can't easily be chan-
neled into marriage and child-rearing, work and respectability. It's a provocative work masquerading as a romantic thriller, a Wagnerian Liebestod
disguised as pulp tragedy. It shows us the transgressive, barely socialized
energies that would flare out in the sixties, which were linked to the dynamic forces of consumption, technological change, and global power. As
the nation emerged from the deprivations of Depression and wartime,
Laurie's tragic, unappeasable hunger for experience, her sense of "I want it,
and I want it now," would become the guiding spirit of a new culture.

This darkly shaded exuberance and vitality is even more marked in the avant-garde arts of the period, especially jazz and painting, and in the Beat movement that followed. This was the moment Charlie Parker, Dizzy Gillespie, and bebop took over the jazz world, with small groups of virtuoso performers replacing the large swing bands of the 1930s. Bebop grew out of a strike in the recording industry between 1942 and 1944, when young men began jamming with each other, developing bold individual styles that had no place in the dance music of the swing era. Here, as in painting, the radical arts in the postwar years took an introspective, experimental turn. Charlie Parker substituted dazzling speed, complex polyrhythms, elusive chord changes, and atonal riffs for the uptempo melodic flow of swing. This kind of jazz depends much more on spontaneity and improvisation. In numbers like "Leap Frog" and "Relaxing With Lee" in 1950, we hear the conversational interplay between Parker's alto sax, Gillespie's trumpet, Thelonious Monk's piano, and Max Roach's drums. Where swing had made jazz social and popular—perfect music to dance to—bebop made it challenging and elusive, difficult and provocative, as well as dangerous for some performers, whose dependence on drugs often became self-destructive.

In smoky late-night clubs in many American cities, boppers created an underground culture out of complex music in the outlaw style of classic American outsiders. The impeccable Duke Ellington and his band had made jazz part of the culture of elegance of the twenties and thirties; Parker and his friends took it back to its darker roots. "He was an obsessed outsider," Ralph Ellison said of Charlie Parker: "Bird was thrice alienated: as Negro, as addict, as exponent of a new and disturbing development in jazz." Ellison was clearly of two minds about Parker's "tortured and in many ways criminal striving for personal and moral integration," but others responded by idolizing and imitating him, and by turning him into a legend after his early death from a heroin overdose in 1955.

At the same time, between 1947 and 1950, Jackson Pollock came into his own in drip paintings of an astonishing beauty and complexity, making way for another band of outsiders who would one day dominate American art. Pollock's kinetic style, which the critic Harold Rosenberg described as Action Painting, linked him to both bebop and the Beats, who also relied on spontaneity and fluid movement over formal restraint or figurative representation. Pollock saw art as a reflection of the inner landscape, the unconscious workings of the mind, which could be drawn out by intuition and association. He seemed to paint from inside the canvas and from deep inside his own mind. His "all-over" method decentralized the canvas and made his work seem random and chaotic, yet his technique demanded enormous discipline and control. Soon a photo spread in *Life* magazine and the films of Hans Namuth trumpeted Pollock's fame to a wider audience, which undermined his precarious stability. His death in 1956, like James Dean's and Charlie Parker's the previous year, made him the epitome of the edgy artist consumed by his own creative intensity. *Pollock,* an earnest and intense movie by Ed Harris, recently consummated this romantic myth by focusing as much on his tormented personality as on his painting.

Thus, at a conservative moment in American art, the arrival of Abstract Expressionism constituted a genuine avant garde, intransigently modern and innovative. But the radical credentials of this art were questioned in a provocative book published in 1983 by the art historian Serge Guilbaut called *How New York Stole the Idea of Modern Art.* He argued that the Abstract Expressionists and their critical supporters, especially Clement Greenberg and other New York intellectuals, were implicated in a process of cultural hegemony, at once dethroning Paris as capital of the art world and delegitimizing the kind of political art, including mural painting and social realism, that had been dominant in the United States before the war. As a result, he claimed, art became complicit with the global and domestic goals of the Cold War, enhancing American power abroad while defusing political criticism at home. By depoliticizing art and turning it towards abstraction, Guilbaut argued, these painters and critics had been engaged in a Cold War mission of imposing a Pax Americana on the art world.

Guilbaut's influential critique was taken up by other art critics and cultural historians, including Frances Stonor Saunders in her widely reviewed book *The Cultural Cold War,* which reveals many details about the CIA support for artists and intellectuals in the postwar years, including a number of overseas exhibitions of abstract art. Her logic suggests that if the CIA supported something, even if the recipients remained ignorant of that support, their work served the interests of American domination. For ideological critics, the political context always determines how we must understand the art. There is no clear evidence that Guilbaut or Saunders ever actually *looked* at a painting to determine whether the work itself was powerful or fraudulent, whether its impact was radical or reactionary, or whether the stylized realism, populism, and regionalism of the Post Office murals should have remained the last word in American art. As an afterthought to her chapter on how the abstract painters were promoted abroad, Saunders adds the caveat that of course "their art cannot be reduced to those conditions . . . There was something in the art itself that allowed it to triumph." What that was she doesn't venture to say. By exporting the Metropolitan Opera as well as the work of abstract artists as markers of creative freedom, the CIA thought it could convince skeptical Europeans that the United States actually had a high culture and a serious intellectual life. If some used art as a weapon in the Cold War, others saw the Cold War as a way of prying loose money to support the arts. While rightly lamenting the secrecy and deception behind this funding, Saunders minimizes the paradox that a branch of the United States government was sponsoring exhibitions of boldly original art that the President himself considered to be meaningless scribbles and many members of Congress saw as a sinister Communist plot.

Guilbaut's book, which came in the wake of a new revisionist historiography on the origins of the Cold War, helped kick off the school of ideological criticism I touched on earlier, which tried to link not only the visual arts but the most disparate cultural developments of the postwar years to the agenda of the Cold War. In this variant of the hermeneutics of suspicion, even the most innocent looking work could be explained in terms of Cold War ideology. The intellectual expression of that ideology was seen in Arthur Schlesinger's liberal anti-Communism, Lionel Trilling's tragic realism, or Reinhold Niebuhr's neo-Augustinian theology. If Schlesinger hadn't published his 1949 book *The Vital Center,* these critics would surely have had to write it for him, if only to prove that there was no middle way, that liberalism itself was the enemy, not simply McCarthyism. Yet all three were acute social critics who often drew radical conclusions from conservative premises about human nature.

On closer examination, postwar culture looks more edgy and unsettling than we once imagined, reflecting powerful and subversive social energies roiling beneath the placid surface of the Truman and Eisenhower years. Undoubtedly there were deeply conservative elements in the arts, not only in popular fiction and music but in more serious writing. Fiction and poetry were often more conventional than they had been between the wars, and, with the exception of southerners like Flannery O'Connor, Carson McCullers, and Eudora Welty, few major women writers emerged then. It was not until the revival of feminism in the late 1960s that a new school of witty, articulate women novelists and social critics would appear, yet another wave of outsiders who would bring a different vision into American writing. In the 1940s and 1950s, most novelists turned away from Joycean or Proustian experiments; established poets retreated from the cutting-edge modernism of Eliot and Pound and the neo-Romanticism of Crane and Stevens to embrace a modest, small-scale academic modernism, learned, densely charged, full of wit and irony, but free to titanic ambitions and audience-challenging technical innovations. The cozy civility and formal dexterity of Auden became a prime influence on younger poets. In criticism as in literature, ambiguity was the watchword; caution and restraint the prevailing mood.

But there was another side to this picture, as I've tried to show here. As we explore the novels, music, art, and movies of the period, the radicalism of the 1960s, which once seemed to surge up out of nowhere, reveals its sources in the turbid cross-currents of the postwar years. Where once I had thought of the 1950s and 1960s as cultural contraries, it became clear that there were vital elements that bound together the whole period from 1945 to 1970 and beyond, a creative reaction against the official values of the period. While seemingly marginal to the business of the hour, artists can serve as canaries in the mine, an early warning system whose message can be understood only in retrospect. Writers, artists, and musicians exposed a deep discomfort at the core of American affluence and power, the same unease laid bare by critics of middle-class conformity such as Riesman and Whyte. Undreamed-of prosperity had created an unprecedented standard of living, so why wasn't it more satisfying? Thwarted politically, social criticism shifted into the cultural sphere; thwarted collectively, American radicalism migrated into the work of individual artists, who had their own vision of what a full life demanded.

For many left-wing critics, this cultural turn looked like a flight from politics, a way of dropping out. The organized left of the 1930s remained the gold standard. They paid no attention to the Hollywood underground though it was largely composed of thirties radicals soon to be blacklisted. They despised popular culture and did not see how the avant garde, so small and marginal, could be the bellwether of social change. What artists explored in the 1940s and 1950s, including drugs, sex, and new forms of self-expression, would become entitlements of the middle class in the decades that followed. Ideological critics of Cold War culture, such as Serge Guilbaut and his successors, were searching for revolutionary art and ideas that would take a conventionally political form and were therefore blind to the *cultural* revolution that actually took place, which would prove far more deep-seated and consequential, not just in shaping the sixties counterculture but in reshaping American life. This cultural radicalism, amplified and commercialized by the mass media, would become the legacy of the postwar years to the rest of the twentieth century.

As we turn back to the major writers of fiction, this continuity may help account for the enduring careers and influence of many of these writers. We should not slight the personal drive, the innate literary gift, the sheer creative stamina that contributed to the longevity of Saul Bellow, Norman Mailer, Gore Vidal, John Updike, or Philip Roth, who were still doing powerful work at the end of the century. But cultural factors also enhanced the staying power of these and other postwar writers who died early, stopped publishing, or burned themselves out, such as J. D. Salinger, Jack Kerouac, Paul Bowles, Tennessee Williams, Flannery O'Connor, Bernard Malamud, James Baldwin, and Ralph Ellison. Like the jazz musicians and abstract painters, they were determined outsiders at a moment when other children of immigrants, blue-collar workers, storefront preachers, and rural sharecroppers were entering the American mainstream. They were the advance guard of the multicultural future though they wanted to succeed as American writers, not as specimens of an oppressed minority. Their work was powered by the appetite, energy, ambition, and unconventionality of strangers in a half-strange land, clamoring to be heard, seeking their place at the table but not by looking or sounding like anyone who was already there.

These writers arrived at a time of momentous change in the economy, demography, and material base of American life. Among the things taken for granted by middle-class Americans by the 1960s that scarcely existed in 1945 or 1950, the historian James T. Patterson lists supermarkets, malls, fast-food chains, air-conditioning, freezers, dishwashers, ball-point pens, long-playing records, four-lane highways, and tubeless tires. The day-to-day lives of most Americans changed dramatically in the postwar years, which saw the beginning of the world as we know it today. Peace and prosperity led to a galloping consumerism and vast technological change, along with new economic and political power in the world. As the American model became the cutting-edge of modernization throughout the world, American art and popular culture also began their long march toward world influence. The writers who began publishing after the war were the first to take account of this new life, especially its psychological effects. Theirs was a world of material comfort and its dissatisfactions, including anomie, alienation, and a nagging sense of weightlessness; of a turn inward towards the self and its problems of identity; a world dominated by the utopian ease and abundance made possible by technology, but also the anxiety set off by its huge potential for destruction; a world that knew the fragility of relationships when moral boundaries have been blurred and sex has become ubiquitous, where advertising and the arts spread images of a better life by making us unhappy with the life we had. In postwar society, material consumption soon translated into cultural consumption, into changes in morality, values, and style. In their focus on the inner life and on the changing world of the middle class, the postwar writers were the first to document this great shift.

For most postwar novelists, this brave new world was not well suited to a traditional fictional approach, the kind of literary realism that held sway from Balzac to Dreiser, which set a large cast of lifelike characters in a closely observed social world. Instead, they grappled with it in a way that still makes sense to us today, not primarily through social realism and reportage but by way of inwardness and self-absorption, an expansion and projection of the ego. Even in Mailer's conventional first novel, we can already see a fascination with power, ego, and will, the murky recesses of the irrational. Eventually Mailer will come into his own by making himself his main character, the sensor who registers the most minute vibrations between his interior life and the larger world. In a more speculative mode, Bellow too will begin to build his fiction around versions of himself without losing his huge curiosity about how different people live their lives. In a series of half-surreal episodes, Ralph Ellison shapes the twentieth-century itinerary of black people around the quasi-autobiographical figure of his Invisible Man; Gore Vidal invents his best character in the cutting patrician persona of his essays. Roth's Zuckerman and Updike's Rabbit, like Chaplin's tramp and Keaton's resourceful Everyman hero, become the indispensable projections of the authors, their alternate lives. By stepping outside themselves, they can at once channel their obsessions and get an oblique angle on their own limitations. They can dream of lives they might have had as they record the inner history of the last half century, decade by decade. By cultivating the self, not entirely without a certain narcissism, these writers found new ways of writing the history of their times, an age of prosperity and therapy when the exigent, imperial self became the obsessive concern of many Americans.

Whatever their limits, which will be noted in the pages that follow, these writers captured the anxiety and insecurity of Americans in their newfound comforts. Amid his recollections of athletic glory, and even his later wealth, Rabbit feels like a loser, a man in decline, for he knows that something is missing. In his obsessive pursuit of WASP women, Roth's Portnoy, trying hard to be crude and vulgar, confesses that "I don't seem to stick my dick up these girls, as much as I stick it up their backgrounds—as though through fucking I will discover America." Flannery O'Connor wickedly pursues the black comedy of educated people marooned among the salt of the earth, in a backwater of humanity where ordinary folks are as cunning as they are self-satisfied. Bernard Malamud plays off cultivated Jews uneasy in their assimilation against ethnic Jews who will never fit in. These resonant themes gave the writers more energy, more purchase on experience than old-stock Americans writing novels of manners in a world that, for them, was changing only glacially. Bellow, Roth, and Mailer especially capture the sexual anxiety of men in the postwar world. The self-absorption of their protagonists, their focus on male grievances, coincides with the emergence of women from the kitchen and the bedroom to demand much more from the world around them.

Once I thought that postwar novelists had perversely turned their backs on society to cultivate their own gardens—the private world of the self and its mysteries. This is a view still held by Tom Wolfe, whose own novels, as colorfully hyperbolic as his essays, are little more than journalistic cartoons passed off as social history. The momentous shifts in American life after the war demanded a different kind of literary imagination, a more surreal technique. The changes in American fiction reflected the transformation of society as a whole. The carnage of the war and the Holocaust turned writers into scholars of violence, specialists in extreme situations. Where Marx had once been their guide to class conflict, they turned to Freud, to existentialism, or even to theology as tutors in the shadowy recesses of the psyche. The new prosperity solved some old economic problems while drawing attention to inner conflicts.

For white male novelists of the postwar years, blacks and women sometimes became projections of the Other, at once desirable and threatening. Their attitudes toward women, always under siege, threatened to strand them in an earlier era. They had to move forward. For a writer like Norman Mailer this meant a turn from the male-centered realism of the war novel to the allegory of *Barbary Shore,* the psychological probing of *The Deer Park,* the egotism and mythmaking of "The White Negro" and *Advertisements for Myself,* the hallucinatory effects of *An American Dream,* the scabrous black humor of *Why Are We in Vietnam?*, and the comically grandiose self-portraiture of *The Armies of the Night* and other works combining fiction and journalism. Mailer's itinerary is extreme but not unusual; Updike, Roth, Bellow, Cheever, Pynchon, Heller, and even Ellison, in *Invisible Man* and in his long struggle to complete his second novel, show the same kind of experimental restlessness, a shift from realism to fable, allegory, and the play of language.

By the early 1970s, in the wake of the new feminism, new women writers were flourishing, bringing along rediscovered ancestors like Kate Chopin and Zora Neale Hurston. The postwar male dominance began to crumble in fiction as it did in society at large. But the novel itself was becoming less important, challenged first by journalism and the personal essay, then, during the explosions of the 1960s, by visual media that could better convey the color and cacophony of politics as theatre. Mailer's generation dreamed of writing the great American novel, but after 1970 this kind of talent was often directed toward moviemaking, starting with Martin Scorsese and his film-school contemporaries. As fiction became less central it grew more self-conscious. The protean transformations of Mailer, his ventures into journalism, coincided with the rise of postmodernism, as fiction lost confidence in its power to encompass the world and reach an audience through the written word. As reality itself turned less credible, realism gave way to magic realism and the comic-apocalyptic extravagance of black humor. With writers like Donald Barthelme, John Barth, and Robert Coover, fiction began probing its own techniques, raising questions about its ability to represent what was real. Soon more personal novelists like Philip Roth, who had arrived on the confessional wave of the 1960s, followed them into metafiction, exploring the interface between autobiography and fiction, confessional writing and fabulation. This dialectic between memory and invention itself grows out of the more interiorized approach of the novelists of the fifties, their fascination with the self and its projections, though which they filtered the social world around them. Roth himself came full circle—moving from the Jamesian realism of his early books and the confessional black humor of his post-*Portnoy* period to the metafictional play of his Zuckerman novels and the historically inflected realism of his books of the late 1990s, such as *American Pastoral, I Married a Communist,* and *The Human Stain.*

Whatever techniques they tried and discarded, the postwar novelists gave us a portrait of society by giving us portraits of themselves, struggling to maintain their precarious balance when the rules of life and art were being rewritten. These writers could be embarrassing about race, dreadful about women, monstrously self-absorbed, oblivious to urgent social problems that had engaged Depression writers, indifferent to politics yet all too entranced with the spectacle of cultural politics, especially in the 1960s when some of them stumbled while others came into their own. What might help account for their endurance, however, is their deep loyalty to art. Like the abstract painters who turned against the populism of mural art, the postwar writers consciously rebelled against their politically committed predecessors, cultivating psychological nuance and linguistic complexity over any social mission. Compared to writers of the thirties, whose work could be too spare and topical, too journalistic, and to many post-sixties writers, who were often seduced by cultural fashion, Bellow, O'Connor, Ellison, Malamud, Cheever, Updike, Baldwin, Mailer, and Roth were faithful to their aesthetic conscience, to the gospel according to James and Joyce, Kafka and Proust, even when the results showed up their own faults of craft or character. They remained loyal to the novel even as its boundaries blurred and its hold on readers diminished. Art may not have made them immortal, but it has given their performance a long and uncommonly interesting run.

WAR AND THE NOVEL: FROM WORLD
WAR II TO VIETNAM

E VEN MORE than World War I, in which American participation
had been brief and casualties relatively light, the Second World
War was a watershed, a turning point, in the social history of the
nation. In the second war there were five times as many American dead,
over half a million in a period of almost four years. This was a total war
effort that mobilized virtually every segment of American society. Men
and boys from sleepy towns in the Midwest, segregated farms and ham-
lets in the Deep South, and large ethnic enclaves in the North were
thrown together in a huge, highly organized fighting force and sent to the
bloody beaches and killing fields of France, Italy, North Africa, and especially the Pacific islands. On V-J Day in August 1945, America had
nearly twelve million men under arms; more than sixteen million had
served in the course of the war.

Novels written about the war invariably emphasize the shock of a new
kind of experience, the social and personal dislocation as well as the shock
of blood and carnage. They show how recruits were forced to adjust to the
army before they had to face the war itself. To many, the hierarchy and discipline of military life cut against the American grain. Individualism gave
way to a harsh, demanding group experience. The men they encountered
and the distant places they were sent catapulted them out of the life they
knew and thrust them into a larger world.

If these soldiers were transformed socially, exposed to other ways of life,
they were also influenced morally by being exposed to killing and dying at
an early age. In battle, young men in the prime of life, at their peak of
health and strength, were faced with danger and death at almost any
moment. The foxholes produced instinctive existentialists, young men
caught between adventure and dread who suddenly became aware of the
fragility of life and their own vulnerability.

The home front was almost as dramatically affected as the men who
went to war. Despite the new mobility made possible by the automobile,
despite the new mass culture of tabloids, newsreels, films, and radio,
despite the gradual migration from towns to cities, many Americans still

lived in isolated, relatively homogeneous communities, including those in the black and immigrant ghettos of large cities. Foreshadowing the new mobility of the postwar years, the war drew many women into the factories, blacks from the South to the war plants of Detroit, and showed other Americans a way of life they had barely imagined and might never otherwise have seen. It sent Japanese Americans from their homes to detention camps, in a perverse echo of the racism of America's foes. Forties films about small-town America, such as *Our Town, The Magnificent Ambersons, Shadow of a Doubt,* and *It's a Wonderful Life,* edged in darkness, were bittersweet elegies to an earlier way of life.

If the poverty of the war zone made men appreciate American abundance, the risk and excitement cut them loose from their solid moorings of class and morality. One of the first significant novels of World War II, John Horne Burns's *The Gallery* (1947), deals with the impact of life in wartime Naples and North Africa on an assortment of Americans who seem at times like innocents abroad confronting Mediterranean decadence, or small-town "grotesques" out of *Winesburg, Ohio,* at sea in a different world. On some, the effect is horrifying; on others, liberating. Of one Red Cross worker we're told, with transparent venom, "She'd never think of the word parasite in the future without modifying it by the adjective, Italian."

An American GI, however, drunk with Neapolitan sensuality at a performance of *La Bohème,* seems happy for the first time in his life: "What was there here in the sweetness of this reality that he'd missed out on in America?" Boozily, lyrically, he sets love and feeling against the power of commerce: "He saw for the first time in his life that the things which keep the world going are not to be bought or sold, that every flower grows out of decay, that for all the mud and grief there are precious things which make it worth while for us to leave our mothers' wombs." Here we feel the heavy hand of the author laying in his themes, as we do when so many of these characters come to a bad end.

If the war made individual Americans less insular and parochial, it also made American culture more cosmopolitan. Americans went abroad, as they had in 1917, but this time foreigners also came to us, as America became the refuge for a vast intellectual emigration that altered many of our arts and sciences. Just as Einstein and other Europeans transformed American physics, surrealists such as Matta, abstractionists like Josef Albers and Hans Hoffmann transformed American painting, helping to create the new abstract art through which New York would displace Paris as the world art capital.

Already in the 1930s, émigré filmmakers, though chafing under the constraints of the studio system, had begun to transform how American movies were made. Literary intellectuals helped spread the influence of Franz Kafka and other European moderns. Such political intellectuals as Hannah Arendt, along with widely read writers like Orwell and Koestler, developed theories of totalitarianism that contributed to postwar anti-Communism. Émigré psychoanalysts helped foster an inward turn that saw Americans shift from the social concerns of the Depression years to the therapeutic ideas of the postwar period.

The writers who drove ambulances in World War I, who fled to Paris for artistic and personal freedom during the 1920s, were disillusioned by the contrast between Wilsonian ideals and wartime brutality. They saw a nation that seemed largely unaffected by the war, a nation of hucksters and boosters dominated by small-town values and middle-class morality. The protagonist of Hemingway's "Soldier's Home" (in *In Our Time,* 1925) returns to a world of boys and girls courting, parents pressuring him to snap back to normal, to look for a job. Always out of step, he cannot talk about what he has gone through, cannot fall back on routines that have gone dead for him. He is far from rebellious; it is just that he cannot seem to make the effort:

Vaguely he wanted a girl but he did not want to have to work to get her. . . . He did not want to get into the intrigue and the politics. He did not want to have to do any courting. He did not want to tell any more lies. It wasn't worth it.

He did not want any consequences. He did not want any consequences ever again. He wanted to live along without consequences. Besides he did not really need a girl. The army had taught him that.

The numb repetition of small words and simple syntax reflects the state of mind of a man deadened by his experience, a man not understood by those around him. He is someone for whom the bright bustle of America, all this active willing and doing, has grown meaningless. Krebs he is called, for crabbed he is. "I don't love anybody," he finally blurts out to his pious, sentimental mother, only to retreat quickly from the flood of her tears. America was no place for those who, having seen the war, had seen through everything.

The suffering and endurance of ordinary Americans during the Depression made such a detached attitude untenable. When the money in Paris ran out, the expatriate writers came home physically; soon enough, they also tried to come home spiritually, though the results did not always feel authentic. Even those writers who had remained in the States, relishing the satiric barbs of H. L. Mencken and Sinclair Lewis, were propelled by the Depression toward journalistic curiosity, radical commitment, and gestures of solidarity with the poor and dispossessed. Hemingway himself signaled his new commitment by involving himself publicly with the cause of the Spanish republic, and having a dying Harry Morgan, his rum-running hero of *To Have and Have Not* (1937), spit out at the end, "No man alone now . . . a man alone ain't got no bloody fucking chance."

One result of this change was to make American literature more insular again, more focused on the struggle for survival at home, and less bleakly pessimistic. The cause of the common man, the bright revolutionary future, made sophistication and formalism seem passé, self-indulgent, and this gave naturalism, moribund since Dreiser's prime, a new lease on life. A handful of writers, such as Nathanael West, preserved the mocking spirit of the twenties but found few readers. Henry Miller, who remained abroad, was as wildly funny in his affirmations as West was in his nega-tions, but the single-minded cry of the flesh kept his work apart from pro-letarian pieties, as it kept it from publication in this country. Another interesting exception, William Saroyan, also wrapped his populism in a prickly individualism. Like Miller he was a kind of anarchist, rejecting the current political formulas for his own common-man vision.

The war put an end to these social commitments and antisocial adven-tures as effectively as it ended the Depression itself. Taking its cue from the cherished myths of the thirties, the war novel substituted the common sol-dier, the ordinary grunt, for the common man, and put the hiking army, wallowing in mud, in place of the bonus marcher, the hobo, the unem-ployed drifter, the migrating family. Reporters such as Ernie Pyle, cartoon-ists like Bill Mauldin, and photojournalists such as Robert Capa and Margaret Bourke-White became the new laureates of the American experi-ence, lending a gritty, heroic cast to the tribulations of the common man.

The war also contributed to the masculinization of American writing. It gave a central place to the Hemingway themes of courage and risk in situa-tions of testing and crisis. In the aftermath of the war, a much more conser-vative view of gender roles became dominant. Depression unemployment often made women the economic and emotional mainstay of their family, and wartime employment brought them into the factories, mills, and war industries. The return of the fighting men, though, left little room for Rosie the Riveter, and the migration to the suburbs kept women domestic as they raised increasing numbers of children. Gender stereotypes returned with a vengeance, replacing the more liberated images of women that had developed between the wars, as Betty Friedan showed in *The Feminine Mystique* (1963). In turn, the major figures in postwar fiction for more than two decades were nearly all male, with rare exceptions, such as Flannery O'Connor, Carson McCullers, and Eudora Welty in the South; the brilliant and brittle Mary McCarthy, who emerged from the bosom of the New York intellectuals; *New Yorker* writers like Jean Stafford, Hortense Calisher, and Shirley Jackson; and Grace Paley, writing in a woman's voice of rare subtlety and delicacy among American Jewish writers. It was not until the sixties sparked a revival of feminism that women reclaimed their vital position in the American novel.

The war also marked a closure for many literary careers. We can scarcely understand postwar fiction without seeing how few writers from the prewar years actually survived the war itself. Some died literally, and others simply lost their creative edge in the changed conditions of the postwar world. West and Fitzgerald died on successive days in 1940, Sherwood Anderson in 1941 (along with Joyce and Virginia Woolf, whose greatest influence in America was yet to come), Dreiser in 1945, Gertrude Stein in 1946, and Willa Cather in 1947. Most of the proletarian writers disappeared after one or two books, some to Hollywood or *Time* magazine, which both remained sympathetic to social melodrama, others into children's writing, historical fiction, or pulp fiction. The rise of McCarthyism made their lot even more untenable.

There was no successor to Henry Roth's *Call It Sleep* – Roth's next novel, really a free-form memoir, would not begin to appear for sixty years – to Daniel Fuchs's Williamsburg novels, to Robert Cantwell's *The Land of Plenty* or Jack Conroy's *The Disinherited*. Committed social novelists who remained prolific were unable to regain the élan of their best work. Steinbeck would never again write anything to match the urgency of *In Dubious Battle* (1936) and *The Grapes of Wrath* (1939); James T. Farrell and John Dos Passos would never equal the social grasp and personal intensity of their Depression trilogies, *Studs Lonigan* (1932–35) and *U.S.A.* (1930–36). Their naturalist methods, which required an immense piling up of realistic details, and a minute verisimilitude, seemed unable to encompass the complexities and absurdities, to say nothing of the social changes, of the postwar world. Along with the expansive, egocentric Thomas Wolfe, who had died prematurely in 1938, their impact on the wartime generation remained great.

Other naturalists lost touch with America by leaving it behind. Living in Europe in the late forties and fifties, Richard Wright remained essentially the author of *Native Son* (1940) and *Black Boy* (1945). His later writing, influenced by European existentialism, became more abstract and lost touch with home – and with his own talent. (The same fate would befall James Baldwin after 1963.) Only the ravages of age or alcoholism and the fragility of genius could begin to explain the decline of the greatest writers of the interwar years, Hemingway and Faulkner, which set in just as their earlier work was gaining them readers, fame, and increasing literary influence. Hemingway's important work ended with his last great stories in 1939 and *For Whom the Bell Tolls* in 1940, though *The Old Man and the Sea* and *A Moveable Feast* would show something of the old hard brilliance.

Faulkner last achieved real power with *The Hamlet* in 1940 and *Go Down, Moses* in 1942, just before he left once more for Hollywood to earn his bread. Most of his later books are sequels that fill in details of the Yoknapatawpha County saga. Despite the Nobel prize that reached them too late, as it eventually reached T. S. Eliot and even Steinbeck, neither Hemingway nor Faulkner did major work on the postwar scene, when young writers revered them, along with Fitzgerald, as the very definition of the modern American novelist.

Finally, the novelists of manners, who had prospered as a conservative counterweight to the radical writers of the Depression, had great difficulty sustaining themselves as postwar writers – outside the best-seller market, where their work continued to thrive. J. P. Marquand, James Gould Cozzens, John O'Hara, John Cheever, and Louis Auchincloss were the diminished heirs to what once had been a major tradition in American fiction. They were the writers from New England and the Northeast who closely documented the lives of the upper and professional classes. In the hands of Henry James and Edith Wharton, this WASP novel of manners was still rooted in the New England moral tradition and the Hawthornean fable. It had not yet devolved into a mere social record or documentation of the status anxieties and sexual or professional problems of a declining elite. Their only real postwar successor was John Updike, a great admirer of Cheever, though he came from a much humbler Pennsylvania background. His brilliant, dexterous prose, scrupulous realism, and bold focus on sex, marriage, and family life gave the novel of manners a different kind of vitality.

By the 1930s, when O'Hara published *Appointment in Samarra* (1934) and *Butterfield 8* (1935), and Marquand, fresh from his success with a Japanese detective, Mr. Moto, turned to serious social comedy with *The Late George Apley* (1937) and *Wickford Point* (1939), American writing was already turning more ethnic and pluralist. John Cheever's published journals refer frequently to the novels of Saul Bellow, for Cheever feels their colloquial and demotic energy eludes him. Writers from the small towns and larger cities of the Midwest had already staked a major claim to national attention in the twenties. Now Southern writers, Jewish writers, and black writers were finding their voice, as they increasingly would after the war. The Depression had weakened the social position of the upper classes and redirected literary attention to the marginal and the dispossessed, so that even a writer as critical of the rich as Fitzgerald was attacked by the literary left and neglected by the magazines that were once so eager to publish his work.

O'Hara, for example, had gone to school with both Hemingway and Fitzgerald, emulating one for his hard-boiled style, built on spare but pregnant dialogue, the other for his gift of social observation. He was more the straight reporter than either of them, however. He shared Fitzgerald's fascination with success but showed little of Fitzgerald's strong emotional identification with his characters. He had very little interest in psychology, not much more in advanced fictional technique, but an insatiable appetite for social and sexual detail. His brief, anecdotal, understated stories were almost the definition of *New Yorker* fiction in the thirties and forties, when they were praised by Lionel Trilling, for their "exacerbated social awareness." But after the war, his novels, once far more disciplined, swelled into an unselective, unrefined record of the material culture of the upper middle class, and critics found it harder to take him seriously.

Ironically, the whole phenomenon of a declining gentry fallen on hard times would gradually lose its basis in social reality during the postwar economic boom, when even the old rich became richer. Yet these writers, caught in a narrowly realist aesthetic, were increasingly trapped in minute social documentation of a numbing and trivializing sort at a time when manners themselves became less important. Affluence was the great economic surprise of the postwar era, since many had predicted that a severe contraction, perhaps even a return of the Depression, would follow the end of war production and the shift to a peacetime economy. Instead, Americans went on an economic binge, stimulated by the savings that had accumulated during wartime and the vast consumer demand that had been pent up since the onset of the Depression. The birth rate soared along with the boom in consumption.

General Motors' immensely popular Futurama exhibit at the 1939 World's Fair was a promise of abundance whose fulfillment was cruelly postponed by the war, then achieved beyond our wildest dreams. (Though many were incredulous, it boldly predicted that there would be a staggering 38 million cars on American roads by 1960. There were actually 74 million.) The show confidently anticipated technological triumphs that were achieved only through wartime military research and were later adapted to peacetime use. Scientific advances ranged from telecommunications and jet propulsion to atomic power and antibiotics. Meanwhile, the economies of Europe and much of Asia were shattered by the war, making the United States the supplier and producer for the whole international system. As Godfrey Hodgson wrote in *America in Our Time,*

In 1945, the United States was bulging with an abundance of every resource that held the key to power in the modern world: with land, food, power, raw materials, industrial plant, monetary reserves, scientific talent, and trained manpower. It was in the war years that the United States shot ahead of all its rivals economically. In four years, national income, national wealth, and industrial production all doubled or more than doubled. . .

In 1947, with postwar recovery under way everywhere, the United States produced about one half of the world's manufactures: 57 per cent of its steel, 43 per cent of its electricity, 62 per cent of its oil. It owned three quarters of the world's automobiles and was improving on that show by manufacturing well over 80 per cent of the new cars built in the world that year. The American lead was greatest in precisely those industries which contributed to the power to wage modern war: aviation, chemical engineering, electronics.

If the American economy provided a basis for world power, it also made possible a consumer society and a new leisure culture that radically altered American life, and this was reflected in American literature and art. Very few postwar novelists could sustain the large-scale social visions of a Dreiser or a Faulkner. *Freud* replaced *Marx* as a catchword not only for writers and intellectuals but for a self-seeking new middle class. In a culture of affluence, in which more and more people were entering the middle class, therapeutic ideas gradually took the place of class consciousness. As American society turned inward, toward the nuclear family and the house in the suburbs, American novels also turned inward, focusing more on private life and individual experience. Novels grew shorter and avoided modernist experiments with time, consciousness, and narrative fragmentation.

A handful of thirties writers, such as Henry Roth, William Faulkner, and Nathanael West, had written their books under the immediate impact of *Ulysses* and *The Waste Land,* as well as the French surrealists and the German expressionists. Henry Miller had been inspired by writers as different as Whitman, Rimbaud, and Céline. The major influence on postwar fiction, however, was Henry James, whose work was just then being revived. James was appreciated less for his ambitious social canvas or his attention to manners than for his formal rigor and his minutely detailed aesthetic and psychological discriminations.

The war novel was the major exception to this Jamesian wave, with its pull toward analysis, reflection, and formal control. If the James revival was a reaction against the proletarian excesses of the thirties and the shocking facts of the war, the war novelists looked back unashamedly to different influences: the social outlook and conservative technique of Theodore Dreiser, John Dos Passos, and James T. Farrell; the autobiographical novels of Thomas Wolfe; and the masculine crucible of Hemingway and other novelists of the previous war. Without the example of such books as *In Our Time, A Farewell to Arms, The Enormous Room,* and *Three Soldiers,* but also of such Depression novels as *Studs Lonigan* and *U.S.A.,* the major novels of the Second World War would be unimaginable. In some essential ways, the war novel was a brilliant offshoot of Depression writing, the last big explosion of naturalism in American fiction.

Unlike popular works of novelized history (like Herman Wouk's *The Winds of War*), which tried to swallow the war whole in one episodic piece of fiction, most serious novels of World War II, even very long ones, dealt with only a handful of incidents, a small corner of the conflict, usually one the writer himself had witnessed. Harry Brown's *A Walk in the Sun* (1944), which became famous for the movie version directed by Lewis Milestone, was a tour de force in the style of *The Red Badge of Courage* that described a grisly day in the campaign to establish a beachhead in Italy. Both Norman Mailer's *The Naked and the Dead* (1948) and James Jones's *The Thin Red Line* (1962) were about the invasion and conquest of a single Japanese-held Pacific island. Yet in unfolding a single action, from the anxieties of landing through all the stages of combat, each novelist managed to portray the whole shape of the war.

But other major novels scarcely dealt with combat at all. Jones's *From Here to Eternity* (1951), still the best of all the novels about the Second World War, is set within the regular army in Hawaii in the months leading up to Pearl Harbor, while Cozzens's *Guard of Honor* (1948) is built around a racial incident at an air force training base in Florida. Mailer, Jones, and Cozzens use flashbacks to fill in the civilian lives of the men in uniform. Circumscribed by the classical unities of time, space, and action, their big novels become microcosms not only of the war but of a larger American society in transition. At its best, the war novel was not simply about the conflict, graphic as it was, but about much of the world that preceded and would follow this war.

Prewar writers, including Michael Gold, Roth, Steinbeck, Wright, and Faulkner, had turned the spotlight on ethnic and regional characters; war writers brought these types together in close quarters under the pressure of extreme conditions, as the war itself had done. Proletarian writers had focused on class conflict in American society; they had drawn special attention to the drifters, the lumpen, the dispossessed of the Depression years, or they had written alarming fables about the dangers of Fascism. War novelists transposed these very themes onto the authoritarian hierarchy of the army. The dictators and plutocrats of Depression fiction were now obtuse, capricious officers; the common man riding the freights became the common soldier hiking through the jungle mud.

Some of the outstanding war novels, such as *The Naked and the Dead,* were actually political novels, novels of ideas. They were written not in the trenches but during the sobering transition between war and peace, between hot war and the cold war. They reflected the writers' fear that victory over Fascism abroad had been purchased at the cost of intolerance and regimentation at home. These war novelists' nightmare was a world threatened not by foreign tyrants and obvious villains but by large, impersonal social organizations. Thus novels like *The Naked and the Dead* led directly to the widely read social criticism of such men as David Riesman (*The Lonely Crowd*), William H. Whyte, Jr. (*The Organization Man*), C. Wright Mills (*Whyte Collar, The Power Elite*), and Vance Packard *(The Hidden Persuaders, The Waste Makers, The Status Seekers).*

American society had been fragmented by the Depression, which exacerbated class consciousness and widened the chasm between the haves and the have-nots. Attacks on the rich were staples of the 1930s, not only in left-wing polemics but in such social satires as Marquand's *The Late George Apley,* screwball comedies like *My Man Godfrey* and *Easy Living,* and congressional investigations into arms profiteering. The pressure to win the war overrode these social divisions, however, as it overcame the Depression itself. For the duration of the war, a sense of unified purpose linked workers and businessmen, Communists and capitalists, farmers and city dwellers, women in factories and men in uniform. To win the war, unions agreed not to strike, businesses accepted price controls, minorities agreed to mute their grievances.

By the end of the war, this artificial unity had turned America into a more patriotic, less tolerant place, more devoted to organizational values and social conformity, more homogeneous in its stated ideals. This helped produce a malaise, an uneasiness that was reflected in the best novels, the darkest films and plays. Since nearly all the war novels were written *after* the war, the writers projected their sense of the postwar world back onto the war, their anger at bureaucracy onto the army, their new fears of nuclear annihilation onto earlier scenes of mortal combat. For all their surface realistic grit, the best war novels were really parables about American life.

Jones's *The Thin Red Line,* a remarkable achievement for a combat novel, shows how a work of limited scope could encompass a large part of the war. Its subject, the invasion and conquest of Guadalcanal in 1942, was a turning point in the morale of Americans in the Pacific, the first offensive action after Pearl Harbor and the first American victory in the Pacific theater. It begins with the landing of men, including some longtime regular soldiers, who have never been in combat, and takes us through every stage of fear, disbelief, exhaustion, camaraderie, battle-tested numbness, injury, unheroic victory, and removal from the war. In Jones's trilogy, the novel is flanked by two books that deal with the prewar military (*From Here to Eternity*) and the postcombat fate of wounded men in a military hospital back home (*Whistle*, 1978).

The last of these, *Whistle*, was a tired novel, written when Jones was already seriously ill, and published posthumously; it reflected the much more downbeat post-Vietnam atmosphere of the 1970s. Full of illness and injury, including the physical and psychological wounds that had lifted the author himself out of combat 35 years earlier, it portrays the war and the larger world from the point of view of the hospital, another "enormous room" like e.e. cummings's World War I detention camp. The war still unfolding far away seems remote and distant but also, in the injuries the men have suffered, an ever-present physical intrusion. The book's links were not with combat stories but with such grim postwar rehabilitation films about damaged human beings as *The Best Years of Our Lives* (1946) and *The Men* (1950), as well as their successors of the 1970s, such as Hal Ashby's *Coming Home*, which turned the spotlight on Vietnam veterans just as Jones's last novel was being written.

The first two novels of Jones's trilogy, *From Here to Eternity* and *The Thin Red Line*, however, are among the most impressive works of American realism. Jones's main rival as a war novelist, Norman Mailer, paid grudging tribute to both books in essays sharply attacking most of his other rivals. In *Advertisements for Myself*, he described Jones as "the only one of my contemporaries who I felt had more talent than myself," called *Eternity* "the best American novel since the war," and said later (in *Cannibals and Christians*) that *The Thin Red Line* could be used as a training manual for an infantry campaign. Perhaps Mailer meant to underline the books' limitations, yet both novels do convey an overpowering sense of actuality.

Though it is as deftly structured as a five-act drama, *From Here to Eternity* unfolds incrementally in the most unforced manner imaginable. Set in and around the Schofield Barracks near Honolulu, where Jones himself had served, the novel creates characters who seem fully alive and a setting that feels like an authentic world. The thirty-year-men we see at Schofield, and later in the concentration camp-like stockade, are refugees from an economically depressed, socially constricted small-town America, as Jones himself had once been. "Most of them had bummed around the country at least once, before they finally enlisted," says Jones. They were "jerked loose from ties by the Depression and set to a drifting that had ended finally in the Army as the last port of call."

Hewing not only to the literary technique but to the social outlook of the 1930s, Jones gives us an outsider's perspective, a grunt's-eye view of the army in *From Here to Eternity,* then of the war itself in *The Thin Red Line.* His achingly proud, taciturn hero, Robert E. Lee Prewitt, a coal miner's son from Harlan County, is a figure out of the proletarian novel, like his mentor in the stockade, Jack Malloy, a veteran of the old Industrial Workers of the World (IWW), who preaches passive resistance. Where the hero of proletarian fiction is usually initiated by some hardened Communist into an understanding of the class struggle, however, Prewitt, as his name indicates, is more of a romantic rebel, doomed, self-destructive, caught between his love of the army and his inability to accept its harsh, often unfair discipline, a Kid Galahad living by his own stubborn code of honor. In his boxing, which he abandons after blinding a man, and his near-magical bugling, which is snatched away from him by officers trying to control or break him, Prewitt is also a sentimental portrait of the artist as the sort of ornery individualist whom no mass organization — and few proletarian novels — could easily accommodate.

Initially a misfit, Prewitt eventually becomes too much the white knight, the prickly hero incapable of compromise. His unbending code of morality makes trouble for others, not just for himself. This stern behavior, which he often regrets, leads to catastrophe in his and other people's lives, including Bloom's suicide, Maggio's imprisonment, and finally his own death. He spoils everyone's lax tolerance for the way things are. There is a laconic stoicism and youthful integrity that make him a figure out of Hemingway — the writer who, along with Stephen Crane, lies across the path of every modern war novelist. Like Mailer, Jones builds on Hemingway's feeling for extreme situations. He explores the special intimacy that develops among men separated from women even as he exposes the corruption of the institutions that bring these men together. Jones's other hero, Sgt. Warden, as ornery as Prewitt, refuses to accept a commission, though it spoils his love affair with his captain's wife.

Though he deals with the regular army, Jones takes a jaundiced, outsider's view of the military character. Officers are nearly always assholes in Jones's novels: petty, ambitious, time-serving careerists who put their own interests first. Their methods parallel those of the bosses and politicians in the civilian world: they exercise power selfishly, arbitrarily, or sadistically. The brutalities of the stockade, as overseen by small-time fascists like Fatso Judson, come more from the chain-gang movies of the 1930s than from the author's insight into Nazi-like violence. The stockade becomes a metaphor for the mass organization's efforts to stamp out resistance and individual identity. Another parable about totalitarianism, *1984,* had been published only a year or two before Jones's novel appeared; Hannah Arendt's book, *The Origins of Totalitarianism,* also came out in 1951. As the Cold War deepened, the whole subject was very much in the air.

Jones's evocations of sadistic brutality bring to mind the striking parallels between *From Here to Eternity* and Mailer's *The Naked and the Dead*. Like Jones, Mailer brought to the army an outsider's viewpoint, in his case that of the middle-class Jew, the Harvard man, the aspiring young literary intellectual. He had joined the army not to fight Fascism (like some of the left-wing writers) or to exit the Depression (like Jones and his characters) but to write the great American novel, deliberately choosing the Pacific theater to avoid the cultural complications of a European setting.

Unlike Jones, though, Mailer was fascinated by everything in his Texas outfit that was not himself — not Jewish, not Ivy League, not liberal or intellectual. He even developed an occasional Texas drawl in imitation of the rednecks who ragged him. His liberal surrogate, the Harvard-educated Lt. Hearn, comes off as honorable but also weak and vacillating. In his clumsy, unbending resistance to evil, he is almost as self-destructive as Prewitt, but his death at the hands of the two fascist types, Gen. Cummings and Sgt. Croft, carries little of the tragic poignance that echoes lyrically through Jones's handling of Prewitt. Mailer's two Jews, Goldstein and Roth, are almost anti-Semitic caricatures of sensitive weaklings, too eager for acceptance, as uneasy in their own skin as in a man's army.

Mailer's real equivalent for Prewitt was his lower-class soldier parallel to Hearn, a tough anarchist named Red Valsen, yet another character straight out of the novels of the thirties. He can still sing "Brother, Can You Spare a Dime?" and he believes "they ain't a general in the world is any good. They're all sonsofbitches." The "Time Machine" chapter that fills in his background is a pastiche out of proletarian fiction and *Studs Lonigan,* a book that influenced not only Mailer's style but also his whole sense of men in groups. (Mailer once described the book as "the best single literary experience I had had.") At the end, in a neat symmetry, Valsen is humiliated by Croft just as Hearn had been humbled by Cummings: this is Mailer's sour epitaph for the humane but naïve liberalism of the Depression era.

In an ironic twist, Cummings and Croft, the figures who represent power rather than conscience, are also confounded. Cummings's chessboard strategy proves as pointless as Croft's superhuman, Ahab-like drive to conquer Mt. Anaka. All their effort, all their brutish cunning, in the end are useless. Instead, the island campaign is won quite accidentally by the doltish Dalleson, a cautious, blundering fool. In tune with the existentialism of the late forties, which had itself been generated by the violence and extremity of war, Mailer's ironic conclusion deflates heroic designs and points to the forces of history and chance over which people have no control. As the novel ends, brilliantly but anticlimactically, a postwar sense of the absurd displaces the prewar social consciousness.

Mailer himself saw very little of the war: as the injured Jones left the war early, Mailer, finishing at Harvard, came to it quite late, while the campaign for the Philippines was being waged and won in 1945. Like many of his characters, Jones joined the army before the war as a way of escaping not just the Depression but the responsibilities of civilian life. "The Jones man is essentially a vagrant," wrote Wilfrid Sheed, a little too sardonically in 1967, "which means that his life has been a compound of freedom and feckless dependency. The army is the ideal nest for him, a place where he can wave his finger at authority and lean on it at the same time."

Jones saw the army and the war from the viewpoint of the thirty-year man, the professional soldier but also a loner who is contemptuous of draftees and officers alike. Mailer, on the other hand, already the political novelist, was fascinated by those who have the power of decision and command. Jones's officers are time-serving careerists and opportunists, organization men stroking their own vanity. The contemptible Capt. Holmes, who gave his wife gonorrhea within months of their marriage, becomes the army's instrument for trying to "break" Prewitt. Like Cummings in *The Naked and the Dead,* he tries to govern by instilling fear and leveling resistance. To him, Prewitt is a pocket of anarchic individualism, a challenge to his power and a passport to his next promotion. Both Prewitt and Mailer's Red Valsen are holdovers from the rural-proletarian thirties, the good soldiers allergic to the Organization, incapable of simply getting along.

Mailer's Cummings, on the other hand, is the grand strategist, the philosophical-minded officer schooled on Carlyle, Nietzsche, and Spengler who sees men as the intractable raw material for his larger designs. He first takes Hearn as his audience, his accomplice, his protégé, only to turn on him (when he resists) with all the venom of a spurned lover. This part of the book, a psychosexual novel of ideas, is a crude rehearsal for Mailer's later fictions about ego, power, and dominance. (Cummings is Mailer's Citizen Kane, as Kane himself was Orson Welles's prototype for his many later versions of overweening power and ego. In a beautiful twist, Welles would play General Dreedle, Joseph Heller's send-up of Cummings, in Mike Nichols's tamely respectful film version of *Catch-22.*)

With its scheming general and its representative platoon stocked with every regional and religious stereotype, the first part of *The Naked and the Dead,* like so many war movies, mirrors the Popular Front fiction and drama of the late thirties. Its "Time Machine" flashbacks are borrowed from the biographical interludes of Dos Passos's *U.S.A.* The novel rises to real distinction only in the latter half, the gripping account of the long patrol dominated by Sgt. Croft, the best character in the book, a purely instinctive, almost animal version of the cerebral Cummings. Here Mailer's interest shifts to the physical and mental testing of men under stress, driven beyond the limits of exhaustion by an obsessive figure. The sensory and visceral details of this part of the story would make it the master text for later writers dealing with jungle warfare, especially the Vietnam War novelists. (Its effect can still be felt, for example, in the opening chapters of Tim O'Brien's *Going After Cacciato* [1978], easily the best of the Vietnam novels.)

Here finally, in this test of endurance, Mailer's ethnic and regional stereotypes come to life as they are cruelly pressed by a single man's will. Mailer's formal sympathies are with the ordinary men but his inner attraction draws him to the Nietzschean overreacher, the kind of character who would help him find his real strength as a writer.

Thus, Mailer and Jones wrote the same novel from opposite points of view. Jones remained the thirties anarchist whose hatred of the organization would take on a new meaning in the Organization Man world of the 1950s, when the social rebel of the prewar years would become the prickly nonconformist of such works as *The Catcher in the Rye* and *On the Road*. Mailer, despite his use of the trappings of the social novel in *The Naked and the Dead*, was already the postwar Freudian and existentialist, more interested in power than in justice, drawn to instinct and will rather than social improvement. In his later fiction and journalism, however, he went on to do some of the best political writing of the postwar era, exploring the erotic rather than the institutional dimensions of power. Jones, on the other hand, like a true thirty-year man, was incapable of adjusting his literary lens to civilian life, though he did write one strong, shapeless, underrated novel, *Go to the Widowmaker* (1967), set largely in the Caribbean, an autobiographical work about masculinity and sexuality perhaps too reminiscent of both Hemingway and Mailer.

Jones's best book after *From Here to Eternity* was his only combat novel, *The Thin Red Line* (1962), essentially a tighter, more disciplined rejoinder to *The Naked and the Dead*. Compared to Jones's limpid and authoritative treatment of the island campaign, with its vivid sense of actuality, *The Naked and the Dead* was the most literary of all war novels; it echoed a score of the best modern writers. Mailer's stereotypes include the vicious sergeant, the college-educated lieutenant, the pompous general, the cringing Jews, the beefy farmboy, the lascivious Southern redneck, the guilt-ridden Irishman, the frightened Mexican, and so on. Filling in their backgrounds clumsily with "Time Machine" chapters, he imitates overripe Southern writing for the redneck Wilson, F. Scott Fitzgerald for the WASP

Hearn, Farrell for the Irishman Gallagher, proletarian fiction for the drifter Valsen. But this is only the beginning of Mailer's anthology of literary echoes: Hearn's sudden death comes from E. M. Forster, Croft's obsession with Mt. Anaka mingles Shelley's "Mont Blanc" with *Moby-Dick,* Martinez kills a Japanese soldier in a scene out of *Man's Fate,* the fetid jungle atmosphere reminds us of *Heart of Darkness,* Wilson's wounded body is borne along and swept away like Addie's corpse in *As I Lay Dying,* Roth's masochistic sense of humiliation is pure Dostoyevsky, Cummings's reflections on war and history echo *War and Peace* – the list could go on. These numerous and classy literary debts, along with the clumsy, mechanical structure of the book as a whole, help explain why many readers have felt some inauthenticity about *The Naked and the Dead,* though it was surely a tour de force for a 25-year-old writer.

Jones's response to Mailer in *The Thin Red Line* is to tell the same story straight, reducing it to the barest essentials. More interested in the psychology of the group than in the individual soldier, he mobilizes a huge cast of characters, including most of the key figures of *From Here to Eternity,* and, in a strange move, gives them all monosyllabic names, paring their personalities down to a few key traits. Thus, Prewitt becomes Witt, Warden becomes "mad" Welsh, and Stark becomes Strange, all mere kernels of the people they once were. Moreover, he ruthlessly purges the Kid Galahad romanticism that had surrounded Prewitt's rebellion and death, his love affair with Lorene, the martyrdom of Maggio in the stockade, the affair between Warden and Karen Holmes. Instead, he substitutes an emphasis on courage and fear, the crushing fear of men new to combat, and, most of all, the utter cowardice of a new, largely autobiographical character, Fife, whose experiences and reactions closely follow the author's own.

Jones's unheroic, often comic view of war and violence partly reflects the period when it was written: the late fifties and early sixties, exactly the time of *Catch-22.* (Jones and Heller had been in a writing class together shortly after the war.) The absurdism of both books, though – far more marked in Heller's – could already be found in the last part of *The Naked and the Dead.* An existential view of war informs Mailer's novel and, more obliquely, creates a feeling of bottomless sadness and futility just beneath the lyrical glow of *From Here to Eternity.* It is at the core of Harry Brown's short novel *A Walk in the Sun,* published before the end of the war: a sense that the conditions of combat, the physical trials, the arbitrariness of instant death, opened up a moral and metaphysical abyss that was as ridiculous as it was tragic, as ironic as it was horrific. This kind of black humor had been a strong presence in war novels going back to Stephen Crane, Jaroslav Hašek's *The Good Soldier Schweik,* and, above all, Céline's

Journey to the End of Night, with its bitter, mocking sarcasm, a tradition Heller would bring to a kind of apotheosis. The interminably dying Wilson, carried along like some intolerable human burden, was but one thread of Mailer's novel; the dying Snowden became the core of *Catch-22,* an image not to be set aside, a continuous reminder of the softness of mere flesh, the fragility of human life.

By the time *The Thin Red Line* appeared in 1962, Heller's book made it look tame. Like Heller, Jones had the notion of writing a "comic combat novel," and many early scenes, such as Bead's gruesome struggle with a Japanese soldier who comes at him when he is emptying his bowels, are bizarre set pieces, strange, unexpected events demonstrating the absurdity of war. At odd moments, the stringent naturalism of Jones's novel seems more like the magic realism of sixties writers like Pynchon and Vonnegut than the verisimilitude of Theodore Dreiser. These later writers, in line with the mocking spirit of the 1960s, belong to a long antiheroic tradition that goes back to Shakespeare's Falstaff, to the Battle of Waterloo as seen in Stendhal's *Charterhouse of Parma,* and to the raw recruits of *The Red Badge of Courage.* This is essentially a comic tradition, though it evokes a disrupted, endangered, and topsy-turvy world. In other war fiction of the 1960s, we find atrocity (the bombing of Dresden in Kurt Vonnegut, Jr.'s *Slaughterhouse-Five*), contingency (the London blitz in Thomas Pynchon's *Gravity's Rainbow*), absurdity (everywhere in Joseph Heller's *Catch-22*), moral ambiguity (Vonnegut's *Mother Night*), and paranoia (in all of the above).

Jones's book is less stylized than any of these, yet odd, unheroic things keep happening, especially in the early stages of the campaign, when the men are going through their clumsy, intense, fantastic rites of passage. The novel turns more conventional as it goes on – it becomes almost straight and documentary – but it never falls back upon the old romantic idea of war. We see that tactics and strategy still matter, as in the old war fiction, that even terrified men, turned numb to fear, can stumble into amazing feats, but also that those who survive come out not as heroes – their heroism is always either savage, unthinking, or quite accidental – but simply as changed men. The crucible of combat has made them different, besides showing them stark, unforgettable things about who and what they are.

Like the war novels of Stendhal, Stephen Crane, and Hemingway, Jones's *The Thin Red Line* is finally a bildungsroman, the tale of how a raw youth all too quickly becomes a man. But by making this a collective story – the story not of a tragic Prewitt but merely of Fife, Bead, Doll, and other truncated characters – and stressing their fear and inexperience, by making the officers such knaves and fools, Jones undercuts all patriotic resonance and conventional machismo. Other combat novels are more harshly antiheroic, but none conveys so well the ordinariness of men in extraordinary situations.

Knowing something about Jones's meager war record, his success in getting *out* of the war, Hemingway had angrily rejected *From Here to Eternity,* much as he turned on all the writers who worshiped and threatened to overtake him. (Jones was the last discovery of Hemingway's own editor at Scribner's, Maxwell Perkins.) Had Hemingway lived to read *The Thin Red Line,* it would surely have confirmed his feeling that Jones was cowardly and neurotic, a recalcitrant outsider to the combat he described. "I spotted him for a psycho and not a real soldier," he wrote to Scribner's in 1951. By 1962, though, Jones was in close touch with the insecure feelings that an earlier Hemingway, free of bluster, had helped him understand. In *The Thin Red Line,* he focused not on the quixotic integrity of a Prewitt but the smell of fear, the horrified sense of disbelief, of smaller characters like Fife and Bead. This does not keep them from becoming swaggering brawlers when they grow inured to battle.

Bead is vetted into combat in the most ridiculous way imaginable, when the Japanese soldier comes at him as he is taking a crap. Clumsily, unheroically, almost involuntarily, he nearly beats the man to death before bayoneting and shooting him, all the while trying to keep his pants on. "My god," he thinks, "how much killing did the damned fool require? Bead had beaten him, kicked him, choked him, clawed him, bayoneted him, shot him. He had a sudden frantic vision of himself, by rights the victor, doomed forever to kill perpetually the same single Japanese." He kills the man clumsily out of a sheer savage reflex of survival, as Jones himself had once done at a similar moment. When he must return to the corpse to look for his glasses, the scene modulates from horrific comedy to existential absurdity:

The faceless – almost headless – corpse with its bloody, cut fingers and the mangled hole in its chest, so short a time ago a living, breathing man, made him so dizzy in the stomach that he thought he might faint. . . . Bead wanted to turn and run. He could not escape a feeling that, especially now, after he'd both looked and touched, some agent of retribution would try to hold him responsible. He wanted to beg the man's forgiveness in the hope of forestalling responsibility. . . . Suddenly Bead had a mental picture of them both with positions reversed: of himself lying there and feeling that blade plunge through his chest; of himself watching that rifle-butt descend upon his face, with the final fire-exploding end. It made him so weak that he had to sit down. . . . Bead saw himself spitted through the soft of the shoulder, head on, that crude blade descending into the soft dark of his chest cavity. He could not believe it.

This passage, with its sense of vertigo and horror, its involuntary empathy, is typical of the serious combat novel, and it makes *The Thin Red Line* especially fascinating as a transitional work, a book anchored half in the documentary spirit of the late forties, half in the surreal climate of the early sixties. Beginning with a meticulous naturalism, the report of a wild and dangerous adventure, these lines modulate into metaphysical irony, a sense of utter disbelief, suggesting that such matters of life and death could not be encompassed by any documentary approach. Along with war novels, works like Malraux's *Man's Fate* had highlighted the sense of fleshy human vulnerability that also would prove crucial to *Catch-22*. (Closer to home, a spirit of grotesque comedy, complete with gothic touches, was an important part of the work of such earlier American naturalists as Stephen Crane and Frank Norris.)

Thus, the war novel, which seemed at first to look backward toward the social fiction of the Depression, also looked forward to the black humor, the anguished sense of alienation of the postwar years. If Mailer and Jones, in their first novels, had looked at the army as the Organization, a possible harbinger of postwar Fascism, soon, thanks to the postwar economic boom, the regimental spirit they feared would emerge in a much blander yet more pervasive fashion. A new sense of community had come out of the war. No doubt it made many Americans feel good to pull together, but to the social critics and filmmakers of the fifties it seemed intolerant, conformist, an "invasion of the body snatchers," an enforced Americanism rooted in the homogeneity of the small towns and new suburbs. The new comic and existential novels about World War II that began appearing in the late fifties, such as Thomas Berger's *Crazy in Berlin* (1958), Heller's *Catch-22* (1961), and Vonnegut's *Mother Night* (1962), along with *The Thin Red Line,* were reactions to that peculiar mixture of social intolerance, boosterish optimism, and metaphysical angst that marks the late fifties.

Some of the changes in how writers saw World War II were based on simple distance and the passage of time. As the impact of the war faded, including the immediate feeling of joy and relief, the deeper horror of the war's aftermath began to seep in: the news of the Holocaust, the new technology of mass destruction that began with Hiroshima, the swift beginnings of the Cold War and the arms race, with periodic crises such as the Berlin blockade and airlift in 1948. Though many Americans felt as righteous in prosecuting the Cold War as in opposing the Nazis, to others our position in the world – even our behavior during the war – became morally ambiguous. What had the Holocaust revealed about human nature, ourselves included? What did it mean for us to have been the first to use atomic weapons? How far would our opposition to Communism carry us? In the new balance of terror, with its mutually assured destruction, what would it mean to "win" a nuclear war?

Eventually, our conflicts over Vietnam crystallized many of these doubts, but World War II became the screen on which these postwar concerns would first be projected. The new war novel of the 1960s was less about the war than about the Holocaust, the Cold War, fear of atomic war, and finally the ongoing war in Vietnam. This second wave reflected a sense of national vulnerability we felt at the peak of our world power, as well as our loss of the moral certainty we had briefly enjoyed – that confident, Wilsonian sense of righteous innocence so deeply ingrained in American history.

The history of these doubts and losses can be traced all through the war writing of the sixties and seventies, both in fiction and reportage, from *Catch-22* and *Mother Night* to Michael Herr's *Dispatches* and Tim O'Brien's *Going After Cacciato.* Indeed, it would not be too strong a statement to say that the history of the whole postwar era could be examined through its changing perspective on war, since the whole period was shadowed by memories of war and by Cold War fears of its recurrence in even more unspeakable forms.

This emphasis on absurdity and moral ambiguity was an intensification of how war had long been portrayed rather than an invention of the 1960s; it can be found already in the 1940s but was deeply rooted in the whole literature of war. There is an ambiguous sense of horror in the vivid violence of the *Iliad,* the antiwar satire of Aristophanes, the "modern" cynicism of Euripides, the savage mockery that runs through Shakespeare's *Troilus and Cressida.* The antiheroic currents in these works spoke powerfully to the forties generation, as many critical writings show, beginning with Simone Weil's classic account of the *Iliad* as a "poem of force." As much a prose poem as an essay, it was widely admired here after it was translated into English by Mary McCarthy. Following the disillusionment of World War I, which undercut all heroic ideals, this existential point of view became the dominant way of writing about war.

Thus Robert Rossen's adaptation of *A Walk in the Sun,* filmed in 1945 by Lewis Milestone, became almost a film noir about World War II. It was based on an extraordinarily direct and simple novel by Harry Brown that tried not only to show how combat felt but also to distinguish it from standard movie heroics. Its emphasis on fear, on the testing of men, its portrayal of their uncertainty and vulnerability, would greatly influence later combat novels, especially Mailer's. The oddity and strangeness of *A Walk in the Sun,* a book that often edges toward the surreal, would become essential to a novel like *The Naked and the Dead,* where some of the major twists of plot serve to deflate the action. Any moderately talented editor could have told Mailer that the triumph of the doltish Dalleson and the final irrelevance of the long patrol, which continues when the battle for the island has already ended, were ridiculously trivial ways of resolving the campaign for the island. Only a silly hornet's nest, not a sense of rational restraint or the limits of human endurance, finally thwarts Sgt. Croft's obsession with the mountain long after it has lost all strategic meaning. Mailer aimed to show how strategy and command fall prey to ego and the need to dominate.

What were simply odd, disorienting touches in Brown and Mailer become the whole novel in *Catch-22,* a World War II fable in a class by itself and one of the most original novels of the whole postwar era. Though one soldier in Brown's *Walk in the Sun* could talk repeatedly about fighting the battle of Tibet in 1956, this surreal touch is grounded in an actual situation: combat weariness, grim pessimism, a sense that the war will drag on forever. Mailer undercuts the characters in his novel with an ironic anticlimax, but he never abandons the view that this is a true campaign, a chapter of a real war. Heller burlesques Mailer's view of the war; for him the war and the army display a pervasive sense of unreality, an element of insanity.

Where Mailer begins his novel with a map of an invented island, Heller begins his with a note on a *real* island that "obviously could not accommodate all of the actions described." Starting (like most combat stories) with the ethnic and regional stereotypes of naturalistic fiction, Mailer thickens his characters with invented histories, psychological profiles, and circumstantial details. Heller, beginning with an even larger cast of the stereotypes, each with a chapter to himself, exaggerates them instead into cartoons, putting them through the paces of stand-up comedy and Road Runner farce.

Similarly cartoonish elements can be found in the ingenious reversals and doublings of Vonnegut's *Mother Night,* in the Candide-like hero and the science fiction trappings of his *Slaughterhouse-Five, or, The Children's Crusade: A Duty-Dance with Death* (1969), and the dizzying multiplication of bizarre plots and oddball characters of Thomas Pynchon's *Gravity's Rainbow,* which wraps the war in comic and paranoid versions of pop-culture myths. This is a novel in which the new technology, including the U-2 rocket, has reduced the characters to ciphers and rendered them almost irrelevant. Pynchon's book is more abstruse and yet more like a comic book view of the war than anything in Heller's and Vonnegut's works. Those older men belonged to the same generation as Mailer and Jones, though they told their stories much later; Pynchon (born in 1937) was not a witness to the war but an inspired, occasionally kitschy fantasist whose overdetermined plots fasten on rocketry and technology as a nexus between sex, extinction, and apocalypse.

Like Vonnegut, Pynchon is interested less in the conduct of the war than in the Nazis, whom he sees through the lens of German Romantic kitsch and post-sixties paranoia and apocalypse, as filtered through writers like William Burroughs, with his dangerous twilight world of the "Zone." What we learn in reading his book is that "this War was never political at all, the politics was all theatre, all just to keep the people distracted . . . secretly, it was being dictated instead by the needs of technology . . . by a conspiracy between human beings and techniques, by something that needed the energy-burst of war" [ellipses in original]. The lesson to be learned from the Germans is that "love, among these men, once past the simple feel and orgasming of it, had to do with masculine technologies, with contracts, with winning and losing." For Nazis like Weissmann, the war, embodied in rocketry, is simply an erotic Götterdämmerung, "a love for the last explosion – the lifting and the scream that peaks past fear," the last big bang. This has little to do with World War II and everything to do with the high-tech war in Vietnam and the sexual-conspiratorial fantasies of the 1960s.

The galloping disillusionment with the Vietnam War all through the 1960s made a revisionist view of World War II inevitable. As reports of atrocities like My Lai began filtering out of Vietnam, survivors of the Holocaust also began to break their near silence of two decades. Their horrendous stories, told in memoirs, documentaries, novels, and fictionalized films, made the old combat novels seem remote and superficial. Starting with a small handful of works by writers like Primo Levi, Elie Wiesel, Hannah Arendt, and Jerzy Kosinski, the Holocaust narrative would eventually displace the combat narrative as our principal vision of the Second World War. As these and other wartime atrocities – and the irrationality and insanity of war in general – became central, as Vietnam shattered our sense of our own purity, it was inevitable that our own behavior in World War II would also be brought into question. The popular view of the war as a simple struggle between good and evil would lose much of its credibility.

By portraying the army in *Catch-22* as a structure of illusion, a vast PR operation, Heller anticipated Don DeLillo's vision of history as virtual reality, the manipulation of appearances. This is an army that would rather move the bomb line than bomb the target, with officers prepared to sacrifice down to their very last enlisted man, officers whose goal is to *look* like officers, to enforce the rules, and to raise the number of required missions rather than to defeat the enemy or win the war. In Heller's war, *every* officer is like Mailer's Dalleson, the comical figure of a total bureaucrat who would rather plan the parade afterward than the battle beforehand, or like Jones's "Dynamite" Holmes, the brutal time server climbing the rungs of promotion and self-promotion.

For Heller, Pynchon, and Vonnegut, writing in a later period, this has become a static war, a war in which nothing happens. This is reflected in the fictional structures they develop – and the individual characters who fail to develop. Both Mailer and Jones, though working close to the events they described – in a sense bearing personal witness – were writing historical novels. The campaigns they worked out had beginnings, middles, and ends; they were microcosms of the war as a whole and sometimes of the whole society that was waging war. In the later writers there is no real sense of unfolding history, no sequential pattern, and little relation between causes and consequences. Their books are circular rather than developmental; they are antihistorical novels. Their characters are pawns rather than agents. No longer hoodwinked by our official war aims, they look to survival, not mastery or heroism, and they are constantly being overwhelmed by larger forces they scarcely understand.

Thus Vonnegut in *Slaughterhouse-Five,* in trying to make sense of his most searing memory – the firebombing of Dresden, which haunted him for 25 years – makes his hero a shell-shocked simpleton, the last of a long line of innocent nobodies caught in the swirling currents of history, politics, and warfare. The book's lugubrious tone can be wearing; its numbing, fatalistic refrain ("so it goes") is repeated when anyone dies, when anything awful happens. This seems to reflect the depressive mood of the author as much as the muted anguish of his Everyman protagonist. By giving us someone who "comes unstuck in time," however, someone whose experiences seem to be happening all at once, whose memories cannot be sorted out or exorcised, Vonnegut at last finds a way of writing about the unthinkable – events that surpass the limits of "realism" and unhinge a novelist's usual approach to character and individuality.

In an aside, the author tells us that "there are almost no characters in this story, and almost no dramatic confrontations, because most of the people in it are so sick and so much the playthings of enormous forces. One of the main effects of war, after all, is that people are discouraged from being characters." This may be too blatant and explicit, yet the word *discouraged* is well chosen: the courage to become a character and lead a coherent life is beyond Billy Pilgrim and his friends. Instead, his role in the book is to show how the shock of history has nullified individual agency. Even after the war, this Pilgrim's "progress" is studded with mental breakdowns, marked especially by a failure to feel, combined with an inability to forget. His behavior seems anesthetized, mechanical, just as Vonnegut's style is nerveless and repetitive. Billy is outwardly adjusted yet inwardly haunted, numb, and mentally disturbed, revealing the survivor mentality that has since become a familiar feature of Holocaust memoirs and oral history.

Vonnegut finally finds a way of telling the story of the Dresden bombing through a "character" who is utterly ordinary yet permanently blighted by it. Thanks to the dubious moral authority of our actions in Vietnam, Vonnegut chooses to focus *his* war on an Allied atrocity; of German ancestry himself, he uses the "good" war to question all war. Billy Pilgrim's later breakdowns convey some of the horror of what was repressed behind the placid and prosperous facade of the postwar world.

Some of the same elements can be found in other post-1960 novels about World War II, such as *Mother Night, Catch-22,* and *Gravity's Rainbow*: a comic-book atmosphere of sheer lunacy and brutality, the reduction of individuals to nonentities by large organizational and technological forces. In the Pavlovian world of *Gravity's Rainbow,* Pynchon's nominal protagonist, Tyrone Slothrop (who bears much of the author's own family history, going back to the Puritans), is wired and conditioned, down to his very erections. In the twilight world of the Zone, he disappears from the novel long before the end, "broken down . . . and scattered." By then, the individual self is barely an object of nostalgia; only a few "can still see Slothrop as any sort of integral creature any more. Most of the others gave up long ago trying to hold him together, even as a concept." Unselved, Slothrop has been dismembered into postmodernism. As Vonnegut dropped into science fiction to unspring our sense of time, sequence, and causation, Pynchon used technology and the pop stereotypes of spy fiction to flatten his characters, to render them absurd and ineffectual.

If Pynchon's characters dash about in circles like experimental rats, Heller's equally two-dimensional characters are the punch lines of jokes, yet they convey a serious point about the war. In the opening chapters of his first novel, *Journey to the End of Night* (1932), Louis-Ferdinand Céline had virtually invented a form of delirious black comedy about war. He gave his hero, Bardamu, whose only goal is to survive, a scabrous ebullience in flaunting his cowardice, his hatred of officers, his loathing of all official and heroic values. Through this first-person protagonist, exploding with rancor and bile, who is hard to distinguish from the author himself, Céline portrays the war as a scene of lunacy and apocalypse, a world saturated with casual death. Instead of the unreliable narrator, Céline creates the hyperbolic narrator, whose nihilistic exaggerations, far from making him less trustworthy, imprint his perceptions like a burning brand. At the edge of madness, he presents himself as the last sane man in the world. For him "this war, in fact, made no sense at all," yet all around him there are madmen determined to fight it: "With such people this infernal lunacy could go on forever. . . . Why would they stop? Never had the world seemed so implacably doomed. Could I, I thought, be the last coward on earth? How terrifying! . . . All alone with two million stark raving heroic madmen, armed to the eyeballs?"

According to Céline, it takes some imagination to understand the horror, to grasp the death happening all around you: "When you have no imagination, dying is small beer; when you do have an imagination, dying is too much. . . . The colonel had never had any imagination. That was the source of all his trouble, and of ours even more so. Was I the only man in that regiment with any imagination about death? I preferred my own kind of death, the kind that comes late. . . . A man's entitled to an opinion about his own death."

Borrowing this tone of slashing anarchic humor, Heller fashioned his own comedy about death, cowardice, and survival. His Yossarian is a more somber variation on Céline's Bardamu, just as Vonnegut's Billy Pilgrim is a doleful, shell-shocked version of Czech writer Jaroslav Hašek's Good Soldier Schweik, the quintessential Little Man caught up in a big war. Despite their real-life origins, as revealed in a 1998 memoir *Now and Then*, Heller's soldiers are not people so much as cardboard cutouts who strike an attitude. Clevinger, for example, is one of those who know everything but understand nothing about the war:

Clevinger knew everything about the war except why Yossarian had to die while Corporal Snark was allowed to live, or why Corporal Snark had to die while Yossarian was allowed to live. It was a vile and muddy war, and Yossarian could have lived without it — lived forever, perhaps. Only a fraction of his countrymen would give up their lives to win it, and it was not his ambition to be among them. To die or not to die, that was the question, and Clevinger grew limp trying to answer it.

In Heller's world, this verbal shell game conveys the existential absurdity. Clevinger is Heller's broad burlesque of Mailer's Lt. Hearn, the Harvard-educated intellectual — reflective, yet also an activist, a doer — whose knowledge masks a real ignorance and whose skills prove essentially useless. "Everyone agreed that Clevinger was certain to go far in the academic world. In short, Clevinger was one of those people with lots of intelligence and no brains. . . . In short, he was a dope." Later, he gets his comeuppance in a chapter that begins: "Clevinger was dead. That was the basic flaw in his philosophy." In Heller's world, death alone provides critical perspective.

In *Catch-22*, Heller brings off a knockabout farce and creates a madcap reality that eventually becomes unbearably poignant and grim. He seduces us with mocking laughter only to take us beyond the jokey one-liners, structuring the book with lightning reversals, comic-book changes of fortune, brilliant riffs of language, and, like Vonnegut, widening circles of disclosure that gradually carry us from comedy to horror. Instead of unfolding chronologically, as if there were a real sequence to the men's wartime experiences, the book is anchored by arbitrary points of reference — Yossarian's stays in the hospital, the number of required bombing missions. In this intricate pattern, characters who are already "dead" in one chapter are still alive in a later chapter, pinned all the more ineluctably to their determined fates. These characters function more as leitmotifs than as real people, since individuality would do little to alter what happens to them. As in Vonnegut's works (but in a more explosive rhythm), everything in the book seems to be happening continuously: throughout, Snowden is dying, the dead man in Yossarian's tent is "dead," and the Soldier in White — faceless, almost bodiless, his being no more than a surreal exchange of fluids — leads his ghostly existence between the animate and the inanimate, between farce and horror.

The characters' "real" life is not necessarily the same as their official life; the man in Yossarian's tent is dead ("his name was Mudd") but has never officially arrived, whereas Doc Daneeka, though alive, has officially died. Heller's satire on bureaucracy — on the insanity of the organizational mind — links the book with his later novels, such as *Something Happened* (1974) and *Good as Gold* (1979), which do for business and government what *Catch-22* had done for the army.

In its way, Heller's book is as literary as Mailer's. The life history of a character like Major Major is a send-up of the biographical baggage in Mailer's "Time Machine" sections. It is built up entirely out of borscht-belt shtick:

Major Major had been born too late and too mediocre. Some men are born mediocre, some men achieve mediocrity, and some men have mediocrity thrust upon them. With Major Major it had been all three. . . .

Major Major had three strikes on him from the beginning — his mother, his father and Henry Fonda, to whom he bore a sickly resemblance almost from the moment of his birth. Long before he even suspected who Henry Fonda was, he found himself the subject of unflattering comparisons everywhere he went. . . .

Major Major's father was a sober God-fearing man whose idea of a good joke was to lie about his age. . . . His specialty was alfalfa, and he made a good thing out of not growing any. The government paid him well for every bushel of alfalfa he did not grow. . . . Major Major's father worked without rest at not growing alfalfa.

Each of these paragraphs goes on like a theme and variations, a comic verbal riff — mercurial, paradoxical, outrageous — with satiric swipes directed at both the army and the larger American society. As Heller builds up Major Major into a major comic nonentity, we laugh at the army yet begin to feel sorry for this useless cog in its silly machinery, which barely leaves room for even the smallest measure of humanity. Major Major's endless trials and humiliations, beginning with his birth and name and climaxing with his promotion to major – which makes him a pariah to the enlisted men – demonstrate Heller's inspired comic adaptations of Dostoyevsky as well as his affinity with schlemiel humor, the serious comedy of victimization that links Jewish jokes to Jewish American fiction.

Heller takes the edge of anxiety built into most combat fiction and makes a comic universe out of it. This is a world saturated with death but made more poignant by his compulsion to joke about it. In this inverted world, for example, Heller's Yossarian prefers the decorum of death in the hospital to the unpredictable turns of death outside the hospital:

There was a much lower death rate inside the hospital than outside the hospital, and a much healthier death rate. Few people died unnecessarily. People knew a lot more about dying inside the hospital and made a much neater, more orderly job of it. . . . They didn't explode into blood and clotted matter. They didn't drown or get struck by lightning, mangled by machinery or crushed in landslides. . . . Nobody choked to death. People bled to death like gentlemen in an operating room or expired without comment in an oxygen tent. There was none of that tricky now-you-see-me-now-you-don't business so much in vogue outside the hospital, none of that now-I-am-and-now-I-ain't.

Alone among these writers, Heller turns a joke into an outlook on life; he transforms anxiety from a stoic situational fear, indigenous to the war novel, into an acrid, cynical sense of vulnerability that becomes the very principle of existence. Thus, *Catch-22* is the apotheosis of the war novel even as it transcends it, since war for Heller is merely a heightened instance of how life will always conspire against you, scheming to do you in. Years later, when Heller himself was stricken with a nearly fatal illness and temporarily paralyzed from the neck down, he was uniquely equipped to milk it for sickly but hilarious comedy in a book appropriately called *No Laughing Matter* (with Speed Vogel, 1986).

Heller's savagely funny sense of the ironies of life was grounded not only in his war experience but in his Jewish outlook and upbringing (as satirized in *Good as Gold*), in his stint as an organization man with Time, Inc. in the 1950s (which formed the basis for *Something Happened*), and in the popular existentialism of the period. It helps explain why *Catch-22*, like other black-humor novels about World War II, remains such a static book. Heller's view of war, like his view of the corporation, the government, and the neurotic Jewish family, is that nothing *can* happen: all involved are stuck in their own rut, perpetual parodies of themselves, acting out roles assigned long ago, a laughable reduction from the fully human. Heller's saturnine outlook, with its conservative sense of possibilities of human development, is reminiscent of haughtier satirists, such as

Evelyn Waugh in *A Handful of Dust,* who entrap their hapless characters in their own pervasive sense of futility.

Something Happened is a postwar pendant to *Catch-22,* using the same comic strategies and verbal riffs in a way that is no longer funny but full of desperation, cruelty, and self-loathing. The nearly anonymous Bob Slocum, surrounded by corporate characters with names like Green, Brown, White, and Black, is merely a voice, ranting at us, suffocating us for nearly 600 pages. A diagrammatic illustration of David Riesman's "other-directed" personality, caught on a middle rung of the corporate fear ladder, Slocum hates his wife and children as much as he hates his job yet is powerless to get away from them. *Something Happened* is as statically uneventful as *Catch-22* is inertly stuffed with reams of "plot." Both are dark books, specimens of gallows humor, but where the earlier book charms us, turning its nihilism into a gradually darkening source of comedy, the later novel, more rigorous in its way, never tries to be ingratiating.

❦

Heller wrote other books of considerable interest without ever matching the brilliance of these first two novels, yet in the sixties and seventies, his cynicism perfectly matched the mood of the times. *Something Happened* was quickly displaced by the work of such writers as Raymond Carver, which achieved the same grim, almost suicidal impact with far greater economy of means. Carver's followers learned to punish readers by withholding from them rather than battering and overwhelming them, and *Something Happened* was set aside as an unpleasant piece of verbal virtuosity that need never be repeated. But *Catch-22* seemed perpetually relevant, especially after Vietnam and Watergate. After Jimmy Carter, American politics took a laughable turn: Ronald Reagan, with his little anecdotes borrowed from old movies, and George Bush, with his fractured syntax and gee-whiz attitudes, could both have been Heller inventions.

The Vietnam writers were especially influenced by Heller's absurdist treatment of war, as well as the magic realism popularized by Latin American writers. Vietnam was exactly the war Heller had anticipated, utterly meaningless to most of its participants yet fraught with a sense of anxiety and waste, the sense of a war machine run amok. The best writers and filmmakers who dealt with Vietnam tried to convey feelings of phantasmagoria that go back in their literary lineage through Heller to Mailer, Harry Brown, and *The Red Badge of Courage.* In Tim O'Brien's best-known novel, *Going After Cacciato* (1978), Cacciato's surreal flight from Vietnam toward Paris is a distant echo of Yossarian's flight to Sweden and Brown's anticipation, there on the Italian coast, of some future Battle of Tibet.

On the other hand, the efforts to deal with combat in Vietnam in a more documentary fashion, such as John Del Vecchio's *The 13th Valley* (1982), proved more earnest than effective. With no clear sense of a front or an enemy or a purpose in fighting, with little prospect of victory and little sense of honor, Vietnam was not a war that would yield to realistic treatment or conventional heroism. Instead, young American conscripts, drenched in monsoon rains and jungle heat, constantly exposed to inept allies and to a tormented civilian population almost impossible to distinguish from the enemy, were saturated with drugs and rock music that meshed with their anxiety but further disoriented their sense of reality.

Every good book or film about the Vietnam War tries to convey its nightmarish qualities, its hellish sense of unreality. Between the ignominious end of the war in 1975 and the early eighties, these long-delayed works probed an untreated wound in the American psyche. Two powerful memoirs, Ron Kovic's *Born on the Fourth of July* (1976) and Philip Caputo's *A Rumor of War* (1977), showed how gung-ho soldiers, passionately committed to the American mission and the American dream, could be transformed into antiwar veterans, maimed in body or mind, who loathed everything our country had tried to do in Vietnam. In *Dispatches* (1977), Michael Herr developed a nervous, explosive, rifflike style, suffused with dread, rhythmically influenced by drugs and rock, to convey a sense, as the best war correspondents had always done, of being there on the ground, being *in* the war:

> The ground was always in play, always being swept. Under the ground was his, above it was ours. We had the air, we could get up in it but not disappear in *to* it, we could run but we couldn't hide, and he could do each so well that sometimes it looked like he was doing them both at once. . . . You could be in the most protected space in Vietnam and still know that your safety was provisional, that early death, blindness, loss of legs, arms or balls, major and lasting disfigurement – the whole rotten deal – could come in on the freakyfluky as easily as in the so-called expected ways. . . . The roads were mined, the trails booby-trapped, satchel charges and grenades blew up jeeps and movie theaters, the VC got work inside all the camps as shoeshine boys and laundresses and honey-dippers, they'd starch your fatigues and burn your shit and then go home and mortar your area. Saigon and Cholon and Danang held such hostile vibes that you felt you were being dry-sniped every time someone looked at you, and choppers fell out of the sky like fat poisoned birds a hundred times a day.

In the edgy flow of his run-on sentences, studded with slang, charged with arresting images, Herr works the feeling of the war into the texture of his prose. His metaphors cut like a knife, and the cutting edge is always fear: "It is a small trench, and a lot of us have gotten into it in a hurry. At the end farthest from me there is a young guy who has been hit in the throat, and he is making the sounds a baby will make when he is trying to work up the breath for a good scream." Herr makes each image count. The "fat poisoned birds" stand for America itself, with its excessive and nearly helpless technology, while the gurgling, choking baby is the hapless soldier, the strangled innocent, a vulnerable human element in that machine.

Soon afterward, filmmakers as different as Hal Ashby (*Coming Home*), Michael Cimino (*The Deer Hunter*), Francis Ford Coppola (*Apocalypse Now*), Stanley Kubrick (*Full Metal Jacket*), Brian De Palma (*Casualties of War*), and Oliver Stone (*Platoon, Born on the Fourth of July*) made movies that tried in different ways to capture the sense of entrapment, horror, and moral ambiguity that had become basic to our view of the Vietnam War. O'Brien's *Going After Cacciato,* on the other hand, was a much more musing and elliptical work that, by going back to the more unconventional novels about World War II, managed to see the Vietnam quagmire in a fresh way. As in *Catch-22* or *Slaughterhouse-Five,* the time structure of O'Brien's novel splinters the relationship between past and present, as if no sequential treatment could do justice to the surreal feeling of the war. The book mixes realistic chapters set in the war with whimsical, picaresque chapters about tracking a missing soldier, Cacciato ("the hunted one"), all the way from Vietnam to Paris – chapters as much indebted to the Road movies of Bob Hope and Bing Crosby as to any literary models. These are punctuated by short, introspective chapters called "The Observation Post," set in the mind of the book's protagonist, Paul Berlin, during a tour of guard duty.

In these inward musings, the whole meaning of the war (and of the novel itself) passes in review. Nothing actually happens in these chapters, though each is carefully marked by a moment in time from midnight to 6 A.M., the period of Paul's watch. In a sense, though, this is where the whole novel takes place – in Paul Berlin's mind, which takes us alternately back into the war, including his own first day of combat, and out of the war, in a reverie about trekking after the missing Cacciato through Delhi, Mandalay, and Tehran to a Paris that is not a place but a "state of mind," a soldier's dream of careless peacetime pleasure. Thus, the book begins exactly where *Catch-22* ends, with Yossarian leaving the war, though it is written not from Yossarian's viewpoint but from that of another man who is trying to imagine why he left, where he has gone, what might have become of him.

Like *Catch-22,* the book has a circular structure. Beginning and ending with chapters that give us a handful of "facts" about Cacciato's disappearance, it weaves backward and forward from grim or funny memories of the war to the larky possibilities of life away from the war. In the long opening chapter, the "factual" chapter, many of the minor characters have already died, but as in *Catch-22,* they live again in flashbacks or as leitmotifs, sometimes comic, often troubling, invariably bizarre. For example, there is Billy Boy Mitchell, who (we are often told) "had died of fright, scared to death on the field of battle." Only much later do we discover that this Snowden-like figure died of fright only after his leg had been blown off by a mine. O'Brien learned from Heller and Vonnegut how to combine the comic with the horrific. He makes war all the more real, as they did, by making his characters less real. They are cutouts, like cartoon figures who have been run over by a steamroller. Caught in a vise that flattens them, squeezes the reality *out* of them, they have been turned into "war stories" – the oddities of what a soldier might happen to remember, or embroider – just as the Cacciato stories are the "battlefield dreams" of "men figuring how, if suddenly free, they would deploy the rest of their lives." Thus, the retrospective and the prospective meet in a multilayered structure of description, fantasy, and reflection, in a book that explores not so much the war itself as the mind of the war – above all, the mind's need to get away from the war.

O'Brien's subject is not simply war but how to write about it, to make sense of it, to find some closure for it. If the postmodern is the realm of the indefinite, the ambiguous, the open ended, then Vietnam epitomized postmodern warfare. O'Brien pursued this postmodern strategy just as effectively in a superb collection of stories, *The Things They Carried* (1990), and in a seemingly more conventional novel, *In the Lake of the Woods* (1994), which deals with the traumatic aftermath of the war, the return of the repressed.

The evolution of the war novel from the late forties to the late seventies is a measure of how the attitudes of American writers changed not only toward war but toward American society. In their own ways, Mailer and Jones were both outsiders, one an intellectual and a Jew who used the war as vehicle for a novel of ideas, the other an aimless Midwesterner, a romantic anarchist who could never quite adjust to the army life he loved and observed with such keen attention. Both were political writers who looked back to the radical causes and literary methods of the 1930s; both wrote under the influence of Hemingway, who treated war as a test of masculinity and courage, of manhood under stress.

For the writers of the sixties and seventies, whether they wrote about World War II or Vietnam, there was no longer even a trace of nobility about going to war. Like many Americans, these writers had lost their faith in the promise of American life; the goals for which we fought no longer had much credibility. The dubious war aims and official lies about Vietnam, the rise of media politics, and the exposure of political malfeasance in the Watergate affair all contributed to a critique of America different from the old political one. The new threat was not Fascism but a public life of sham and unreality.

For such a theme, the outrageous exaggerations of the black humorists and the magic realism of the Latin American writers proved more useful, more authentic and honest, than did the tightlipped, brutally restrained realism of Hemingway. Tim O'Brien's constant concern in *Going After Cacciato* is the relationship of the observer to the thing observed, the fine line between fact and fantasy, memory and dream. Vietnam is the war that eludes those who fought it and even those who write about it. Sequence and order elude Paul Berlin; chronology puzzles him. "Focus on the order of things," he says to himself in one of his musings; "sort out the flow of events so as to understand how one thing led to another, search for that point at which what happened had been extended into a vision of what might have happened. Where was the fulcrum? How did it tilt from fact to imagination? How far had Cacciato led them? How far might he lead them still?"

Some of these sentences might have come from books of the early sixties, such as Pynchon's *The Crying of Lot 49,* but Vietnam and Watergate seemed to have confirmed them. As postmodernists were fond of pointing out, the culture of the image, the reign of "virtual reality," had taken hold. From a sixties viewpoint, Yossarian and Cacciato, like their predecessor, Holden Caulfield, are rebels against authority, tender misfits who step outside the official frame. By the late seventies, however, rebellion had been transformed into isolation, skepticism, and unbelief, as if society were no longer real enough to rebel against.

Compared to the World War II novels, the books about Vietnam take place in a vacuum. The sense of the world back home that Mailer and Jones tried to provide, that even Heller and Vonnegut evoked in a more comical and formulaic fashion, had been completely dissipated. It appears only as the false promises that soldiers unlearn in the hellish context of the war itself. In the world we see here, patriotism is little more than the illusion that unhinges us, that seduces us toward destruction. The Vietnam stories, fiction and journalism, film and memoir, are all about disillusionment, loss of faith, a grim awakening. In these works, we cut through seeming knowledge to find uncertainty, cut through a tissue of lies to reach the heart of darkness. The characters find that they have risked their lives for what they were taught in grade school. The greatest illusion, it seems, is that their leaders were honorable, their cause was just, and that this society can ever command anyone's unambiguous loyalty.

3

❧

THE NEW FICTION: FROM THE HOME
FRONT TO THE 1950S

T HERE WERE OTHER war novels besides those set in the armed forces
or at the front, novels that dealt with World War II more obliquely
or were set on what was then called the home front. A number of
these books anticipated the direction of postwar fiction more acutely than
did the combat novels. Though ambitious young writers like Norman
Mailer and James Jones dreamed that the war could provide material for the
Great American Novel, the naturalist methods of the early war novels were
discarded when American society, without reverting to isolationism, turned
in upon itself during the Truman and Eisenhower years. The new writers
were influenced less by the war than by rapid onset of the Cold War and of
nuclear weapons so soon after the shooting war, which fostered anxieties
that America's victories abroad might otherwise have laid to rest, and by
the new therapeutic culture of psychoanalysis, which gradually replaced the
social consciousness that had driven much of American literature and visual
art during the Depression. As American power and prestige expanded outward across the world, at home artists and writers looked inward, sometimes boastfully, often fearfully, to explore the existential dilemmas of
selfhood. Europe had been broken as a dominant political and economic
force, but strands of European culture, from modernism and surrealism to
existentialism, had migrated to America. As America entered an era of
prosperity and international dominance, American artists and writers grew
pessimistic and introspective, like troubled prophets brooding darkly at the
banquet of national celebration.

Two first novels published toward the end of the war foreshadowed the
conflicting directions that would be taken by later fiction writers. In contrast to the gargantuan size of some of the combat novels, Chester B.
Himes's *If He Hollers Let Him Go* (1945) and Saul Bellow's *Dangling Man*
(1944) are hardly longer than novellas. Both are first-person novels that
end with the narrator's induction into the army; both are preachy, self-concerned, argumentative. Here the similarity seems to end, for though the
two books emerge from newly articulate ethnic groups – the blacks and
Jews who would have the greatest impact on postwar fiction – their char-

acters find different ways of coping with their lives. Himes and Bellow were almost archetypes of the outsiders who had already begun to play significant roles in American fiction before the war. Both writers came of age against the background of the Depression. Bellow was born in Lachine, Quebec, Canada, in 1915, grew up in a lower-middle-class Jewish family in Chicago, the scene of some of his best fiction, and studied anthropology at the University of Chicago and Northwestern University. Himes, whose parents were schoolteachers, was born in Jefferson City, Missouri, in 1909 and dropped out of Ohio State University after one semester. Arrested for armed robbery in 1928, he served eight years in an Ohio penitentiary, which turned him into a writer. He published his first story in *Esquire* in 1934 while still in prison.

If He Hollers Let Him Go, his first novel, could not have been written without the incendiary example of *Native Son,* the book that dramatically undermined America's illusions about racial harmony. These misconceptions had not been seriously challenged by the more genial, more accommodating writers of the Negro Renaissance, who were strongly supported by white patrons, or even by such powerful prewar works as James Weldon Johnson's *Autobiography of an Ex-Colored Man,* Jean Toomer's *Cane,* Langston Hughes's *The Ways of White Folks,* and Zora Neale Hurston's *Their Eyes Were Watching God.* Himes's hero, Bob Jones, is a more reflective, better educated version of Richard Wright's Bigger Thomas, a man seething at the daily slights his color imposes on him. He has worked through two years at Ohio State by waiting on tables, and his girlfriend Alice is the light-skinned daughter of a wealthy, prominent black physician. He supervises a black crew as a "leaderman" at a wartime shipyard in Los Angeles, a position of responsibility that he loses early in the novel for cursing out a white Southern woman who calls him nigger. His almost uncontrollable fury over the way he is treated as a black man propels him to the brink of rape and murder. His rage is a new tonality in African American writing.

Like Bigger Thomas, Bob Jones careens through the novel boiling with anger, ready to explode, struggling constantly with his fear and hatred of the white world. Though he destroyed himself, Bigger achieved some kind of purgation and freedom through violence, and finally through self-acceptance, dispelling a nameless force that had oppressed his every waking moment. In the same way, Bob Jones dreams constantly of striking an arbitrary but massive blow that will somehow liberate him. But unlike Bigger he is a highly self-conscious character, analyzing his own situation acutely, bitterly. Each time he moves to act out his violent fantasies, he sees with perfect lucidity exactly how it will ruin his life.

Bob Jones is pulled in every direction: toward the accommodation that works so well for his girlfriend and her middle-class family, toward the white men and women he would like to kill or rape yet would also like somehow to emulate, and toward the generous and gentle black woman whose house he shares, who is kinder to him than anyone else in the novel. Nursing a baby, nurturing the men around her, she stands for the honest, authentic life he never succeeds in creating for himself.

With all these figures, Bob's fantasies are almost entirely sexual. His girlfriend, who could pass for white, lends him dignity and class while trying unsuccessfully to soften his edges and make him over. The white woman is the classic bitch of film noir, pure poison, a perfect male nightmare. ("When I thought about Madge that cold scare settled over me and I began to tremble. Just scared to think about her, about living in the same world with her. Almost like thinking about the electric chair.") Though she treats him like dirt, he is drawn to her whiteness, her pure cracker hatred of him, until she finally ruins him by accusing him (falsely) of rape. In contrast, his poor black woman friend, living with another man, stands for sex mainly as nurture and domesticity – which is not nearly enough for him.

Chester Himes would later become famous in France, and finally in America, for his detective novels published in the *Série noire,* but *If He Hollers* is already a classic hard-boiled novel, acrid, taut, atmospheric, and menacing – a cross between Richard Wright and James M. Cain, between a social novel about black rage and a seedy romantic thriller. The *Postman* aura of Los Angeles noir lends a mood of fatality to Bob Jones's obsession with race. His girlfriend warns him that "you're insanely belligerent" and "if you continue brooding about white people you are going insane," but he is hooked on his daily dose of fear and humiliation, which gives the book its amazing psychological intensity.

If He Hollers was exactly the kind of pulpy protest novel that critics of the forties and fifties would belittle or ignore. James Baldwin cut his teeth as a writer by reviewing many of these books including Himes's *Lonely Crusade*; he finally denounced the whole genre in his celebrated attack on Wright and Harriet Beecher Stowe ("Everybody's Protest Novel," 1949). But such novels, often written by beleaguered survivors of the proletarian movements of the thirties, would lead an underground life all through the postwar years in cheap paperbacks, well below the dignified purview of "literature."

As a social novel about race and sex, status and prejudice, written in the low-life proletarian mode influenced by Hemingway, *If He Hollers* seems to look backward. *Dangling Man,* on the other hand, cast as a journal, with its action entirely internalized and reflective, anticipates the more private world of postwar fiction, drawing away – but not *too* far away – from the old social and political themes, much as its protagonist detaches himself from all his former commitments. *Dangling Man* even begins with an attack, in the same spirit as Baldwin's, on the "era of hardboiled-dom," which the writer identifies with the active masculine style of both the Depression and the war years. As he uses it, however, the term also embraces the politics of the Communist Party, which has ostracized the narrator for dropping out, and the larger ethos of America itself, the literary and social code embodied by Hemingway, "the code of the athlete, of the tough boy – an American inheritance."

By keeping a journal, the narrator, Joseph (a name out of the Bible by way of Kafka), will pursue a slightly subversive, European mode of self-interrogation. *Dangling Man* gives an American accent to the gloomy, cerebral fiction of ideas that would help displace the kind of naturalistic social novel that loomed large in American writing from the 1890s through the 1940s. In its different incarnations, this introspective approach would become the major current in postwar fiction. For all their differences, though, the Himes and Bellow books were two rivulets from the same source, Dostoyevsky's *Notes From Underground,* the master text for all modern portraits of the thwarted, angry, alienated outsider chewing nervously on his own bitter thoughts.

Dostoyevsky's feverish portrait of a self-tormenter proved irresistibly attractive to black and Jewish writers alike. To blacks it provided some wonderful metaphors for marginality – the whole notion of the underground, for example, and the closely related theme of someone who feels invisible, who is not even noticed by those whose very being oppresses him, as Dostoyevsky's protagonist is elbowed aside by a man on the street who does not see him, for whom he simply does not exist. (Richard Wright and Ralph Ellison performed their variations on Dostoyevsky's themes in "The Man Who Lived Underground" and *Invisible Man,* respectively.) Jewish writers like Bellow, on the other hand, would be most taken with the anxiously brilliant, unstable, fretfully intense manner of the man who translates his marginality into neurosis. Looking for slights and quarrels, brooding endlessly about revenge, the Underground Man messes up his relations with everyone around him. He gnaws away at himself with paranoid imaginings and overwrought self-analysis, living in his agitated mind more than in the actual world. *Dangling Man* hardly measures up to Dostoyevsky's original, but in its musing, low-key fashion, almost stripped of novelistic action, it is an impressive sketch for Bellow's best later novels, *Seize the Day* (1957), *Herzog* (1964), and *Humboldt's Gift* (1975).

Even before his journal opens, Joseph, waiting for his army service to begin, has gradually separated himself from the life around him, quitting his job at a travel agency, distancing himself emotionally from wife, friends, and family. With his induction delayed, he has been "dangling" for months, and in the course of the book he quarrels with nearly everyone around him, very much like Bob Jones in *If He Hollers*. Joseph lives in the *pensées* of his journal, where his life contracts to the reports he makes of it. Finally, at the end of his rope, he puts himself up for immediate induction, canceling his burdensome freedom and solving his problems in one stroke. The self-examination he touted in the opening paragraphs has run its course.

It would be far too easy to reduce these two versions of Dostyoevky to black and Jewish stereotypes, to say that the core of Bob Jones is his emotional violence, his sexual fantasies, his constant sense of humiliation, whereas Bellow's Joseph, almost a caricature of the pure intellectual, turns everything in his life into ideas. In fact, Bob Jones is a virtuoso of self-analysis, though he also behaves like a man under unbearable pressure, and Joseph, for all his philosophical distance, is almost as irritable and quarrelsome as Himes's alter ego. But Himes's book, though it is an intense exploration of Jones's mind, also has an explosive and timely social subject – race. Joseph's mind, on the other hand, runs toward the metaphysical: his ruminations anticipate Bellow's later reflections on the self and the universe, on the general condition of man. They are the meditations of a restless intellectual who is essentially a version of Bellow himself, as all of Bellow's protagonists after Herzog would be.

In contrast to Himes's focus on race, and even to the ethnic punctuation of Bellow's later books, there is only one passage in *Dangling Man* that explicitly treats Joseph as Jewish. This comes when Joseph tries to account for his touchiness, but even here the word *Jew* is never mentioned: "I have known for a long time that we have inherited a mad fear of being slighted or scorned, an exacerbated 'honor.' . . . We are a people of tantrums." But he goes on to attribute such behavior to a previous self, the "old Joseph," still ethnic and benighted: a social being who had yet to transcend these petty feelings, the very feelings that are the subject of Himes's book.

For all the delirious extremity of its mental atmosphere, *If He Hollers* – like Himes's longer, more diffuse, more ambitious second novel, *Lonely Crusade* (1947) – is firmly set in wartime Los Angeles, with its mixed population of Southerners drawn to the defense industry, working side by side with blacks and women taking advantage of unheard-of job opportunities. It is a workplace full of newcomers thrown together in a racial and sexual tinderbox, under wartime production pressure as well as a new federal antidiscrimination order. Like the shipyard itself, Bob Jones is less an individual than a social emblem for Himes. Along with many other Californians he is a man from elsewhere, tossed into a bubbling urban cauldron.

In the course of the war, the issue of race and prejudice rapidly came to a head in American life. The racial rhetoric of the Germans and Japanese, the racism directed *at* the Japanese, and the string of nasty incidents at military bases and in neighboring towns raised the level of racial tension in America. Though blacks made up only ten percent of the population, they made up sixteen percent of the still segregated armed forces. Many of the bases were in the South, where the presence of black soldiers provoked whites, just as their frequent mistreatment evoked violent anger among blacks back home, who felt that their contributions to the war effort were being discounted. To many blacks, they were fighting for the rights of others abroad while their own rights were being violated at home. There were a number of racially motivated murders that led to black protest marches; even small clashes and rumors of racial incidents affecting black soldiers mushroomed into serious race riots in Detroit and Harlem. The war exacerbated the fever about race in a world already hot with violent conflict.

In "Notes of a Native Son" (1955), one of his best essays, James Baldwin vividly described the 1943 Harlem riot, which coincided with the death of his preacher stepfather. He recalled how the funeral procession had moved somberly through the surreal devastation of the ghetto. Ralph Ellison used a similar scene for the dramatic climax of *Invisible Man.* The zoot-suit riots in Los Angeles, in which white soldiers and sailors beat up young Mexican Americans, come up as part of the background in *If He Hollers,* along with the federal antidiscrimination efforts. The transplanted Southerners in the novel feel personally aggrieved that in California they cannot simply lynch Bob Jones – for disrespecting a white woman with dubious morals and low credibility.

In *Lonely Crusade,* set in 1943, Himes casts a wider net. Though much of the novel focuses on the hero's attraction to white women and his betrayal of his long-suffering black wife, Himes also deals unflinchingly with black anti-Semitism and with the duplicity of Communists doing union organizing, who feel free to sacrifice their own or even sabotage the cause if they cannot control it. Both the Communists and the law *do* try to frame or lynch the protagonist, Lee Gordon, but their vicious antics, devoid of moral principle, help make a man of him. Embittered from the beginning, hating himself as much he hates and fears white people, yet cursed by an internal, prickly sense of pride, he ultimately recoils when other blacks use race to excuse failure and justify violence. Gradually (if not wholly convincingly), he develops an Orwellian commitment to basic human decency, and at the end of the novel, as the police try to smash an organizing march, he picks up the fallen banner of the union, perhaps at the cost of his life. To redeem himself, he must take up the standard of something larger than himself.

❦

This sense of a larger society, superficially unified by wartime goals but wracked with internal tensions, is completely missing from *Dangling Man*. Joseph has stepped away from all this. He belongs with the alienated intellectuals: his detachment, his "dangling," defines his position or lack of one. The shocking force of Himes's novels is grounded in a social psychology, not an individual one; it is focused on the lurid intersections of race, sex, and the desperate need for manhood or respect. Bellow's novel looks to a different kind of fiction in which the important conflicts will be personal or cosmic, not social. This longer view makes Joseph quite conservative – in his taste in clothes, for example – since "he wants to avoid the small conflicts of nonconformity so that he can give all his attention to defending his inner differences, the ones that really matter." The thirties romance of political commitment and even of an assertive bohemian individualism seems distant and distracting. Bellow's fundamental conservatism came through early.

Like Bellow's later intellectual protagonists, including Herzog and Mr. Sammler, Joseph preaches a sense of metaphysical limits as well as of individual obligations. Through Joseph's jottings in his journal, Bellow argues that "we suffer from bottomless avidity," from an exaggerated "Sense of Personal Destiny." We ask ourselves, "shall my life by one-thousandth of an inch fall short of its ultimate possibility," for "we have been taught there is no limit to what a man can be." Bellow would pick up this theme again in his next novel, *The Victim*. "Everybody wanted to be what he was to the limit," he says. "You couldn't expect people to be right, but only try to do what they must. Therefore hideous things were done."

Ironically, the economy of growth and abundance that developed after the war did more than anything to dispel the sense of limits that had been built up during the Depression and enforced by wartime rationing. The surge of consumerism would convince social thinkers and political leaders that we had genuinely transcended social conflict, that only Communists and fellow-traveling liberals still believed that there were significant class issues in American life. This emphasis on consensus went back to the war. Wartime propaganda had fostered an artificial unity – a resurgence of Americanism and a suspicion of dissent – that did much to drive class issues out of American politics. Harry S. Truman's successful populist campaign in 1948 as an underdog candidate was the last hurrah for the rhetoric of the New Deal, though the Democrats would still cling to it with diminishing force in future elections. This was the year that Truman, over intense opposition, finally integrated the armed forces. A strong civil rights plank became part of the Democratic platform, provoking a Dixiecrat rebellion led by diehard segregationists like J. Strom Thurmond of South Carolina.

Yet all through the late 1940s, before McCarthyism took hold, there were powerful novels and films, still rooted in the naturalism of the 1930s, that dealt with race, anti-Semitism, and the darker side of urban life – sometimes boldly and honestly, yet often luridly and formulaically. Ira Wolfert's *Tucker's People* (1943), Ann Petry's *The Street* (1946), Willard Motley's *Knock on Any Door* (1947), and Nelson Algren's *The Man with the Golden Arm* (1949), like Himes's *Lonely Crusade,* upheld a waning style of urban realism identified with Richard Wright and James T. Farrell; they conveyed a feeling for the stifled and oppressed, for the mean streets of the neighborhood; they exposed the traffic in power and corruption, the difficulty in preserving one's humanity.

Meanwhile, the crackling films noirs of the late forties, including work by such directors as Edgar G. Ulmer, Nicholas Ray, Joseph Lewis, John Huston, Billy Wilder, Robert Siodmak, and Jules Dassin, translated the harsh outlook of hard-boiled fiction into memorable film imagery: shadowy, menacing interiors; rain-swept, dimly lit streets; seductive but treacherous women whose behavior still reflected the sexual tensions and fantasies of the war years. For all their stylized urban settings, a mood of cynicism and paranoia ran through the ingeniously twisted plots of these films, which were dominated by themes of official corruption, moral depravity, and personal betrayal. Though made in Hollywood, they became a kind of official nay-saying counterculture of the late 1940s.

There were other dissenting notes in the upbeat social climate of the era. After the war, there was a short-lived vogue of social problem stories focusing on outsiders and victims. Sometimes these victims seemed interchangeable, as when the murdered homosexual in Richard Brooks's novel *The Brick Foxhole* became the murdered Jew in Edward Dmytryk's effective film noir adaptation, *Crossfire* (1947), and the psychologically damaged Jewish veteran in Arthur Laurents's play *Home of the Brave* became a black man in the film version. Even the Western could be turned into a timely parable about race relations. Delmer Daves's *Broken Arrow* (1950), made from a screenplay by Michael Blankfort – soon to be blacklisted, like many other Hollywood leftists who worked on these films – centers on the lethal hatred and warfare between white men and Indians. The conflict is eased by the mediation of a brave white scout (Jimmy Stewart) who, rather too easily, gains the trust and friendship of the fierce Apache chieftain, Cochise (Jeff Chandler) and the love of an Indian woman.

After evoking troubling issues, these stories too often tilted toward pat conclusions and happy endings. *Broken Arrow* preached mutual respect, the brotherhood of man; it gave the individualism of the Western hero a liberal twist. The films about disabled veterans like *The Best Years of Our Lives* and *The Men* preached adjustment over brooding resentment, socialization (at all costs) over prickly individuality. They made short work of the surly loner who, for whatever understandable reasons, nurses his hurt and anger, like Himes's Bob Jones, or stays outside the norms of the group, like Marlon Brando's embittered paraplegic veteran in *The Men*. In many of these films, like *Home of the Brave* and *The Men*, a doctor serves as a therapeutic mediator to bring these men back into harmony with the group. Eventually, this defense of community and conformity became the dominant "social ethic" of the 1950s, as critical observers like William H. Whyte and David Riesman would show in their widely read works of social criticism.

៙

Besides the early work of Chester Himes, novels touching on racism and anti-Semitism after the war included books as different as Faulkner's *Intruder in the Dust* (only the second Faulkner novel made into a film); Laura Z. Hobson's popular but superficial *Gentleman's Agreement*, which became far better known as a film, directed by the ubiquitous Elia Kazan and starring Gregory Peck; Sinclair Lewis's *Kingsblood Royal*; and the young Arthur Miller's 1945 *Focus*, published before his success as a playwright. Both the European and Pacific war had sensitized the public to racial issues, which figured significantly in such war novels as James Gould Cozzens's *Guard of Honor* and Irwin Shaw's *The Young Lions*, written from sharply opposed conservative and liberal viewpoints. Saul Bellow's second novel, *The Victim* (1947), arose from the same set of forties concerns, which also produced such landmark studies of prejudice as Gunnar Myrdal's *An American Dilemma* (1944), the classic study of American race relations, as well as T. W. Adorno's *The Authoritarian Personality* (1950) and Hannah Arendt's *The Origins of Totalitarianism* (1951), both dealing with anti-Semitism. Beginning with its title, *The Victim* is almost a parody of the literature of social protest. But like *If He Hollers*, it also confronts the ethnic identity that was so muted and oblique in Bellow's first novel.

The strong concern with victims and outsiders in the postwar years also created an opening for writers to deal more frankly with homosexuality, another issue heightened by wartime changes in living patterns. Two of the literary sensations of 1948, both by writers in their early twenties, were Gore Vidal's *The City and the Pillar,* an unexpected best-seller, and Truman Capote's first novel, *Other Voices, Other Rooms,* an exercise in style that, along with his early stories, catapulted him to sudden fame. Neither book is a problem novel that reduces the homosexual to society's victim. Both are coming-of-age fables, psychological parables, that substitute sensibility and point of view for social protest. Though Vidal's book is strictly realistic, even oversimplified, and Capote's is often shimmeringly surreal to the point of being opaque, both anticipate the 1950s fascination with troubled adolescents that would soon be exemplified by J. D. Salinger's *The Catcher in the Rye* and films like *The Wild One, Blackboard Jungle,* and *Rebel Without a Cause.*

Already in the early forties, Malcolm Cowley, who had once been a strong defender of radical and proletarian writing, anticipated this turn toward the personal and the psychological. Looking back in 1943, he observed that "the social realism of the 1930s had proved to be a less fertile movement than many writers had hoped. . . . People had begun to feel the need of books with more warmth, inwardness, and freedom." Warmth and freedom, however, were not the emotions that echoed most strongly after the war, but rather a gloomy inwardness, spiced with a strong sense of fatalism. This mood showed itself in the cynicism of the films noirs, which gave a deep psychological twist to the urban realism of the Depression, often showing the hidden links between cops and criminals, victims and villains. Other films noirs (such as Nicholas Ray's *In a Lonely Place*) concentrated on psychologically damaged war veterans; still others *(They Live By Night, Gun Crazy)* dealt poignantly with thwarted, doomed young outlaw couples, a theme that carried over from such grimly deterministic Depression-era works as Edward Anderson's Bonnie-and-Clyde novel *Thieves Like Us* and Fritz Lang's second American film, *You Only Live Once* (both from 1937).

Like Himes's books, Bellow's second novel, *The Victim,* gives us a literary variant on the nightmarish urban atmosphere of film noir. At the most superficial level, Bellow's protagonist, Asa Leventhal, feels put-upon and harassed by the anti-Semitic Kirby Allbee, who accuses Leventhal of depriving him of his job years earlier and putting his life on a downhill slide. At the same time, Leventhal feels responsible for a sick nephew, since his sister-in-law is desperate, irrational, and his brother is unaccountably out of town. These two threads of "plot," such as they are, barely serve to hold the novel together. Set in the stifling atmosphere of a sweltering New York summer, *The Victim* is a Kafkaesque novel about a man who (like Himes's self-lacerating heroes) feels deeply uncomfortable in his own skin.

If Joseph anticipates the intellectual surrogates of Bellow's late novels, Asa Leventhal foreshadows the blocked feelings, the sense of entrapment and asphyxiation of the hapless Tommy Wilhelm in *Seize the Day*, whose whole life comes unstuck in just twenty-four hours.

Such Russian writers as Dostoyevsky and Gogol had focused obsessively on clerks, bureaucrats, and minor functionaries who lived pinched lives, hounded by their superiors and their creditors, tormented even by their families (if they have families). Jewish writers as different as Sholom Aleichem and Kafka were strongly drawn to these stories, which often transformed the social disabilities or frantic insecurities of their luckless protagonists into morose shaggy-dog comedies of survival. Thanks to the Kafka vogue right after the war, agonizing versions of such Little Man stories reappeared among Jewish writers like Arthur Miller (in *Death of a Salesman*), Bernard Malamud (in his short stories and in *The Assistant*), and Bellow. (*Seize the Day* would be Bellow's masterpiece in this suffocating yet spiritual "Russian" vein.)

These tales shifted the attention of Jewish writing from typical Depression subjects; exploited workers and poor immigrants gave way to lonely salesmen, loveless clerks, and long-suffering shopkeepers. The postwar writers moved away from social problems toward metaphysical concerns about identity, morality, and man's place in the larger scheme of the universe. In some sense they were all Holocaust novels, starting with *The Victim*, though the murder of Europe's Jews is scarcely mentioned in them. It was as if the Nazi genocide had eclipsed not only the social outlook of the Depression but the social character of anti-Semitism itself, offering us instead a terrible glimpse into the human heart.

The details about the Holocaust that became known only in 1945 no doubt account for some key differences between *Dangling Man* and *The Victim*, which climaxes with Kirby Allbee, the down-at-heels descendant of America's WASP patriciate, turning on the gas in Leventhal's kitchen, perhaps hoping to kill them both. (He "tried a kind of suicide pact," Leventhal tells someone, "without getting my permission first.") Asa Leventhal and Allbee are alter egos, each the oppressor, each the victim. Just as *Dangling Man* is a more lighthearted version of *Notes From Underground*, *The Victim* crosses *The Double* with a plot borrowed from another Dostoyevsky novella, *The Eternal Husband*, a story of early middle age, about a "worn-out man" who discovers his own inadequacies.

To make sure we understand the doubling effect, Bellow reminds us that "it was supremely plain to [Asa] that everything, needlessly everything without exception, took place as if within a single soul or person." Much like the characters who are cruelly paired in Malamud's fiction, Asa and Allbee are doppelgängers who plague and harass one another as if each is the suppressed part of the other's being. Bellow's point, never fully conveyed by the murky details of the story, is that we all have the capacity for cruelty, for self-exculpation, and that we are all inseparably responsible for one another. Thematically, *The Victim* reminds us of many less imaginative postwar works that yoke Freud's pessimism to notions of sin and human imperfection coming down from Paul and St. Augustine by way of Reinhold Niebuhr. Bellow refuses to see even the Holocaust as a tale of good and evil. Avoiding any easy division into victims and villains, Bellow's fable turns the protest novel inside out.

Besides Dostoyevsky, the other main influence on *The Victim* was Kafka – not the Kafka who was then seen too simply as a prophet of totalitarianism but the Homer of Jewish insecurity, the lyric poet of the soul's profound uneasiness with itself. Asa is dominated by a nameless malaise, a vaguely unhealthy nervous excitement. Analyzing everything, brooding about what people think of him, Asa begins "to feel unsure of his ground," to fear that "the lowest price he put on himself was too high." Just as Kafka's characters are complicit with all that oppresses them, with the terrible circumstances they feebly protest, Asa never understands why he permits intolerable demands to be made of him, why he allows Allbee to insinuate himself into his life, even to move into his home.

Kafka showed Bellow how to give a dreamlike credibility to the improbable and implausible, but Bellow uses this device to develop a moral theme – that men are accountable to each other, that debts must be paid – to wives, to children, even to strangers:

After all, you married and had children and there was a chain of consequences. It was impossible to tell, in starting out, what was going to happen. And it was unfair, perhaps, to have to account at forty for what was done at twenty. But unless one was more than human or less than human . . . the payments had to be met.

This refers to Leventhal's brother, who manages somehow to be absent while his young son is dying in a hospital, but Allbee, too, belongs to this "chain of consequences." A reflux from the past, he is like the intrusive Trusotzky, the Nemesis figure in Dostoyevsky's *Eternal Husband*. Allbee is not only a buried part of Asa himself but also the Other, the accuser, the figure with whom he must somehow come to terms. In Bellow's novels, early and late, all human debts must eventually be paid. During the same period, in such much-admired stories as "A Tree of Night," "The Headless Hawk," and "Shut a Final Door," the precocious Truman Capote was developing a glossy gothic version of the same haunting motif, but without Bellow's moral weight.

Bellow developed this doubling pattern in rather academic terms; his ideas seem independent of the novel's minimal plot. In later years, Bellow was fond of saying that in these two books he was paying his dues to get into the club — that *Dangling Man* was his master's thesis, and *The Victim,* his doctoral dissertation. By then, however, he had become a voluble critic of the "cant of alienation," the "Wasteland outlook"; he was perhaps embarrassed to have begun his career with two such pinched, depressive books. But *The Victim* was as prophetic of postwar fiction as *Dangling Man.* It helped shift fiction from the social subject to the private subject, from naturalism to the Hawthorne/Kafka mode of fable, from politics to themes of personal growth and identity.

This was the moment when a publisher, under pressure from a leading book club, subtracted Richard Wright's political history from his autobiography and turned *American Hunger* into *Black Boy,* yet another story of growing up. It was a moment when the two most ambitious postwar political novels, Robert Penn Warren's *All the King's Men* (1946) and Lionel Trilling's *The Middle of the Journey* (1947), shifted the emphasis from their political protagonists (based on the charismatic figures of Huey Long and Whittaker Chambers) to their ambivalent observers, instinctive metaphysicians who are more engrossed with sin, fate, and human destiny. In these two books, as in Norman Mailer's *Barbary Shore* (1951) and *The Deer Park* (1955), we can see the novel of ideas swerving from the stresses of politics toward the mysteries of personality and moral choice.

In such quasipolitical novels, the public world is still part of a dialogue with the troubled reflections of the private man. But in many of the most widely discussed books of the late forties, touted by critics as the "New Fiction," the public world disappears completely and we are plunged into a vortex, a metaphysical abyss. Even in *The New Yorker,* that weekly offshoot of the novel of manners, long famous for its flippant and lighthearted view of life, such writers as Jean Stafford, John Cheever, Shirley Jackson, and Hortense Calisher began turning away from the social text toward an interior castle of personal trauma and dysfunction, the familiar terrain of such young Southern writers as Carson McCullers and Eudora Welty. Closely linked to them in sensibility were the daring new gay writers, Vidal, Capote, Paul Bowles, and Tennessee Williams, who managed at once to be outlaws and celebrities, media favorites and cultural villains. Consciously posing for a group portrait as a new literary generation, they were friendly rivals then, mainly Southern but not exclusively regional, mostly homosexual but also immensely gifted at portraying indelibly original female characters.

Ten years before Norman Mailer turned from fiction to brilliant self-projection in *Advertisements for Myself,* Vidal and Capote, cultivating an aura of notoriety and sexual ambiguity, began promoting their work by projecting their own personalities. The feline, sybaritic figure lounging on the jacket of *Other Voices, Other Rooms* eventually became the fey talk-show personality that would completely displace the writing. A new culture of outrage and provocation was waiting in the wings. Vidal was another performing self who would later make a specialty of literary feuds and cutting attacks beginning with his well-publicized "feud" with Capote. The challenge, as he said in one novel, was to capture the spotlight and hold it forever. Ultimately, like his despised rival Mailer, he would prove more consistently gifted as an essayist than a novelist. Reviewing Williams's memoirs, introducing Bowles's or Williams's stories several decades later, he would become the historian and publicist of the group, rehearsing their happier moments, retelling old stories in which he always comes off well, angling for a place in literary history.

The difference between *The City and the Pillar* and *Other Voices, Other Rooms* is somewhat like the difference between Himes and Bellow. Where Vidal, still under Hemingway's influence, is flat and literal, Capote grows shadowy and metaphorical; where Vidal is concrete, Capote's early work trembles, not always convincingly, with dark symbolic relationships, doublings, in the manner of *The Victim* (though borrowed more directly from Carson McCullers, especially from *The Member of the Wedding,* 1946). Just as *If He Hollers* was almost a handbook of bruising racial encounters, filtered through the pores of a thin-skinned black protagonist, Vidal's novel was a Baedeker of gay life, from growing up in Virginia to making one's way in the armed forces, or in the demimonde of Hollywood, New Orleans, and New York. With the war as a distant background, Jim Willard explores each of these fugitive scenes, trying to find his identity and come to terms with his homosexuality. But the author's real purpose is to enlighten the audience on the range of homosexual behavior, feelings, even terminology:

Jim discovered their language, their expressions. The words "fairy" and "pansy" were considered to be in bad taste. It was fashionable to say that a person was "gay." A person who was quite effeminate, like Rolloson, was called a "queen." A man who could not be had, who was normal, was called "jam." The rough young men who offered themselves for seduction but who did not practice were known as "trade"; sometimes they prostituted themselves for money; more often, however, they were homosexuals who had not yet realized it themselves. Among the homosexuals there was a saying that "this year's trade is next year's competition."

Vidal's ambition to become the Virgil of homosexual underworld is admirable, even courageous. (Many years later, Edmund White and Armistead Maupin would take on a similar role in exploring the more uninhibited gay scene of the 1970s.) Vidal aims to show his readers that homosexuals are anything but monolithic: like straight people, their personalities, their sexual styles and social practices, vary immensely. Jim is cast as the innocent, as yet uncertain of his identity, who encounters gay characters ranging from effeminate queens to famous writers to seemingly virile Hollywood stars. This documentary aspect of the book is the fictional counterpart of the first Kinsey report, *Sexual Behavior in the Human Male,* a study that caused a sensation when it appeared just a few months later, in part because it revealed – and perhaps exaggerated – the extent of homosexual experience among American men. But such an instructional approach, though socially admirable, does real damage to the novel. Vidal permits characters to lecture each other over drinks on the origins of homosexuality and the dominance of castrating women in American culture. Most of *The City and the Pillar* is written in a numbingly simple declarative style, punctuated by Dick-and-Jane dialogue in which everyone sounds alike and no one, not even a sailor, ever curses or uses slang.

Vidal had begun his career with *Williwaw* (1945), a spare war novel written under the Hemingway influence, and this uninflected manner persists in *The City and the Pillar,* but without Hemingway's wealth of reverberation and implication. After Jim's idyllic sexual initiation and his stints in the navy and in Hollywood, a vague malaise settles over the second half of the novel, in which very little occurs. Unhappiness is the one common denominator among the people Jim meets and sleeps with. Their unfulfilling lives are meant to build up a 1940s gay equivalent of *The Sun Also Rises,* with its wounded or dissatisfied expatriates living aimlessly, for pleasure, but cut off from their own feelings. But this part of the book falls flat, drifting forward on a style so muted, so lacking in color or emotional atmosphere that it takes us nowhere.

As an acute observer of the literary scene, Vidal was very much aware of the stylistic options available to him; but he must be pulling our leg, or his character's, when he has a woman say: "You know, I'm really thrilled to see Henry James coming back. I think we are all tired of those short ungraceful sentences of the thirties. It will be nice to read books with lovely long sentences about *real* people." Henry James *was* coming back, but not in this novel. Someone else responds that "it takes something more than long sentences to create great literature" and that there is "a lot to be said for the staccato style." This allows the author to have it both ways while satirizing the literary chitchat of the moment.

The real failure of the novel comes not from its style, however, which Vidal himself later renounced, or its documentary approach, and certainly not from its sympathetic portrayal of the problems of homosexuals, but from its basic timidity, especially if we compare it to a genuinely outrageous later book like *Myra Breckinridge* (1968), the work of a more freewheeling era. Gore Vidal set out in *The City and the Pillar* to show that homosexuals, far from being strange or exotic creatures, could be as ordinary as anyone else. Just as Laura Z. Hobson cheated in *Gentleman's Agreement* by making the victim of anti-Semitism a gentile in disguise, Vidal's protagonist is a handsome, tennis-playing young athlete from Virginia, an all-American boy out of an Andy Hardy movie. But Jim is an anachronistic figure: in the Freudian climate of postwar America, Andy Hardy was turning into James Dean. Jim is unhappy with his life and turned off by the subterranean gay cultures he encounters. "He liked young men his own age who, like himself, were not effeminate or unnatural." As in so many of his later novels and essays, Vidal wants to be transgressive and popular at the same time. Attracted only to the most civilized outcasts and scoundrels like Julian the Apostate or Aaron Burr, he is always courting outrage while exercising a safe kind of daring.

To take *The City and the Pillar* seriously as a work of imagination, not simply a documentary of gay life, we would have to accept the unconvincing premise that Jim Willard's goal in life is to recapture the magic of a single adolescent experience with a heterosexual friend. According to Vidal's memoir *Palimpsest* (1995), the friend was based on the only man he ever really loved, a brilliant young athlete named Jimmie Trimble who was later killed in the war. A nostalgically remembered scene of awkward initiation has since become a commonplace of gay fiction, but the weight it is forced to bear in *The City and the Pillar* damages the novel's credibility.

The tangled memory of Jim's thwarted infatuation is meant to make him a gay figure with whom everyone else can identify — not someone motivated by simple hatred of his father, fear of women, or strong repugnance toward their bodies. In a wildly improbable and lurid conclusion that Vidal rewrote two decades later, Jim is reunited with his old friend eight years afterward and kills him when his sexual overtures are rejected. (In the 1965 version, he merely rapes and abandons him.) Thus, Vidal's first searching critic, John W. Aldridge in *After the Lost Generation* (1951), complained that as a character Jim was not a person but *only* a homosexual, simplified to make a social point, as in the contemporaneous protest novels about blacks and Jews, in which the characters were often merely social types.[1]

Later, in novels like *Burr, 1876,* and *Lincoln,* Vidal would bring a stylistically richer version of his no-frills approach to well-researched but thinly imagined historical fiction. He began in 1964, after a decade away from fiction, with a distinguished novel about Julian the Apostate, probably inspired by Robert Graves's crisply written Claudius novels. Vidal portrays Julian as a genuinely civilized figure in a society of power-hungry Caesars, a tolerant, enlightened classicist amid small-minded Christians.

But Vidal also tried, to match the disillusioned wit of Henry Adams, and starting with *Washington, D. C.* (1967) he began writing a sardonic history of America in fictional form, achieving commercial success by appealing to a more disillusioned age. At best his transparent style followed Graves in wiping away the cobwebs and museum clutter from the historical novel. Trying to write a fictional chronicle of American politics, he could do no more than assemble a collection of venal politicians – plotters, scoundrels, and corrupt scalawags – faceless avatars of the American empire whom he attacked repeatedly in his witty essays. Simply as a storyteller, he did more justice to Burr and Lincoln and American politics than to Jim Willard and homosexuality. His novels tried to serve both the Hollywood-fed imagination of the mass audience and the patrician cynicism of his own political outlook. He exploited the roguish charm of his heroes as pendants to his own public personality, which he cultivated on talk shows, in occasional movie roles, and in many cutting and entertaining essays.

Vidal himself had made an effective but quixotic run for Congress from New York in 1960, doing well as a Democrat in an entrenched Republican district. He drew upon his Washington background and his knowledge of the mechanics of American politics in a hit play and film, *The Best Man* (1960; 1964), then in *Washington, D. C.* The novel holds a special place in his fiction because it is so autobiographical, saturated with his own boyhood in Washington during the New Deal era. Vidal had politics in his blood. His maternal grandfather was a blind senator from Oklahoma, Thomas P. Gore, and his father was a New Dealer who had become well

---

[1] In his afterword to the 1965 revised version, Vidal argued that the novel had always been misunderstood, since the character had been intended as a *negative* example: "I intended Jim Willard to demonstrate the romantic fallacy. From too much looking back, he was destroyed, an unsophisticated Humbert Humbert trying to re-create an idyll that never truly existed except in his own imagination. Despite the title, this was never plain in the narrative." This intention was belied by the autobiographical emotion that Vidal invested in Jim, feelings that still echo through Vidal's 1995 memoir, where he even looks forward to being buried near his boyhood friend. In the novel, the incident is portrayed lyrically; the afterword comes more from the more cynical, technically adroit older writer half acknowledging the weaknesses of the book.

known as a star athlete and coach at West Point and as an aviation pioneer. Taking us from the beginning of FDR's second term in 1937 to the heyday of McCarthyism in the 1950s, *Washington, D. C.* includes portraits of his adored grandfather as a "flawed idealist," his mercurial mother and handsome father, and his own callow but sharply observant younger self, with secondary characters based on such familiar legends of the Washington scene as Alice Roosevelt Longworth and the closeted columnist Joseph Alsop. The novel is powered by Vidal's essayistic intelligence, his insider's knowledge of Washington life, his moral seriousness, and his smoothly adroit handling of the levers of conventional fiction. It even recaps, more realistically, the sexual initiation portrayed so lyrically in *The City and the Pillar* without pursuing the earlier novel's homosexual theme. But *Washington, D. C.* loses strength when its central character, a rising young politician and fake war hero, turns into a hollow pastiche of John F. Kennedy. Vidal had a family connection to Jacqueline Kennedy – they shared a stepfather – but he had grown to detest her husband after being banned from the White House in the early 1960s. The personal thrust of his need for revenge undermined the fiction, but the book did initiate Vidal's unique chronicle of American history, which he would carry through six additional novels, from *Burr* (1973) to *Empire* (1987), *Hollywood* (1990), and *The Golden Age* (2000).

❧

The best contrast to the well-meaning but pedestrian treatment of homosexuality in *The City and the Pillar* can be found in the stories of Tennessee Williams and the fiction of Paul Bowles. Born in the same year, 1911, Bowles and Williams were more than a decade older than Capote and Vidal, and both had significant careers outside their work in fiction. Something of a prodigy himself, Bowles, as a protégé of Aaron Copland, Virgil Thomson, and Gertrude Stein, found success as a composer before turning to fiction, whereas Williams was the most renowned American playwright of the late forties and early fifties. (This helps explain why his fiction went virtually unnoticed as he was doing his best work.) Neither had the genius for self-promotion of Vidal and Capote, though they were bolder, more dangerous writers.

All four writers were dependent on style to the same degree that many thirties writers depended on *not* having a style, on not embracing the merely aesthetic during a time of social suffering. Vidal's style – crisp, direct, intelligent – was the most readable and least original of the four, serving him better in the essay form than in the novel, carrying us along on the intimately conversational yet mandarin flow of his voice, entertaining us with the twists and turns of his clever mockery and self-regard. Yet

Vidal would later be generous to the writers of the late forties – Williams, Bowles, John Horne Burns, even Mailer – who shared his moment of literary history. Introducing Williams's collected stories, for example, he says incisively: "These stories are the true memoir of Tennessee Williams. . . . Except for an occasional excursion into fantasy, he sticks close to life as he experienced or imagined it. No, he is not a great short story writer like Chekhov but he has something rather more rare than mere genius. He has a narrative tone of voice that is totally compelling."

Aside from telling us how much Vidal learned from Williams, this puts a finger on the paradox of Williams's neglected but wonderful prose fiction. At a time when the well-made story was the dominant mode – thoroughly plotted, oblique, full of irony and complexity – Williams's memory stories and anecdotal fragments were a sharp departure, almost doomed to be undervalued. They seem dreamed or hallucinated rather than formally composed. At moments they feel like erotic reveries, written solely for the writer's own satisfaction. Frequently Williams loses interest in them a few pages before the end and simply races to a conclusion. They are storyteller's stories, pieces of an ongoing life, and they resist all closure, yet they are kept afloat by a remarkable vividness: it is virtually impossible to put them down. Even Williams's late, eccentric *Memoirs* (1975) have this mesmerizing, irresistible quality: they are the inimitable sound of one man talking.

Like many of his fine autobiographical sketches (such as "'Grand'" and "The Man in the Overstuffed Chair"), the *Memoirs* clarify the handful of intense relationships that lay behind both the plays and the stories: the overbearing mother captured so well in *The Glass Menagerie,* the alcoholic and mercurial father who mocked his son as a sissy, the maternal grandparents, the Reverend and Mrs. Dakin (his beloved "Grand"), the sister who was his inseparable companion until adolescence separated them and a frontal lobotomy destroyed her mind, and the young girl who was the other female companion of his childhood. These early connections eventually gave way to his life as a writer and his discovery of his homosexuality, to travel, love affairs, cruising, addictions and breakdowns, and always an iron devotion to the daily call of his work. When Williams had nothing new to write (Gore Vidal reports), he simply sat down in the morning to retype something he had already done.

The later forties were a time of fictional experimentation. As Bellow reflects the impact of Kafka and Dostoyevsky, as the early Vidal uses the spare manner of Hemingway without its suggestive depths, so Williams and Bowles reflect opposing facets of the work of D. H. Lawrence, early and late. In Williams's hands, Lawrence's vision remains earthy, lyrical, and celebratory, whereas Bowles explores the dark side, the sense of drugged self-surrender in the pursuit of the primitive. In "The Mattress by the Tomato Patch" (1953), Williams too easily creates a female Zorba, the woman as life force, strong and indestructible compared to the men around her, whereas in the weakest part of his masterwork, *The Sheltering Sky* (1949), Bowles yields to a masochistic fantasy of erotic surrender, sexual enslavement, and the descent into madness, all motifs from Lawrence's later work, including *The Plumed Serpent, St. Mawr,* and "The Woman Who Rode Away."

The common coin of the New Fiction was the allegorical fable, which the writers used as a Freudian vehicle for tapping into the unconscious, but like all *literary* fables, they worked best with an abundance of realistic detail. Good fiction is nothing if circumstantial, full of what Irving Howe calls "gratuitous detail." Bowles became famous (or notorious) for his remarkably concrete horror stories – "A Distant Episode," "The Delicate Prey," "Pages from Cold Point" – in which frightful events were narrated in a detached, neutral, almost clinical manner. He dedicated his first collection, *The Delicate Prey and Other Stories* (1950), to his mother, "who first read me the stories of Poe."

Williams worked entirely from experience as rearranged by memory and fantasy. As Vidal remarked, he spent "a lifetime playing with the same, vivid ambiguous cards that life dealt him." He reworked his stories tirelessly, sometimes in new versions, often as plays, seeking fresh emotional truth as he rearranged details, bringing a different intensity to each transformation. For him, writing was an act of recovery that began with the experience of unhappiness and loss. In one of his most autobiographical stories, "The Resemblance between a Violin Case and a Coffin" (1949), he describes a young man's loss of his childhood as he grows alienated from his beloved sister and feels the first confused promptings of his own homosexuality:

And it was then, about that time, that I began to find life unsatisfactory as an explanation of itself and was forced to adopt the method of the artist of not explaining but putting the blocks together in some other way that seems more significant to him. Which is a rather fancy way of saying I started writing. . .

Williams sees art as a way of reassembling blocks of experience to yield new structures of emotional meaning. Yet this passage itself, so typical of Williams, is a rather clumsy piece of "explaining" that sounds more like an excerpt from an essay than lines from a story. If Williams seems gauche and uneven, this is inseparable from the marvelous spontaneity of his writing. As he compares an idyllic past with the conflicts and losses that came afterward, Williams endlessly wrestles his experience into meaning, not by any literary strategy, certainly not through form, but by whatever means language affords – sometimes discursively, often confessionally and self-accusingly, always emotionally. Williams writes out of an intense yearning to retouch and reshape a handful of unforgettable experiences.

Williams's stories feel at once repetitious and strikingly different. Two stories about his sister, "Portrait of a Girl in Glass" (the source for *The Glass Menagerie*) and "The Resemblance between a Violin Case and a Coffin," are like an artist's rendering of the same scene or the same model at different moments of recollection. As a writer, Williams is driven by a relentless dissatisfaction, or simply an inability to let anything go; for him to finalize his memories would be to cast them aside. Thus, "The Mysteries of Joy Rio" (1941), about furtively looking for love in the balcony of an old movie theatre, is transformed twelve years later into "Hard Candy." Because they belong to the culture of the closet, haunted by a mixture of fear and desire, pleasure and embarrassment, Williams's stories of gay sex seem strikingly complicated, brave, and (unlike *The City and the Pillar*) unformulaic. "Two on a Party" (1951–2) must be one of the best stories of the hustling life ever written. Entirely unpredictable, it portrays the bond of affection between a male hustler and slightly older prostitute who team up and go looking for trade together. Above all, it is suffused with Williams's own comic affection for marginal characters and their sordid, insecure lives, over which he never sits in judgment.

Another of his best stories, "There Players of a Summer Game" (also 1951–2) – the source for his play *Cat on a Hot Tin Roof* – takes place in a completely different world, a Peter Taylor world of rich social memory, in which money and class are no defense against emasculation, cancer, alcoholism, or unhappiness in love. An unhappily married man has an affair with a recently widowed woman, but it ends badly for both of them when his determined wife gets the upper hand. The story centers on this strange love triangle fraught with social disapproval, personal weakness, and even a kind of vampirism. Williams's special touch is that this is all observed from the point of view of two children who mainly remember the period as a magical summer, not as the misfortune that adult life might have in store for them as well.

Williams's darker material foreshadows the whole Grove Press school of underground writers – such as John Rechy in *City of Night* (1963) and Hubert Selby, Jr. in *Last Exit to Brooklyn* (1964) – yet his work is as fluent, unforced, and forgiving as theirs is violent and sensational. Occasionally his work comes closer to theirs, as in the famous "Desire and the Black Masseur" (1946), one of his rare horror stories in the lurid vein of Capote, Bowles, and the last pages of *The City and the Pillar.* Williams's stories scarcely underline his personal links to the Southern gothic manner of Eudora Welty and Carson McCullers that are writ large in the early Capote. Like many writers who dramatize the conflicts of the closet, Williams deals frequently with sexual confusion, guilt, and repression, but "Desire and the Black Masseur" is one of his rare fictional excursions into sadomasochism and allegory. Bowles, on the other hand, explores the edges of civilization as a twilight zone in which these dark and forbidden needs are repeatedly acted out. Where Williams naturalizes homosexuality and its conflicts into a narrative of lyrical recollection, Bowles is the first of the transgressive writers whose bleak nihilism and lurid atmosphere open doors for the James Baldwin of *Giovanni's Room* and *Another Country* and the William S. Burroughs of *Naked Lunch*.

Each of these writers came from seriously dysfunctional families. Williams's parents were hopelessly mismatched, as he never tires of showing in his work. Vidal's and Capote's mothers were alcoholics; Capote's mother quickly realized that her unreliable husband would never manage to support her, and she farmed her son out to her family for years until she remarried and brought him north. In "The Frozen Fields" (1957), a rare autobiographical story, Bowles, the precocious son of a well-to-do Queens dentist, portrays his father as a sadistic tyrant bent on crushing and humiliating him, and shows up his mother as a woman too weak to stand up for him. The summers the boy has spent on his grandparents' farm are an "enchanted world" to him, an escape into his own imagination, but the presence of his father threatens him, "because it was next to impossible to conceal anything from him, and once aware of the existence of the other world he would spare no pains to destroy it."

His father objects when the family fusses over the boy and showers him with Christmas gifts, and he in turn imagines his father's being carried off by a wolf who embodies the terrifying forces that lurk outside the safe circle of society. In a horrendous scene, his father – who is concerned (as Williams's father was) that the boy was too sensitive and unmasculine – forces him to take a walk in the snow and, in a fit of anger, rubs the snow in his face and down his neck. "As he felt the wet, icy mass sliding down his back, he doubled over. His eyes were squeezed shut; he was certain his father was trying to kill him. With a desperate lunge he bounded free and fell face-downward into the snow."

Deftly, the story takes an existential turn typical of Bowles. Instead of fighting his father, the six-year-old boy, "his mind empty of thoughts," takes a mental leap into a land of unfeeling, where he finds his freedom. "An unfamiliar feeling had come to him: he was not sorry for himself for being wet and cold, or even resentful at having been mistreated. He felt detached; it was an agreeable, almost voluptuous sensation which he accepted without understanding or questioning it." Nearly every wrinkle of Bowles's imagination can be found in this story. If the father stands for the despotic power of respectable society and the patriarchal family, the wolf is the lure of what lies outside the town gates, outside the limits of the conscious mind. Between these two extremes Bowles gains the almost inhuman detachment of the sensitive yet fatalistic observer. As he says of his surrogate, Port Moresby, who is observing an ugly quarrel in *The Sheltering Sky*, "He was determined to remain wholly on the periphery of this family pattern; the best way of assuring that, he thought, would be to have no visible personality whatever, merely to be civil, to listen."

This detachment became not only Bowles's social mask but his literary physiognomy as well. Along with Poe and Lawrence, Conrad's *Heart of Darkness* is the tutor text of all Bowles's best work. Bowles was drawn to Morocco and then into the Sahara just as Mr. Kurtz and then Marlow in *Heart of Darkness* were drawn into the Congo, fathoming the limits of civilization in themselves and those around them. "I think one is always writing about oneself," Bowles once wrote, but added that "writing is, I suppose, a superstitious way of keeping the horror at bay, of keeping the evil outside." Williams writes in order to get in touch, to actualize his memories, fantasies, and desires more vividly in his mind, on paper, or on stage. Bowles, on the other hand, felt the pressure to *dis*engage, to outline his fantasies with a cool precision very far from the adjectival vagueness of Conrad's portentous evocations of the horror of the unknown.

Bowles's stories and novels reject the father without sentimentalizing the wolf. The wolf crystallizes everything that is violent, primitive, and devouring yet still somehow attractive to him. Modern literature is full of versions of the wolf, Rilke's sleek panther, for example, or Kafka's leopard, which every day invades the courtyard of the temple to drink up the blood on the altar. Kafka's leopard, the force of the irrational, can scarcely be resisted but it can somehow be domesticated, included in the ceremony, made part of the ritual. Freud's system, though less fatalistic about the power of the unconscious, in effect aims at achieving the same result. For Bowles, however, the wolf – the irrational, the primitive, the unconscious – represents the irresistible attraction of letting go.

Bowles's protagonists seek the outer limits of a civilization they detest; deliberately or unconsciously, they yield themselves up to forces that will dissolve or destroy them. "A Distant Episode" could be the title of many of Bowles's stories, just as "The Delicate Prey" describes their lurid, sadomasochistic material, which the writer develops in the crisp, neutral style of an anthropological observer. The title "Pages from Cold Point" could almost be a motto for this detachment, though it also refers to the chilling, predatory traits of the characters. In a remote part of a Caribbean island, a young man, by all appearances a paragon of innocence, seduces and black-mails his own father, who is himself a repressed homosexual with some buried scandal in his past. In "A Distant Episode," a professor, a linguist, has his tongue cut out by nomadic tribesmen who imprison him and make him their mascot and buffoon. In "A Delicate Prey" a trusting young mer-chant traveler is robbed, mutilated, raped, and then murdered by a desert outlaw, whose crime is then grotesquely avenged by the victim's kinsmen.

Whether the narration is oblique, understated, and brilliantly sugges-tive (as in "Pages from Cold Point") or graphic and lurid (as in "A Distant Episode" and "The Delicate Prey"), Bowles's strategy is the same. His sup-posedly "civilized" characters, like Mr. Kurtz in Conrad's story, are drawn to the heart of a void, a solitude, which then enfolds and envelops them, exposing their secret wishes and vulnerabilities. Port and Kit Moresby in *The Sheltering Sky* have come to Africa, just as Paul and Jane Bowles had done, to find a resonant backdrop for their own estrangement. Obscurely, they hope to overcome the sexual dissonance, the failure of feeling, that has overtaken their twelve-year marriage, but they have also brought along a companion, Tunner, as a distraction, a defense against intimacy, and he makes it harder for them to find each other. Even before he seduces Kit on a nightmarishly crowded train, the boringly normal Tunner, with his casual, conventional masculinity, serves as a buffer between them, making it almost impossible for them to be alone. His sharp will accentuates their vague aimlessness, their immense fatalism.

It is not at all clear what the couple is seeking in Morocco as they move ever more deeply into the Sahara, even as Port falls dangerously ill with typhoid. Bowles himself was making the same journey as he wrote the book, turning to drugs to write the difficult scene in which he knew Port would have to die. For Port, as for Bowles, Africa is a way of sloughing off the decadence of the West, with its residue of oppressive morality. "Pages from Cold Point" begins with a Spenglerian vision of decline keyed to the nuclear age – "Our civilization is doomed to a short life. . . . The bigger the bombs, the quicker it will be done" – but this vast claim will be quali-fied by our sense of the narrator's personal failings as a husband, brother, and father. Kit's problem is that she wants Port, wants him back, but can-not empathize with what Port needs, since it diminishes and frightens her. Part of him is oriented to the void rather than to humankind. At a key moment, they cycle out at sunset to some remote rocks overlooking an empty landscape, which highlights the gap between his longing for the abyss and her inescapable fears:

It was such places as this, such moments that he loved above all else in life; she knew that, and she also knew that he loved them more if she could be there to experience them with him. And although she was aware that the very silences and emptinesses that touched his soul terrified her, he could not bear to be reminded of that. It was as if always he held the fresh hope that she, too, would be touched in the same way as he by solitude and the proximity to infinite things. . . . And now for so long there had been no love, no possibility of it. . . . The terror was always there inside her ready to take command. It was useless to pretend otherwise.

In such ruminative passages, Bowles steps not only beyond the descriptive, detached manner of the stories but also outside the novel itself, providing discursive touches of motivation that are otherwise elusive; they seem to come from his own mind and marriage. Early critics like John W. Aldridge complained that the characters "move without motive from sensation to sensation" and that Port "is driven by a compulsion which neither he nor we can formulate," but this ignores the *kind* of novel Bowles is reinventing: the prewar existential novel (like Sartre's *Nausea* and Camus's *The Stranger*) in which hollowed-out characters, devoid of feeling and clear motivation, move obscurely through vacant landscapes of alienation. (This helps explain why *The Sheltering Sky* became a cult book in Europe, and why Bernardo Bertolucci would eventually direct a faithful film version, with the aged Bowles in a cameo role.) Long before the French discovered this way of developing the theme, Hemingway in *The Sun Also Rises* and *In Our Time* had created a pared-down, shell-shocked style of the unspoken, with characters drifting aimlessly, almost devoid of affect or purpose, a style that relied heavily on inference and suggestion. More convincingly than Gore Vidal, Bowles creates a 1940s equivalent of Hemingway's mood of postwar disillusionment.

The Sheltering Sky remains powerful and convincing as long as Bowles stays with the Moresbys' marriage, their descent into the Sahara, and Port's illness and death. In the predatory Lyles, mother and son — vicious, bigoted, thieving, paranoid, and probably incestuous — Bowles provides the reader with a comically horrible foil for the Moresbys. Early in the novel, Bowles distinguishes between tourists and travelers, between mere sightseers collecting experiences and true voyagers who submit to the alien strangeness of their surroundings. Armored in their Mercedes, following the same route as the Moresbys, bickering over their hotel bills, the Lyles are contemptuous of the Arabs and impossible to each other. The Dickensian solidity of these sharply drawn characters contrasts very effectively with the growing metaphysical vagueness of the Moresbys. The underlying strain in the Moresby marriage is set into high relief by the satirical intensity of the Lyles' incessant quarreling.

As the Moresbys leave the last vestige of European influence behind, Port's health deteriorates, as if in direct consequence of his descent into the Sahara. While her husband falls into fever and hallucination, Kit is increasingly drawn to the exotic and sinister Arab men around her. Feeling imprisoned by his illness, tied to a person she now scarcely recognizes, she is gradually transformed, seeking out the self-obliterating transcendence he had sought for himself. Distracted but no longer fearful, she yields to the primitive void all around her. While Port dies, she is off with Tunner, but afterward she wanders into the desert, where she is picked up by a tribal caravan.

Repeatedly ravished, lost in an erotic haze, Kit willingly becomes the kind of sex slave we encounter in Victorian orientalist pornography, such as *The Lustful Turk*. As Port yields himself to death, to the gray emptiness he had perceived behind the blue, sheltering sky, Kit takes on his vast fatalism: instead of remaining the character we knew, she acts out the author's fantasy of masochistic submission, which also lay behind the cocky professor's enslavement and humiliation in "A Distant Episode." Both characters surrender themselves with huge relief and resist only when their submission ends. When the professor's numb stupor begins to pall, he angrily rebels; similarly, Kit recoils and grows disoriented when her rescuers, including the persistent Tunner, manage to bring her back into civilization, a return that she (or her madness) is unable to accept. Like some late Lawrence characters, they have known the ecstasy of self-surrender and self-immolation. A return to sanity and the trials of individual existence feel unbearable to them.

So long as the book rests on its autobiographical foundation – the strange marriage of Paul and Jane Bowles – it remains haunting and resonant. Despite Paul's nihilism and fatalism, his recoil from Western civilization, despite Jane's lesbian promiscuity and neurotic fears, the two were a devoted and dependent couple. Their life together, difficult as it was, seemed to liberate and inspire him, and he did little significant writing after her death in 1973. Especially during this short period in the late 1940s, his fantasies and memories were chillingly concrete. The same cannot be said of the other most celebrated practitioner of the grotesque during this period. Capote's early stories and novels show up the weaknesses of postwar gothic in its most banal and aestheticized form. For the celebrity journalism of the period, in the pages of such glossy magazines as *Life* and *Vogue,* Capote himself became the precocious, sexually ambiguous child who appears throughout his early fiction. But Capote's writing was more authentic than his clippings, not as a designer version of gothic horror but as growing-up stories that anchor the New Fiction in a child's-eye view of the world. Capote was a fashionable tourist in the lower depths but his work was only a step or two away from the imperishable adolescent complaint of *The Catcher in the Rye* and the kinky Old World lust of Nabokov's *Lolita,* with its refined attraction to the robust vulgarity of youth.

More chic but less touching than these later works, entirely lacking their comic concreteness, *Other Voices, Other Rooms* (1948) and the horror stories in *A Tree of Night and Other Stories* (1949) give us fragile fantasy without resistance, sexual anxiety and dysfunction without solidly grounded detail. Whether they deal with orphaned children in search of their parents (as in *Other Voices*) or impish children as evil spirits, wreaking revenge on the adult world (as in "Miriam"), whether they are set in the rural South, a land that time forgot, or in fashionable New York, Capote's fiction is spun out like a gossamer web from the viewpoint of the child who is not quite ready to grow up, whose fantasies recoil from sexual differentiation and adult behavior. (Capote developed a mellower, more benign version of this Peter Pan fantasy in *The Grass Harp,* 1951.) Even when the protagonists are adults, as in "The Headless Hawk" or "Shut a Final Door," they are people who never really grew up, who certainly never resolved the conflicts that plagued them as children. Haunted by mysterious doubles representing suppressed parts of themselves, locked in emotional isolation, as little able to give as to receive love, they come to grief like shipwrecked vessels on the raw, unintegrated parts of their own personalities.

If Bowles is always writing variants on Conrad's *Heart of Darkness,* the distant ancestor of Capote's early fiction is Hawthorne's greatest story, "My Kinsman, Major Molyneux," the archetypal American coming-of-age fable. Both Bowles and early Capote are also literary descendants of Poe, but Bowles is astringently precise and detached where Capote remains watery, vague, and self-pitying. In the light of its theme, a young man's search for his father, Capote's style in *Other Voices* is far too mannered and involuted, too lyrical. As Alfred Kazin wrote not long after it was published, "I am tired of reading for compassion instead of pleasure," adding, "This demand on our compassion is not limited to the quivering novels of sensibility by overconscious stylists."

There is something exquisitely artificial about Capote's early fiction, as if he were too young to have experienced any of the things he wrote about except for the feelings behind them. Aldridge complained in 1951 that "the real world behind the nightmare which Capote gives us has been refined almost completely out of existence. . . . Joel, the central figure in *Other Voices, Other Rooms,* is neither a boy nor a caricature of a boy. He is a creation entirely of Capote's talent for the grotesque." The same point could be made about James Purdy's more accomplished but strangely airless growing-up stories of the 1950s and 1960, such as "63: Dream Palace" and *Malcolm.* Like *The City and the Pillar* and several of Williams's best stories, *Other Voices, Other Rooms* is about discovering and coming to terms with one's homosexuality. But its reliance on gothic devices and its hothouse atmosphere and stylistic extravagance seriously undercut the genuine feelings of loneliness, homelessness, and personal confusion that give the novel some authenticity. We have the testimony of writers like Cynthia Ozick and Alfred Chester about its powerful impact on them when the book first appeared, but its affected manner made it largely an exercise in style, a throwback to the decadence and aestheticism of the 1890s.

Like McCullers's *The Member of the Wedding,* Capote's novel centers on the dreamy world of a young adolescent. Thirteen-year-old Joel Harrison Knox journeys from New Orleans to a remote, moldering mansion called Skully's Landing in search of his lost father, Edward Sansom, who turns out to be a drooling, helpless, mentally incompetent cripple rather than the strong Samson figure he desperately seeks. Instead, he finds a tomboy, Idabell, who rejects his very tentative sexual advances, and his stepmother's cousin Randolph, a Wilde-like transvestite who, despite his own miserable experiences, enables Joel to accept his own inchoate homosexual identity. This is curious, since identity itself is portrayed by Capote as fluid and mercurial: the book's title refers metaphorically to different identities and alternative selves. In a rather willed conclusion, we see the sensitive boy turning unconvincingly into the precocious author: "'I am me,' Joel whooped. 'I am Joel, we are the same people.' And he looked about for a tree to climb: he would go right to the very top, and there, midway to heaven, he would spread his arms and claim the world." But this has nothing to do with the sad and uncertain boy we have known, only with the ambitious claims registered by the author's style. It does nothing to resolve the deep sense of lovelessness and homelessness that give Capote's early stories their bleak and horrifying edge.

What enabled the self-destructive author to survive as long as he did — he died shortly before his sixtieth birthday in 1984 — was not the newly integrated personality he asserts at the end of the novel but, as in Bowles's case, the writer's steely detachment, even cruelty, in the face of his own lurid material. Admirers of his later journalism, such as Mark Schorer, applauded Capote's "progression from the wholly private psychic world into the world of objective social realities." Though Capote removed the trappings of gothic fantasy and childlike bewilderment and, beginning with *The Muses Are Heard* (1957), became a solid reporter in the best *New Yorker* manner, real life would provide him with material even more garish than his youthful fantasies. Capote the reporter, still the bright, attentive child, became indistinguishable from Capote the voyeur, the social butterfly, the malicious gossip, the cold melodramatist.

Looking always for *le mot juste,* he set down all he saw and heard in a neutral manner that concealed his own wounds. "From a technical point," he later wrote, "the greatest difficulty I'd had in writing *In Cold Blood* was leaving myself completely out of it." The two psychopathic killers in *In Cold Blood,* however, are found versions of the confused waifs and grimly haunted adults of his early fiction, and Capote, for all his surface detachment, identifies with them far more than he identifies with their "innocent" victims. Similarly, the gossipy, back-biting world of his last, unfinished novel, *Answered Prayers,* is a keenly observant child's malicious report on what society is. Capote himself had the killer instinct, and, like the precocious child accustomed to being forgiven and rewarded, he was amazed when his tale-bearing was not applauded by its victims.

Other Voices, Other Rooms today seems like a passing phase for its author and a minor moment in American fiction, yet it epitomized many of the qualities of the New Fiction that would develop in the decades after the war. Its emphasis on inwardness and style foreshadowed much of the psychological fiction of the 1950s, just as its focus on a boy's coming of age anticipated the direction of the new youth culture that would lead through the Beats to the counterculture of the 1960s. Capote himself was a fastidious writer who famously described *On the Road* as typing rather than writing, yet his phantasmagoric treatment of homosexuality paved the way for Burroughs and the Beats. Adept at manipulating the publicity machinery, Capote himself became very much an insider despite his homosexuality. Nevertheless, the figure of the delicate young outsider in his early work anticipated the sensitive, alienated misfits – young, black, gay, Jewish, or simply unhinged by contemporary life – who would establish a main line in American fiction from Salinger to Vonnegut, a line that joined the underground writers to the more acclaimed and established talents.

The major alternative to the New Fiction would be offered by one of its early practitioners, Saul Bellow, who, along with such black writers as Ralph Ellison, would take the new style of personal fable in a more social, moral, and ethnic direction, away from the violent aestheticism and lurid primitivism foreshadowed by Capote and Bowles. The nightmares of the black and Jewish writers seem more historical, less purely personal, for they were grounded in real traumas, the cultural legacies of their people. They certainly had no sense of a lost innocence; like Kafka, they felt they were born guilty, born under a curse or at least a burden. They understood how their quest for identity had strong social roots, but they were as concerned with survival as with identity, and they looked more to be integrated into society than simply to transgress its norms.

If the new gay and bisexual writers were the immoralists of postwar fiction – bold in exploring a dangerous new terrain, lyrical in evoking both a lost innocence and a utopia of personal freedom – Jews and blacks were the moralists, weighing the inexorable cost of the historical horrors and psychic traumas their characters had experienced. There was no Jewish equivalent to the emotional poetry of Tennessee Williams's plays, to the willed horror or sense of loss in Capote's evocations of childhood, or to Bowles's shocking variations on Poe and Conrad. Since they were intellectuals as well as fiction writers, Bellow and Mailer would respond strongly to the effects of politics, war, the Holocaust, and the bomb, as the more self-concerned Capote and Williams did not. Their ruminations about history and personality, about all the catastrophic twists of modernity, would give their own work a deeper moral and metaphysical cast that would in turn be reflected in the work of the many younger writers whom they would strongly influence.

4

###

ON AND OFF THE ROAD: THE
OUTSIDER AS YOUNG REBEL

ESPITE the emergence of writers who were moving in new directions, the late 1940s was hardly a stellar period in American fiction. Very few major novels were produced. Most of the important
books, as we have already seen, either dealt with the war or reflected its
aftermath, since very few events altered American life as much as this
global conflict. Many novels that were much acclaimed at the time, such as
The Naked and the Dead, All the King's Men, The Young Lions, Guard of Honor,
and *Other Voices, Other Rooms,* seem flawed or dated today; in some cases their
authors (Mailer, Capote) went on to make their mark in strikingly different
styles. The plays of Tennessee Williams and Arthur Miller and the hard-
boiled films noirs of the era seem stronger today than the fiction of the
period. The work of some novelists who were just beginning to write then,
including Mailer, James Jones, Saul Bellow, Flannery O'Connor, Ralph
Ellison, and James Baldwin, still feels vital and impressive today, yet their
work belongs primarily to the literary scene of the next decade.

Nevertheless, the forties were the testing ground for everything that
happened in American writing for the next twenty years. As the
American economy moved from Depression and war production to affluence, consumerism, and worldwide geopolitical dominance, writers
turned away from economic and social concerns to engage more with
spiritual and personal issues. The radical politics and progressive social
views that were so important between the wars lost favor, despite Harry
S. Truman's unexpected victory over Thomas E. Dewey in 1948. With
much of the world's economy in ruins, America entered a period of
booming economic growth and relative social peace, marked by
expanded job opportunities, a high birth rate, migration to the suburbs,
new upward mobility and, thanks to the GI Bill of Rights, a vast expansion of higher education. To some it seemed that American society had
entered a new golden age, but very few writers shared this expansive outlook. Instead, they reflected a deep sense of malaise that contrasted with
the surface buoyancy and optimism.

The cultural mood, influenced by the horrors of war, grew receptive to European existentialism and crisis theology. For many intellectuals, the sense of sin and evil in Søren Kierkegaard and Reinhold Niebuhr, which found a secular equivalent in the psychology of Freud, supplanted the pragmatic social hope and faith in reform that marked the work of John Dewey, though Dewey himself lived until 1952. In fiction, the social novel of the 1930s gave way to stylized fables that brought forth the prismatic figure of the outsider, the misfit, the madman, or the primitive. As America's official values grew more conservative, this outsider character would give a radical edge, a mood of brooding alienation, to work that no longer had any clear public agenda. It would link this new fiction with the Beat poet, the abstract painter, the Method actor, the jazz musician, and the youth-oriented rocker. As economic growth leaped ahead dramatically in the two decades after the war, this outsider character emerged in fiction, poetry, movies, and music as one of the great nay-saying figures in American culture.

Not all thirties writers were naturalists or Marxists, but nearly all of them, even those who were modernists influenced by James Joyce and Marcel Proust (including John Dos Passos, William Faulkner, and Henry Roth) saw the texture of society, of city life, or of America as a whole as their inescapable subject. For them, the marginal characters who mattered to their fiction were *social* misfits, immigrants moving haltingly into a new culture, Wobblies laying down their idealistic challenge to American capitalism, poor white trash like the Snopeses making a new order out of their own predatory needs. The writers who followed in the forties and fifties, however, were influenced more by *Heart of Darkness, The Interpretation of Dreams,* and *Civilization and Its Discontents* than by *The Communist Manifesto* and *Das Kapital.* They were obsessed more with Oedipal struggle than with class struggle, concerned about the limits of civilization rather than the conflicts within civilization. Their premises were more Freudian than Marxist.

Auschwitz and Hiroshima had set them thinking about the nature and destiny of man, and relative affluence gave them the leisure to focus on spritual confusions in their own lives. Just as the burgeoning consumer society sanctioned a new selfishness, so the growing therapeutic culture, buoyed by affluence, invited a focus on "relationships" that would have seemed a luxury or irrelevant to earlier generations. At the same time, the beginnings of the Cold War and the development of McCarthyism, which aimed to root out the remnants of Depression radicalism, encouraged writers to turn away from politics to domestic problems and personal relations. The war itself had brought ordinary Americans together, heightening their patriotism and their intolerance of dissent. The crusading, provincial, and suspicious atmosphere of the Cold War contributed to a new conformity and materialism. This in turn deepened the spiritual malaise of the post-war years and made some of the best writers feel even less at home in America than the radicals of the 1930s, who put a noble *idea* of America and a belief in its promise and possibility at the center of their work.

Thus, at a moment when America seemed more triumphant than at any time in its past, when we had just fought and won a "good war" and much of the world (including our leading economic and political competitors) lay in ruins, a deep streak of disaffection set in. As advertising became more pervasive, as television began to enter every home, some serious artists felt swamped by the growth of mass culture, though others welcomed it as an expression of the native energy. During this period, Robert Hughes wrote, "the real artist was the one who worked against the grain of American vulgarity, who aspired to a European complexity and subtlety and felt alienated at home." Artists also felt politically alienated. Communism and Fascism were the gods that failed, yet to many writers, American society seemed disoriented, confused; they sought a vantage point outside it. This is reflected in the brutal fantasies of pulp fiction, which exploded in the 1950s from such writers as Jim Thompson and Mickey Spillane, and in the dark patterns of film noir, where the outlook is often so bleak, the milieu so dark and corrupt that the appointed czar of the film industry threatened to forbid the export of American movies for fear of tarnishing our image abroad.

The Catcher in the Rye, which J. D. Salinger had been working on since the last days of the war, seemed a harmless and beautifully crafted book about adolescence when it first appeared in 1951. But with a baby boom developing in tandem with a spending boom, adolescence would prove to be a more potent and far-reaching subject than many realized at the time. Meanwhile, Marlon Brando arrived on the stage as one of Tennessee Williams's dangerous primitives in *A Streetcar Named Desire,* but in his first film, *The Men,* he played a paralyzed war veteran, surly and morose, who must be coerced — by his peers, by doctors, by women — into rejoining the community. Brando's acting combined sullen toughness with hints of strong emotion, a smoldering physicality with a bruised sensitivity. At once masculine and feminine, his style, like Salinger's, helped usher in a new mood of youthful rebellion.

Within a few years, in *The Wild One* (1953), Brando was playing the leader of a motorcycle gang that terrorizes a small community. By then much of America was up in arms over a new youth culture, marked by supposedly antisocial comic books, media violence, and juvenile delinquency. The older generation in small towns, cities, and newly affluent suburbs found their values rejected by their own children. With a surge of

economic growth, social and geographical mobility, and consumer spending, more Americans were moving into the middle class. As the fruits of
plenty and of world power dispelled memories of deprivation that went
back to the Depression, many of the young turned away from the ethic of
upward mobility, finding their parents' lives stodgy, unadventurous, and
materialistic. Soon the culture industry discovered a potent new market
among adolescents. They made films and songs *for* the young, not simply
about them, and rock 'n' roll became the official music of adolescent rebellion, much to the horror of the older generation. In films like *The Wild One*
and *Blackboard Jungle,* the sociological study of delinquency turns into an
anthem of generational revolt. The pride of the fifties was the nuclear family, nurturing, wholesome, and patriarchal, celebrated in such television
sitcoms as *Father Knows Best.* But movies like Nicholas Ray's *Rebel Without
a Cause* (1955) exploded such families as dysfunctional – distorted by
neglect, parental discord, and repressed sexuality – with adults unable to
understand the simplest needs of the young. The kids in the movie, led by
a very insecure James Dean, must form a more nurturing alternative family
among themselves. In the hands of "sensitive" new actors like Brando,
Dean, and Montgomery Clift, maladjustment itself became a form of
rebellion, even if its goal was obscure. Asked what he was rebelling against
in *The Wild One,* Brando answered famously, "Whad'ya got?"

❧

Soon the widespread concern over juvenile delinquency, which led to congressional hearings like those on organized crime, gave way to the media's
fascination with the antics of the Beats. *Time* saw them as good copy, combining moral titillation with public spectacle. But besides their promo-
tional gifts, which were reminiscent of earlier avant-garde movements
such as Dada and surrealism, the Beats conveyed to their young followers a
new social spirit, communal, antinomian, and sexually liberated. Among
the Beats, the values previously associated with advanced art were played
out in bohemian enclaves of voluntary poverty and spirited exhibitionism.
With the beginnings of the civil rights movement and later the Vietnam
War, student protest activities burgeoned on a scale unseen since the Great
Depression. This new radicalism in turn helped fuel the rise of the sixties
counterculture, whose focus on community, poverty, drugs, and sexual
experimentation acted out a criticism of American values and behavior,
ranging from puritanism and competitive individualism to anti-
Communism and the worship of technology.

Artistically, the Beats had strong links to two movements whose perma-
nent achievements would prove greater than their own. One was jazz,

which was undergoing a revolution in the forties, turning from large swing bands playing dance music to the amazing virtuosity of bop artists like Charlie Parker, Dizzy Gillespie, and Thelonious Monk. It was their improvisational freshness, complexity, and spontaneity that the Beats would try to recreate in their prose and poetry. The other movement was abstract expressionism, the reigning avant-garde of the late forties and early fifties, whose gestural, performative manner and large spiritual ambitions also influenced the Beats. For these artists, painting was an act, an event, an experience rather than a crafted, finished object or the direct representation of a recognizable image. "What was to go on the canvas was not a picture but an event," said Harold Rosenberg, the critic who coined the term Action Painting. The purpose of art, as Meyer Schapiro wrote in 1957, had become "more passionately than ever before, the occasion of spontaneity or intense feeling." In the work of such abstract painters as Jackson Pollock, the tangible buildup of the paint on the canvas reminds us constantly of the physical action and movement that put it there. "The work of art," said Schapiro, defining the abstract aesthetic, "is an ordered world of its own kind in which we are aware, at every point, of its becoming."

In both jazz and abstract painting, as in Beat writing, the fluidity, energy, and subjectivity of the creative process become signifying elements of the work itself. This self-consciousness points to the Americanization of modernism in the postwar years. Challenging the more conservative culture of the fifties, these kinetic arts supplanted traditional forms with a vehement expression of personal energy; they became part of a growing counterculture that appealed strongly to alienated intellectuals and to the rebellious and discontented young.

Many contemporary observers described the fifties as the Age of Anxiety. Because of the Cold War, the widespread fear of nuclear annihilation, the Korean War, and finally the war in Vietnam, American society had remained, psychologically at least, in a wartime frame of mind. To all this, a large segment of the young said no, first through the music, then eventually with drugs, political protests, campus rebellions, and freer sex. By and large they were children of affluence, moved by the guilt and boredom that comes with privilege, not the anguish born of deprivation. Even their leaders, many of them children of thirties radicals, abandoned the rhetoric of class conflict that had fired up their parents. The colorful circus of generational conflict appealed to the media far more than the quiet persistence of class conflict. From the surly Brando and the troubled James Dean to the raucous Abbie Hoffman and the clownish Jerry Rubin, the restless young exposed a widening fissure in American life that novelists and filmmakers were among the first to exploit.

Novels and films rarely found a public language to deal with social conflicts over race, war, McCarthyism, Communism, or any other issues that
divided an otherwise triumphant America in the decades following World
War II. By integrating the armed forces and supporting civil rights legislation, the Truman administration had briefly put race at the top of the
American agenda, provoking a Southern revolt, but the brief vogue of
social protest films and novels in the late forties effectively died by 1950,
and the tough, shadowy style of film noir lasted only a few years longer.
The public lost interest in the problems of the returning soldiers, especially when most of those veterans, taking advantage of the education
offered through the GI Bill of Rights, began to thrive in the booming
postwar economy. By the 1950s, as anti-Semitism diminished, thanks to a
spasm of guilt over the Holocaust, race and poverty became subjects few
still cared to discuss. Some social scientists and historians, often former
radicals, began emphasizing consensus rather than conflict, status anxieties
rather than class divisions, and portrayed America as a country that had
largely solved its most pressing problems.

Novelists and filmmakers, on the other hand, were drawn to stories that
reflected the darker side of American life. The fifties saw a vogue of low-
budget horror and science-fiction films that reflected pervasive anxieties
about the Cold War, nuclear war, and the blight of timidity that spread in
this atmosphere of fear. These works expressed such themes as the fear of
invasion by an alien force, fear of the invisible, delayed effects of nuclear
radiation, and (in the case of Don Siegel's *Invasion of the Body Snatchers,*
1956) fear that, beneath a veneer of normality, the Cold War itself would
undermine American traditions of dissent and individuality.

Again and again, such novelists as Ralph Ellison, William Gaddis, and
Thomas Pynchon would deal not so much with the contour and clash of
personalities, like most earlier novelists, but with the loss of personality
in a world that trivialized individual differences. Some of this effacement
of personality had already been a theme of war novelists such as Norman
Mailer and James Jones, who saw the repressive and brutal aspects of
army life as an intimation of postwar fascism. But McCarthy, the kind of
figure their novels anticipated, proved to be a demagogue and a clown
rather than a Fascist, and the threat came more from what William H.
Whyte, Jr. called the "social ethic," the spirit of suburban and corporate
conformity, than from political repression. Although Mailer would argue
in 1957 that the concentration camps and the atom bomb had visited
untold psychic havoc on the postwar world, the new prosperity had a
deadening effect at least as widespread as any anxious concern about survival. The fifties were at once a period of complacency, of getting and

spending, and an age of anxiety, a time for doubt and self-questioning, as shown by works like David Riesman's *The Lonely Crowd* and Hannah Arendt's *The Origins of Totalitarianism.* With such writers as Riesman, Whyte, Vance Packard, C. Wright Mills, John Kenneth Galbraith, and finally Paul Goodman and Betty Friedan, social criticism became a major growth industry in an apparently self-satisfied society. Much of the fiction of the fifties, including such popular novels as Sloan Wilson's *The Man in the Gray Flannel Suit* and Cameron Hawley's *Executive Suite,* belongs to this vein of critical self-examination.

It is hard to think of J. D. Salinger as any kind of radical. His best-known hero, the superbright young prep-school dropout, Holden Caulfield, and Holden's even brighter and cuter sister, Phoebe, live comfortable middle-class lives on New York's Park Avenue, where Salinger himself spent his adolescent years. The son of a prosperous Jewish cheese importer and a Scottish-born mother, Salinger was born in 1919 and, after an indifferent academic career, served in the army from 1942 to 1946. Before he joined the literary community surrounding *The New Yorker* in 1948, the army was the family to which he became most strongly attached. From the breakdown he describes in his 1953 story "For Esmé – With Love and Squalor," it appears that the emotional problems he experienced during the war impelled him to look for a way to recapture the lost innocence of childhood and adolescence. His work would become one of the literary keys to a world in which adolescence was becoming an overriding concern.

Though earlier writers like Henry Roth in *Call It Sleep* (1934), Jean Stafford in *The Mountain Lion* (1947), and Truman Capote in *Other Voices, Other Rooms* (1948) had written intensely lyrical growing-up stories, Salinger was the first to tap emotionally into the new youth culture created by America's growing adolescent and college-age population after the war. The economic boom enabled Americans to keep young people out of the job market for a much longer period; meanwhile, increasing affluence turned the young into consumers with cultural values distinct from those of their elders, whose needs had been shaped by immigration, depression, and war.

The stresses of the period from 1929 to 1945 had created a cautious, culturally conservative middle-class generation whose values, at least initially, were invested in home, family, and maturity. Thanks to the GI Bill, returning soldiers received college degrees that gave them an advantage in the increasingly specialized postwar economy. But the massive influx of blacks and Hispanics into the large cities drove newly affluent whites to garden suburbs organized around single-family homes, shopping malls, and the automobile. When many of their children took up rock music and Beat styles, with their roots in the ghettos and in black culture, they were embracing the milieu and the values their elders had left behind.

Salinger's work is the most polite, well-bred version of adolescent rebellion, yet it is founded on a sweeping dismissal of grown-up life as inauthentic, pompous, and moralistic. Holden Caulfield is the first of a long postwar line of fictional naifs who see through everything, whose lives are an epic of thwarted sensitivity, who feel stifled by the hypocrisy of adults, the stupidity of their peers, the betrayal of those they trust, and the manipulations of all figures of authority. In the course of the novel he is misunderstood, patronized, verbally abused, beaten up, even propositioned by a trusted teacher, all described in the same bright-eyed tone of shocked wonderment and premature sophistication.

Like dozens of later novels from *On the Road* and *Slaughterhouse-Five* to *Portnoy's Complaint* and *Bright Lights, Big City,* Salinger's *Catcher in the Rye* is not a growing-up novel but a *not*-growing-up novel, focusing on a young man's refusal to assume the social responsibilities the world is too eager to impose on him. All these novels go back in different ways to *The Adventures of Huckleberry Finn,* one of the *ur*-texts of postwar fiction, with its emphasis on the inner life of troubled boyhood, and Huck's need to escape the corruptions of the adult world. This had a special point in the fifties, when *maturity* and *adjustment* were cultural watchwords, bolstered by a pop Freudianism. To Holden Caulfield, everyone from his teachers to the actors he sees on the stage are "phonies." Thrown out of yet another school, Pencey Prep – modeled on a well-known military academy where Salinger himself had spent two years – Holden is a genteel urban Huck Finn who dreams of taking to the road but instead, in his few days of adventure in New York, is actually in the midst of having a breakdown. The book thus brings together three of the main tropes of the fifties counterculture: the youthful misfit, the road, and mental illness as a form of social maladjustment and intuitive wisdom.

Where the growing-up novel, even in the hands of a writer as unsentimental as Jean Stafford or Nabokov, often expresses itself in nostalgia for a lost world, Salinger's stories rediscover the vernacular of childhood and youth as a language of endangered innocence. A wicked satirist with a cool eye and a perfect ear, Salinger lampoons the vulgarity and duplicity of adults while endowing his powerless young with amazing verbal virtuosity. Some of Salinger's best and worst stories, from "De Daumier-Smith's Blue Period" and *Catcher in the Rye* to the five long stories about the Glass family published in *The New Yorker* between 1955 and 1965, are essentially extended comic monologues that cleared a path for the picaresque writers of the 1960s, including Roth in *Portnoy's Complaint,* who, with some impetus from Céline, helped bring this tradition to its climax. One of Truman Capote's early mentors had called *Other Voices* the "fairy Huckleberry Finn," but *The Catcher in the Rye* was more truly in the colloquial Huck Finn tradition. Only Salinger successfully captured the exact accent and rhythm of the adolescent voice and sensibility; only in his work did the young recognize themselves as they were or as they dreamed of being.

Unlike the writing of Twain or Ring Lardner, Salinger's theme is spiritual: his young people and his sainted dead (especially Seymour Glass) are eternal innocents who cannot adjust to society or accept its compromises. "A Perfect Day for Bananafish" (1948) is the prototype for Salinger's later, more garrulous fiction. The main character besides Seymour Glass is an infinitely wise, articulate child named Sybil. He meets her on a Florida beach, and she provides him with a momentary respite from his gossipy wife Muriel ("Miss Spiritual Tramp of 1948," according to Seymour), whom we see polishing her nails and chatting with her mother on a long-distance telephone call. Caught between an unrecoverable innocence and a vulgar vitality, Seymour commits suicide – the founding moment of the Glass dynasty. Holden Caulfield and the shell-shocked soldier in "For Esmé – With Love and Squalor" are spiritual descendents of the martyred Seymour, while Holden's bright sister Phoebe and the young Esmé belong to the oracular mode of the bright young Sybil.

As we see in the later Glass stories and occasionally in Beat writing, such fictions can easily turn precious and narcissistic, reposing on a sentimental vision of the elect, but with little sense of the society that frustrates their needs. Salinger's later work needs more Muriel and less Sybil, more of the world's variety and less obsession with saintliness. In Holden Caulfield's sojourn in New York, though, Salinger still has his ear tuned to wider frequencies: roommates, parents, prostitutes, college boys, taxi drivers, elevator operators, spoiled mentors, all the people who fail Holden on his way down. The key to Holden is that at sixteen he is still virginal, pre-sexual, like the falling children he dreams of rescuing as "the catcher in the rye." He has a grown-up mind trapped uneasily in an adolescent's awkward body. Holden's problem with sex is a more concentrated version of his problem with the adult world: that it seems unspiritual, crude, a violation of the perfect sympathy he feels only with children:

If you want to know the truth, I'm a virgin. I really am. I've had quite a few opportunities to lose my virginity and all, but I've never got around to it yet. Something always happens. For instance, if you're at a girl's house, her parents always come home at the wrong time – or you're afraid they will. Or if you're in the back seat of somebody's car, there's always somebody's date in the front seat – some girl, I mean – that always wants to know what's going on *all over* the whole goddam car. I mean some girl in front keeps turning around to see what the hell's going on. I came quite close to doing it a couple of times, though. . . . The thing is, most of the time when you're coming pretty close to doing it with a girl – a girl that isn't a prostitute or anything, I mean – she keeps telling you to stop. The trouble with me is, I stop. Most guys don't. I can't help it. You never know whether they really *want* you to stop, or whether they're just scared as hell. . . . Anyway, I keep stopping. The trouble is I get to feeling sorry for them. . . . They tell me to stop, so I stop.

This sexual embarrassment is the material of stand-up comedy, but it is more than a riff: it remains wonderfully in character. Holden's adventures in New York are really a series of Jewish jokes, at once sad, funny, and self-accusing. Like Philip Roth, Salinger is an inspired mimic. When Portnoy complains that he feels caught in the middle of a Jewish joke, he's following in Holden's footsteps. Though little of Salinger's work belongs explicitly with the Jewish American novel, there is a touch of the schlemiel about Holden's fumbling adolescent self-consciousness, about the way he is prone to disaster, doomed to disappointment at every turn. Holden's haplessness arises from a mixture of anxiety and good-heartedness; his failures attest to his nobility and single him out for a special destiny.

As Twain did with Huck Finn, Salinger concentrates on the flow of Holden's voice, the starts and hesitations that echo his behavior. Voice – volatile, immediate, and seductive – was the secret weapon of fifties writers against the postwar resurgence of gentility and good form. Where more formal writers depend on a stable sense of identity, the picaresque narrator, like the jazz performer or Action Painter, seems to be making himself up as he goes along. Holden is not only a great storyteller but also a compulsive fibber and fantasist, living more easily in the identities he assumes than in the ones imposed on him. He lies out of an excess of imagination, and as a way of avoiding unpleasant confrontations. He is verbal and judgmental but never grasping or deliberately cruel. He understands sex only as violation – as a way of using someone and spoiling what is perfect about them. For Salinger, this makes him not just confused and unhappy but morally superior to the world around him. Holden foreshadows a counterculture that will be less about sex than about innocence; its ideal would be a kind of sainthood and spiritual election in a fallen world.

The youthful rebels and misfits who followed in the fifties and sixties were generally less funny than Holden and far less attentive to the nuances of a world they found oppressive. Their cultural or moral revisionism takes the place of the social revolts of previous decades; it aims to escape the demands of society rather than to change society. Their unorganized protests occur not in a Depression world of crisis, suffering, and upheaval but in a triumphant world of postwar affluence and economic growth, a world they find soulless rather than exploitative. They are truly rebels without a cause. The terms of their radicalism are existential, not political; they seek inner satisfaction and identity, not social justice. Thus James Baldwin and Ralph Ellison reject the work of their mentor, Richard Wright, as "protest novels" or as works that fail to do justice to either the richness of African American life or the hollowness of the larger society.

If the protest novel, in Baldwin's sense, was political, propagandistic, and its moving force was a burning rage at injustice, the new kind of novel of the 1950s was not only personal, it was lyrical. Lyrical novels were not so much critical of society as indifferent to it, in flight from it, subjecting it to a dismissive mockery. These novels were often colloquial, written in the first person (like *Huckleberry Finn*), loosely structured, seemingly spontaneous. Their heroes, always in flight, lay claim to the Emersonian freedom to create and remake themselves that many Americans consider their birthright. The alternative to the lyrical novel in the 1950s is the ironic novel, tightly patterned, intricately written, in which such freedom proves to be a delusion, because society will never permit it and life itself makes it unattainable. Here the protagonist, much less identified with the author, becomes an object lesson in frustration or failure.

Versions of the lyrical novel include the road novel, the adolescent novel, the adventure novel, the first-person picaresque. The sensitive protagonist is always trying to escape from social regimentation, from the nuclear family, especially from the domesticating power of women, and trying to find his own path within an overorganized society. The ironic novel, on the other hand, often took the form of the Jamesian social fable or the Kafkaesque metaphysical parable. It centered on plots that created a sense of entrapment or futility, on characters caught in webs of circumstance not of their own making, or in contradictions set deep within their own personalities. Fatalistic works like Bellow's *Seize The Day* or Malamud's *The Assistant* show us a world not at all shaped to a person's needs or likely to bend to his will.

The ironic novel belongs to the conservative, quiescent strain of American thought after the war: the darkly shaded Freudianism of such critics as Lionel Trilling, the sense of sin of theologians like Reinhold Niebuhr, the anti-utopianism of historians like Arthur Schlesinger, Jr. and Richard Hofstadter, the critique of liberalism and progressivism of the work of these and other writers and thinkers, including Schlesinger in *The Vital Center* (1949), Niebuhr in *The Irony of American History* (1951), and Hofstadter in *The Age of Reform* (1954). As Morton White showed in *Social*

Thought in America (1949), the darkly shaded mood of existentialism had displaced the spirit of progressivism; the influence of Dewey had given way to the ghost of Kierkegaard. In Trilling's *The Liberal Imagination* (1950), a sense of modernist complexity and tragic realism undermines the old faith in reform. Nearly all these intellectuals remained liberals, but their social faith had a tragic, anti-utopian cast.

This recoil against liberal optimism was influenced by both the failures of Communism in the 1930s and the barbarities of Fascism in the 1940s. It was a neoliberalism that had little confidence in human nature and the benign power of the human will; it looked back not to Emerson but to the founding fathers, with their suspicion of democracy and irrationality and their insistence on checks and balances to keep human nature at bay. Its literary roots were more European than American, for its outlook was grounded not in Emerson, Thoreau, and Whitman but in the social determinations of the realistic novel and the ironies of literary modernism.

The ironic novel, the kind of novel in which people are defined by who they ineluctably are, not by what they want or need, became the specialty of Jewish writers such as Saul Bellow and Bernard Malamud, of Southerners like Flannery O'Connor, and blacks like James Baldwin, writers who came from groups that had known defeat and oppression and had experienced the direct impact of history on their collective and personal lives. The idea of man's unbounded freedom had little resonance for them except as a misguided form of hubris. It didn't belong to their own experience. The goal of their characters was survival, decency, the chance to get along: the recognition of their humanity, not the giddy intensities of self-invention. People in their novels who do try to reinvent themselves, like Tommy Wilhelm in *Seize the Day* (1956), are invariably thwarted, humiliated, even destroyed, though not without moments of tragic self-understanding. Lyrical novelists, on the other hand, brought American fiction closer to native traditions of transcendentalism and pragmatism. Emerson's work was their scripture, Whitman and Twain their literary inspiration. The oral richness of American humor spoke to them more strongly than the ironic reverberations of Kafka or Freud or the social structures in Balzac and George Eliot. Their novels, so often autobiographical, were personal effusions more than social canvases, though they were scarcely free of ironic details, and often conveyed a sharp sense of the social limits they fiercely resisted. These were utopian novels, dreamers' novels, even when (as in *The Catcher in the Rye*) their well-meaning characters came to grief. They appealed most to young people, and in the fifties and sixties they became an important vehicle for an emerging counterculture as well as a momentous turn in American fiction.

The novel that had the greatest impact after *The Catcher in the Rye* was Jack Kerouac's *On the Road,* completed the same year *Catcher* appeared (1951) but not published until six years later. In the interim, Kerouac wrote nearly a dozen books in what became his autobiographical saga, the Duluoz legend, but none would be as readable as *On the Road,* nor would any of his other novels match its mythic status as a founding text of the Beat movement. Born in 1922 in the mill town of Lowell, Massachusetts, where his French Canadian father worked as a printer, Kerouac did not even speak English until he was five or six, and his later celebrations of the American heartland were the work of a keen observer rather than a confident insider. For Kerouac, Lowell and his mother's home represent a Catholic tradition of family values, while the great empty spaces of the West, which he discovers for the first time in *On the Road,* offer undreamed-of possibilities of freedom that leave him feeling ecstatic but deeply ambivalent.

Kerouac's more traditional first novel, *The Town and the City* (1950), was written in the expansive autobiographical mode of Thomas Wolfe. A high school football star, Kerouac had left Lowell in 1939 for a year of prep school in New York before taking up an athletic scholarship at Columbia. After a disastrous hitch as a merchant marine in the U.S. Navy, he returned to New York, where his real life in the city began. In his first novel, the hometown and the large nuclear family based on Lowell were set off against the exciting bohemia of the city, peopled by characters based on Allen Ginsberg, then still a Columbia freshman, and William Burroughs, the Harvard-educated black sheep of a wealthy St. Louis family — Kerouac met both of them in 1944. Their world, on the fringes of the university, attracted the young writer, essentially an autodidact, to whom art was as darkly appealing as sin. This alternative family offered the hope of self-transformation through a new kind of community: close-knit but transgressive, morally adventurous, marginally criminal, and wonderfully creative.

The Town and the City is a benign version of the "revolt from the village" novels of the 1920s, typified by Sherwood Anderson's *Winesburg, Ohio* (1919) and Sinclair Lewis's *Main Street* (1920), in which the writer's autobiographical surrogate tries to flee the stultifying intimacy of the small town to seek fulfilment in a wider world, usually the big city. The genre was ill suited to Jack Kerouac, who, just beneath his bohemianism, had a deeply conservative cast of mind, as his later life would repeatedly show. It was only by escaping *from* the city that he found the subject that truly ignited his literary imagination.

On the Road is based on a series of cross-country trips that Kerouac himself had made, mostly with Neal Cassady, between 1947 and 1950, at the very moment other Americans were rediscovering the mobility they had lost during years of Depression and wartime. There would soon be an explosion of cars on the road, sped along by the sleek new highways of Eisenhower's Interstate Highway System, the major federal achievement of the 1950s. Best-selling books like Whyte's *The Organization Man* (1956) would show that Americans were becoming a rootless people, thanks to migrations from rural areas to cities, from cities to new towns and suburbs, and from stable manufacturing jobs to corporate white-collar positions that repeatedly transferred them to different parts of the country. Though *On the Road* seemingly turned its back on the world of marriage, families, and jobs, it was very much in tune with the new mobility that peace and prosperity afforded to many Americans in the 1950s. The jobless, penniless drifters of the Depression were turning into the white-collar transients of the postwar world; Cassady and Kerouac, one rootless, the other restless, were pushing their way past a door that was already swinging open.

The genius of *On the Road* was to attach the new restlessness to the classic American mythology of the road, and to use it to express a subversive set of values – exuberance, energy, spirituality, intensity, improvisation – that would challenge the suburban and corporate conservatism of the 1950s. The road represents the expansive, footloose spirit of America after the war yet also the need to escape from the constraints of the new domesticity and work ethic. Dean Moriarty, Kerouac's hero, based on Cassady – his name combines James Dean with Sherlock Holmes's chief villain – is everything from a charismatic con man and cocksman to a "HOLY GOOF" with the tremendous energy of "a new kind of American saint." As a self-made man, he is much better at holding down a job and supporting a family than the pampered Kerouac, raised on mother love. But this saint lives for kicks and preaches a gospel of irresponsibility that makes everyone around him miserable, especially the long-suffering women. In the eyes of Sal Paradise, the fearful but enamored narrator (based on Kerouac), the kinetic Dean, fleet runner, legendary driver, virtuoso lover, is everything he himself is not: comfortable in his own skin, free of moral hang-ups and family ties. Where Sal, like Tom Sawyer, never breaks the umbilical cord connecting him to his aunt, Dean is a modern Huck Finn who was "actually born on the road" and grew up with his wino father on skid row in Denver, an abused child and orphan who learned early on to fend for himself.

In *On the Road,* the likable but impossible Dean is the daemon who presides over the Road; he is the tutelary spirit of the West, even of the pioneers Kerouac also had in mind as he repeatedly tried to tell the story of his "life on the road." He runs and drives like a figure out of Greek myth or black magic. The American tradition of the Road is built into the scale of the continent itself, the endless migration made possible by the frontier and the great open spaces of the West, a migration that extends the "westering" movement that first brought the colonists to the New World. In biblical and Christian imagery, this westward movement is always renovating and apocalyptic, offering the promise of a fresh beginning, a new life, as John Steinbeck understood when he took his family of Okies on a biblical trek across the desert to a green and promising land. In *On the Road,* as in early Westerns like *The Virginian* and its many film offshoots, the East represents a stale, unhealthy, ossified civilization, an indoor civilization out of touch with nature, while the West is a brave new world, full of explosive energies and dangerous possibilities.

Road novels and movies were especially important in the 1930s when so many Americans were uprooted by the Depression. From *I Am a Fugitive From a Chain Gang* (1932) and *Wild Boys of the Road* (1933) to *U.S.A., The Grapes of Wrath,* and *Sullivan's Travels* (1941), the hobo and the drifter became icons of the era, staples in fiction, photography, and Depression journalism as well as film. Even earlier, Whitman had eulogized the open road as the emblem of a truly American freedom and Mark Twain had turned the Mississippi into an escape route that rescues Nigger Jim from slavery and Huck Finn from the brutality of his drunken father and the tyranny of small-town respectability. As the novel ends, Huck decides famously "to light out for the Territory" when the adults threaten to "sivilize" him. Jack London had collected the memories of his tramping life in the 1890s into another apotheosis, rich with hobo slang, *The Road* (1907). "I became a tramp – well, because of the life that was in me, of the wanderlust in my blood that would not let me rest," wrote London, whose adventurous ways had already made him a legend. "I went on 'The Road' because I couldn't keep away from it; because I hadn't the price of the railroad fare in my jeans." Immensely literary and self-conscious about his work, Kerouac responded strongly to plebeians like London and to vernacular writers who experimented with the American idiom, including Twain, Sherwood Anderson, Hemingway, Ring Lardner, Nelson Algren, and William Saroyan – the same writers who most impressed the young Salinger. Most of these were writers whose work emerged out of the great oral tradition of American humor, storytelling, and mimickry.

In Kerouac's work, going on the road is less a matter of economic need, as it had been during the Depression, more a myth of rebirth, as in literary and religious parables. Almost from the beginning, the narrator feels eerily estranged from himself: "My whole life was a haunted life, the life of a ghost. I was halfway across America, at the dividing line between the East of my youth and the West of my future." This is not so much a destination as a dream of pure movement, directionless, propulsive, unreflective. To the more conventional Sal, Dean's "frantic" travels eventually come to seem "maniacal" and "completely meaningless," but at certain times they make him ecstatic; their manic intensity projects him into a realm of pure spirit. Kerouac himself was afraid of driving, terrified of flying, uncomfortable with women, afraid of falling under the tracks of trains – all the spheres in which Dean, with his amazing physical dexterity and con man's irresistible charm, performed with such ease and confidence.

At about the same time Kerouac was mythologizing Cassady, the publicity apparatus of American culture, especially *Life* magazine, was mythologizing another rugged son of the West, Jackson Pollock. He was hard drinking, taciturn, intensely physical, and often worked on a grandiose American scale. He had studied with Thomas Hart Benton but then gone his own way, though the swirl and flow and size of Benton's compositions influenced his work. Though he rejected the stylized realism of the thirties muralists, he said he wanted to create "large, movable pictures that will function between the easel and mural." Keeping the canvas on the floor so that he could get *into* it, throwing paint at the canvas and letting it drip, sometimes adding tactile, angular bits of gravel and pebbles, he created a thickly layered grid, a complex impasto of paint that was almost a road map of the energy and intensity he had put into it. (Like Kerouac he was attracted by the improvisational energy of jazz.) For Pollock, the canvas itself was his way of being "on the road," of taking off on an explosive free-form adventure of his own. Until one drunken night on New York's Long Island in 1956, he wrapped his car around a tree, killing himself and one of the women with him. Like James Dean in his silver Porsche the previous year, he was yet another casualty of the road.

At about the same time, another great visual artist, the Swiss-born photographer Robert Frank, also took to the road to create a document of American life. When his pictures were collected in *The Americans* (1959), with an introduction by Jack Kerouac, they not only captured the look of postwar America but reshaped the legacy of Depression photography. Where Walker Evans and Dorothea Lange had portrayed an America suffering extreme privations with exquisite dignity and determination, Frank showed the world a casual, backwater America, tending its small-town rituals, caught up in the undramatic business of everyday life.[2] Unlike their Depression counterparts, Frank's "Americans" had multiple histories, not just one big brush with History. In line with their subjects, his pictures

---

[2] Frank, working with Alfred Leslie, memorialized the downtown world of the Beats and the New York painters with the same random attention in a largely improvised film, *Pull My Daisy* (1959), that was pulled together by Kerouac's inspired narration.

had a drab throwaway look that broke sharply with the artful composure of previous American photography. They seemed to have a deceptively amateur quality, as if the image just happened to come together, like some of Kerouac's prose of which Paul Goodman complained that "nothing is told, nothing is presented, everything is just 'written about.'"

But unlike Frank's sad, eerie images of an American wasteland, Kerouac's novel has a figure at the center to energize his portrait of America. At first Sal relishes the simple pleasure of being with Dean, the sense of putting all entanglements behind him, of leaving even himself behind. He feeds on Dean's explosive energy, his sheer physicality. Dean is the spirit of the West, life in the raw; he is the orphan boy without a superego, ready at any moment to pull up stakes and jettison his life. Friends, jobs, wives, children mean something to him only so long as he feels impelled to stay with them. A kind of centaur, perfectly fused to his four wheels, Dean believes in movement simply as a way of going with the flow, cutting any knot that binds him and complicates his life.

"Whooee!" yelled Dean. "Here we go!" And he hunched over the wheel and gunned her; he was back in his element, everybody could see that. We were all delighted, we all realized we were leaving confusion and nonsense behind and performing our one and noble function of the time, *move*. And we moved!

As time goes on, however, Sal, with his Catholic feeling of guilt, his middle-class sense of family, recoils from Dean's habit of simply picking up and moving on. Like Dean's wives and girlfriends, Sal flinches from the irresponsibility that attracted him in the first place. In one memorable scene, many of the women in Dean's life, wives of his old buddies, have their say: we see the Pied Piper from the point of view of those who were left behind, who nail him for living solely for "kicks." To Sal, as to these jealous upholders of civilization and domesticity, Dean's energy has become more like madness than exuberance; it evokes Sal's deep-seated anxieties as much as his sense of wonder. For him, Dean's sainthood and irresponsibility are all mixed up. Dean is like the unfathomable Gatsby seen through the grudgingly respectful eyes of Nick Carraway; he's the obsessed Ahab conjured up in lightning flashes by his chronicler, Ishmael.

Curled up in the back of the car, expecting an imminent smash-up, Sal tries to sleep. Soon, in Dean's hands, his mortal fear gives way to resignation:

As a seaman I used to think of the waves rushing beneath the shell of the ship and the bottomless deeps thereunder — now I could feel the road some twenty inches beneath me, unfurling and flying and hissing at incredible speeds across the groaning continent with that mad Ahab at the wheel. When I closed my eyes, all I could see was the road unwinding into me. When I opened them I saw flashing shadows of trees vibrating on the floor of the car. There was no escaping it. I resigned myself to all. And still Dean drove.

As Dean's character thickens into moral ambiguity, Kerouac's prose becomes less wide eyed and innocent, more Melvillean. This "road unwinding into me" is also the Buddhist or Tao road of cosmic submission, the tranformation of fear into individual purpose. "What's your road, man?" he imagines Dean saying to him, "– holyboy road, madman road, rainbow road, guppy road, any road." The enigma of Dean, the message of Dean, even Dean's style – these are what the book is all about. Soon after he completed *On the Road,* Kerouac would write another book, *Visions of Cody* (1973), his most free-flowing and experimental work, simply to fathom his friend's character.

The run-on spontaneity of Cassady's talk and letters influenced Kerouac's writing much like the improvisational flow of jazz riffs, which Kerouac worked hard to imitate in language. Kerouac's "spontaneous bop prosody," as Allen Ginsberg called it in the dedication of *Howl and Other Poems,* was yet another version of the "road," the flow, the book's organizing metaphor. So was the physical manuscript of the final version, which Kerouac produced on a single long roll of paper in three weeks of nonstop composition in April 1951. As he wrote to Cassady a few weeks later: "I've told all the road now. Went fast because road is fast . . . wrote whole thing on strip of paper 120 foot long (tracing paper that belonged to Cannastra.) – just rolled it through typewriter and in fact no paragraphs . . . rolled it out on floor and it looks like a road" (*Selected Letters,* 22 May 1951). Truman Capote quipped that Kerouac's style was not writing but typing. Yet Kerouac's typing, with its uncensored, unshaped remembering, was one of the few spheres in which he could match the speed and intensity of Cassady's driving, running, screwing, and verbal riffing. His style, shaped by this nonstop flow of memory, reflects the aimless spontaneity of their cross-country travels.

Kerouac's three-week marathon was his literary breakthrough. *On the Road* is somehow a great book without being a good novel. Too much in the book happens mainly because it happened, with little dramatic buildup or consequence; too many minor characters are there just because they really were there at the time. Even the style often falls into cliché; the much-edited syntax, the punctuation "improved" by the publisher, too often goes lame. There is a gushing adolescent enthusiasm that does not entirely belong to Kerouac's narrator, Sal: "I licked my lips for the luscious blond." "The nights in Denver are cool, and I slept like a log." On apple pie and ice cream: "I knew it was nutritious and it was delicious, of course." But neither the clichés nor the publisher's insistence on conventional punctuation really damages the *lilt* of Kerouac's prose or the propulsive energy and feeling behind it. Shapeless at its worst, incandescently evocative at its best, Kerouac's prose became a landmark in the poetics of improvisation that gave the counterculture its distinct character. At its frequent best, this style, influenced by eruptive writers like Céline, would free up countless others, beginning with his friends Ginsberg and Burroughs, and then Norman Mailer, all of whom were still working in a far more conventional vein in 1951. If we compare Burroughs's straightforward *Junkie* to *Naked Lunch* or Ginsberg's formal early poems to *Howl,* Kerouac's influence on them becomes immediately clear. Kerouac taught writers from Ginsberg to Bob Dylan to go with the flow, to avoid censoring outlandish images, to tap their fantasies as they shaped their memories, and to ride the shape of their own breath, as the surrealists preached, the Buddhist masters taught, and jazzmen instinctively practiced. The flow of this style, the cascade of details that Kerouac recalled astonishingly well – Ginsberg called him "The Great Rememberer" – meshes with Dean's kinetic personality to give the novel its unusual kind of strength.

Ultimately, *On the Road* was more important as a myth, as a cultural marker, than as a novel. As Holden Caulfield became the first literary protagonist of the new youth culture, Dean Moriarty would become the patron saint of the counterculture, to be followed closely by the Ginsberg of *Howl,* the Mailer of "The White Negro" (1957), the Paul Goodman of *Growing Up Absurd* (1960), and, among literary characters, the ultracool Randall McMurphy in Ken Kesey's fable *One Flew Over the Cuckoo's Nest* (1962) and many others throughout the 1960s. (Before his death in Mexico in 1968, Cassady himself would drive the bus for Kesey's perpetually stoned group of Merry Pranksters, as tediously recorded in Tom Wolfe's sixties chronicle, *The Electric Kool-Aid Acid Test* [1968].) Thomas Pynchon's *V.* (1963) zanily crosses the offbeat drifter world of Kerouac with the precise plotting of Conrad and Graham Greene. In later years, Ginsberg would mythologize Kerouac as a Beat legend, as Kerouac had mythologized Cassady, and as Norman Mailer, the promising but reserved young novelist, would revamp himself into a hip adventurer, an existential legend, in "The White Negro," "The Time of Her Time," and *Advertisements for Myself* (1959).

Because of Kerouac's sense of himself as an outsider, *On the Road* is ultimately a sad book rather than merely an exuberant one. Where Mailer mythologized blacks as figures of impulse and violence, Kerouac, in the most notorious passage in the novel, projected his loneliness onto the black ghetto of Denver, imagining it as a scene of warmth and belonging from which he feels excluded. Sal is disappointed with Dean, cut off from everyone else, locked in his own shyness and inhibitions. Feeling abandoned, he dreams of exchanging worlds with "the happy, truehearted, ecstatic Negroes of America." They represent the vitality, spontaneity, and human connection he himself had despaired of achieving except in fugitive moments, as in the brief affair with a Mexican girl described so touchingly in *On the Road.* For Kerouac himself, this sense of being stranded and cut off was prophetic, for the success of the book made his world a living hell.

Kerouac was deeply ambivalent about the fame he had sought and found, which made him feel even more isolated. Nearly all his important work was written before *On the Road* was published. His chronicles ranged from early love affairs retold in strikingly different styles in *Tristessa, Maggie Cassidy,* and *The Subterraneans,* which brought out some of his tenderest writing, to accounts of the Beats themselves, his substitute family, in books like *The Dharma Bums,* written quickly to capitalize on the success of *On the Road,* and in *Desolation Angels* (1965), his last good book.

In his final years – he died of alcoholism in 1969 – he became almost as reclusive as Salinger. The two writers also shared a deepening interest in Buddhism, and both obsessively devoted their later energies to shaping a family saga. Like the fictional Holden Caulfield, who idealizes his dead brother Allie as a dreamy legend, Kerouac wrote worshipfully of an older brother, Gerard, whose death in childhood left him feeling half amputated, a mere survivor. *Visions of Gerard* (1963) was the peculiar shrine he erected to this departed saint. Kerouac played off another childhood legend in *Dr. Sax* and described a nervous breakdown brought on by fame, drink, and drugs in *Big Sur.* Publishers showed little interest in his carefully composed Buddhist scrapbook, *Some of the Dharma,* an ambitious collage of poems and meditations that did not appear in full until 1997. The last book he published in his lifetime, *Vanity of Duluoz* (1968), was a more directly autobiographical version of *The Town and the City.* As Salinger's last published story, "Hapworth 16, 1924" (1965), was written in the precocious voice of a seven-year-old Seymour Glass, Kerouac's posthumously published *Pic* (1971), an early experiment in first-person storytelling, was narrated in dialect by a black boy of ten.

It would be foolish to extend the parallel between Kerouac and Salinger too far. Even with the solipsistic excesses of his Glass stories, Salinger remained a fastidious writer in the *New Yorker* mode, crafting each sentence as if it were his last. Kerouac was in every way a looser, more spontaneous stylist, a good travel writer with an evocative sense of place, experimenting with different techniques from book to book, running the gamut from solid naturalism to undifferentiated stream of consciousness depending on the subject and his state of mind. One of Kerouac's most improbable admirers was a younger *New Yorker* writer, John Updike, mandarin stylist, heir to Nabokov in lexical playfulness and metaphoric dazzle, yet also a conscientious realist, dutiful husband and father, and protégé of John Cheever as chronicler of the suburban middle class. In a 1971 interview excerpted in *Picked-Up Pieces* (1975), Updike singled out Salinger, Kerouac, and the virtually unknown Harold Brodkey, his Harvard contemporary, for having broken the mold of the well-made story they had inherited in the 1950s.

According to Updike, "It's in Salinger that I first heard, as a college student in the early Fifties, the tone that spoke to my condition," something he had not heard in the short stories of such hard-boiled or "wised-up" writers as Hemingway, John O'Hara, or Dorothy Parker. "Salinger's stories were not wised up. They were very open to tender invasions. Also they possessed a refreshing formlessness which, of course, he came to push to an extreme, as real artists tend to do."

He goes on to praise Brodkey's work for going "deeper into certain kinds of emotional interplay than the things written by older writers" and Kerouac because "there is something benign, sentimentally benign, in his work." When the interviewer expresses astonishment at any link between Updike, the polished craftsman, and the fluent Kerouac of the printer's roll, Updike insists that "Kerouac was right in emphasizing a certain flow, a certain ease. Wasn't he saying, after all, what the surrealists said? That if you do it very fast without thinking, something will get in that wouldn't ordinarily."

Updike's comments are virtually a manifesto for the lyrical novel by someone not usually associated with the first-person picaresque or with any kind of countercultural self-assertion. They suggest that Kerouac's and Salinger's importance even to the most buttoned-up writers was not simply a matter of form or style but a whole approach to experience. The arrival of the sensitive male in American fiction followed quickly on his appearance in film and drama. The formal breakthrough of the writer also represents the physical freedom many young people were seeking in a transitional era of severe but rapidly eroding moral constraints. American society still stigmatized sex and stressed the value of home, family, and work, but this was a rear-guard position within a growing culture of consumption and abundance. "Maturity" was the albatross of the postwar generation; Salinger and the Beats helped their readers see beyond it, to find the sensitive child, the thwarted adolescent in themselves. This in turn connected them to the newly emerging values of personal fulfilment, individuality, and unlimited consumption.

In remarks in *Esquire* in 1945, Salinger himself had criticized the hyper-masculine war novels for showing "too much of the strength, maturity and craftsmanship critics are looking for, and too little of the glorious imperfections which teeter and fall off the best minds. The men who have been in this war deserve some sort of *trembling melody* rendered without embarrassment or regret. I'll watch for that book." Here, Salinger speaks rather self-consciously for those for whom the war was a trauma rather than a triumph, a desperate challenge or a breakdown rather than an adventure. His aim is to write the emotional history of the war genera-tion, to give us characters who, in Updike's revealing phrase, are "very open to tender invasions."

Salinger, Kerouac, and Updike thus represent in their different ways the inward turn of the postwar novel, its feminization, so to speak. They look beyond masculine worlds imagined by Hemingway, the social map minutely drawn by John O'Hara. They look beyond sophistication toward the lost innocence of childhood, the paradise approximated by sex or drugs, the freedom associated with the road yet also the tenderness of fam-ily life. Families are their subject yet families also bring out their most ambivalent feelings. Families represent at once the remembered scene of childhood, the site of tender relationships, and the maturity trap they are anxious to escape. Sometimes they reject home and marriage only to exper-iment with new families, as with Kerouac and his Beat friends or Updike's Rabbit in *Rabbit Redux,* whose house becomes a kind of sixties communal pad, an irregular family, after his wife has left him.

Transgressive writing had flowered briefly with such homosexual authors as Tennessee Williams, Gore Vidal, and Paul Bowles in the late forties, but in the fifties and sixties a dream of freedom, a sexual and moral utopianism, beckoned to nearly every important American writer. Saul Bellow's chilling novella *Seize the Day,* a masterpiece of ironic fiction, dra-matizes the failure of one man's bid for freedom, but it is preceded and fol-lowed in Bellow's work by two wildly lyrical novels, *The Adventures of Augie March* (1953) and *Henderson the Rain King* (1959), essentially road novels exploring the limits of both well-made fiction and social conven-tion. Ralph Ellison's great *Invisible Man* (1952) is the most surreal of auto-biographical novels. Its form takes on the classic picaresque pattern of Voltaire's *Candide* or Nathanael West's *A Cool Million,* in which the eter-nally hopeful hero, like a rubbery cartoon character, repeatedly takes it on the chin from a crude and brutal world. *Invisible Man* carries us through Ellison's Oklahoma childhood, his encounter with the South and the ideas of Booker T. Washington at Tuskegee Institute, his arrival in Harlem in the late 1930s, and his disillusioning attachment to the Communist party.

For the anonymous protagonist, as for many other black migrants, this road takes him nowhere, toward a Dostoyevskian underground room where he nurses his final cynicism. The strategy of his patrons is simply to manipulate him, to wear him out with the appearance of movement and progress: "Keep this nigger boy running."

Even compared to Bellow and Ellison, Updike is the most improbable of road novelists, the one most anchored to suburban life and a conventional literary career. At a time when so many young couples married so they could have sex and conceived children largely because they were married, Updike and his first wife were raising four children while still in their twenties. His literary mentor, John Cheever, seemed every inch the country squire, the well-mannered *New Yorker* stylist with the moral weight of his New England Puritanism behind him. But early on, Cheever began writing, in a deceptively light tone, about seriously dysfunctional families – emasculating mothers, failed fathers, murderous fraternal rivalries – and from *Falconer* (1977) to his posthumously published *Journals* (1991), he raised the curtain on a secret life of dark bisexual hedonism and marital misery on an epic scale. Another errant son of New England with a troubled family history, Robert Lowell, made the breakthrough much earlier and more daringly in the autobiographical prose and verse fragments of *Life Studies* (1959), contrasting his famous family name and genteel but impoverished background with his tortured mental history.

Compared to Cheever and Lowell, Updike's family origins were strictly lower middle class. His father, memorably portrayed in *The Centaur* (1963), was a high school math teacher and his mother, the central figure in *Of the Farm* (1965), was a frustrated writer who actually began publishing fiction late in life. Born in 1932 and raised in rural Pennsylvania, Updike attended Harvard on a scholarship and spent a year in Oxford as an art student before joining the staff of *The New Yorker,* where he became a lifelong contributor. His alter ego in fiction, Harry "Rabbit" Angstrom, is his notion of what he might have become had he never left southeastern Pennsylvania. The two main settings of Updike's fiction are the Pennsylvania towns where he grew up (the suburb of Reading he calls Olinger or Mt. Judge) and Massachusetts shore towns like Ipswich (called Tarbox in his novels) where he brought up his growing family after 1957.

Updike's work blends social chronicle with invention and autobiography, but like most lyrical novelists, his writing has a deeply personal core. Besides *The Centaur* and *Of the Farm,* two of his most effective and heartfelt works, he wrote remarkable sequences of stories about his boyhood and youth (collected in his *Olinger Stories,* 1964); his travels and his life as a writer (transmuted into *Bech: A Book,* 1970); and his first marriage, separation, and divorce (brought together memorably in *Too Far to Go,* 1978), collections that read like loosely sutured autobiographical novels. His first great commercial success, *Couples* (1968), was an epic of suburban adultery lightly salted with spiritual longing. But the core of his work can be found in the life history of Rabbit Angstrom, a sensual man trapped in marriage, family, responsibility yet always hungering for something beyond, a perfection he once experienced as a high school athlete.

Free of the showy stylistic filigree of Updike's early work and the lumbering, pedantic manner of some of his late books (such as *Roger's Version,* 1984, and *Memories of the Ford Administration,* 1992) and written in the vivid immediacy of the present tense, the Rabbit novels become Updike's personal history of America over four decades. His scenes from a marriage are keyed to the mood of the country at large: rebellious but frustrated in the late fifties, apocalyptic in the late sixties, smugly materialistic in the late seventies, disintegrating by the late eighties. Since Rabbit is not an intellectual, not a writer but a sentient animal who lives most in his body, the novels are full of vividly observed details, a flat poetry of the ordinary that gave rise to the Kmart school of fiction (by such lower-middle-class writers as Bobbie Ann Mason) in the seventies and eighties. But the Rabbit novels, especially *Rabbit, Run,* are also the history of a spiritual quest that does not always mesh well with Rabbit's unreflective nature. Though Rabbit eventually becomes prosperous, making love to his wife in a bed of Krugerrands in *Rabbit Is Rich* (1981), the novels unfold a long history of decline, foreshadowed from the first page of *Rabbit, Run.*

The Rabbit tetralogy begins and climaxes with the same scene: a bit of sandlot basketball in which the sometime star athlete tries to turn the clock back, to show the kids (and himself) that he still has the moves. In *Rabbit, Run,* eight years out of school, already past his prime at 26, Rabbit impresses the kids, who have no idea who he is; in *Rabbit at Rest* (1990), ailing, fat, out of shape, he reaches for the rim one last time but suffers a massive heart attack that has been coming on for two decades. Yet the subject of the books, especially of *Rabbit, Run,* is not Rabbit's fall so much as his inchoate quest, his effort to shape his life to the fleeting glimpses of glory he once had — occasionally still has — as an athlete and lover. Though Rabbit's instinctive middle-American conservatism seems a world away from the Beats, we can see here how Updike, a serious Christian, was influenced by Kerouac in crafting a fable about the frustrating constraints of family life, the deadening spiritual limits of adulthood, maturity, and civilization itself.

Along with Richard Yates's neglected *Revolutionary Road* (1961), *Rabbit, Run* is the classic novel of middle-class disappointment in the late Eisenhower years, when the social confidence of the fifties was breaking up, when John F. Kennedy was building his presidential campaign on a sense of national malaise, on the contrast between Republican stagnation and his own well-projected vigor. Although his opponent, Vice-President Richard Nixon, accused him of "downgrading America," he offered a new beginning, with a historic sense of passing the torch to a new generation. Though his private life did not become public till long after his death, he and his young wife even then conveyed a sense of sexual as well as political potency that contrasted with the avuncular Eisenhower and the devious, sinister Nixon. Updike, like Mailer before him, like Philip Roth, his exact contemporary, also projected a sense of male energy at bay, caught in a world swamped by mediocrity and routine.

Rabbit, Run is built on images of blockage, frustration, baffled vitality. *On the Road* had begun with the end of Sal's marriage, the start of his life on the road. Updike's novel begins with Rabbit married two years, with a son at home, a child on the way, a crummy job, and a wife who drinks too much, who watches children's programs on television, and no longer attracts or responds to him much in bed. "Just yesterday, it seems to him, she stopped being pretty." Her pregnancy "infuriates him with its look of stubborn lumpiness." In one recurring metaphor, Rabbit feels meshed in a "net" that keeps tightening around him, "a net he is somewhere caught in," not the hoop of his glory on the court but a web of routine and responsibility. He "senses he is in a trap." Surrounding the town there are still "hundreds of acres of forest Mt. Judge boys can never wholly explore," a dark wood just outside the line of civilization, the mountains where Rabbit continues to run as the novel ends.

Work and marriage have made Rabbit claustrophobic; his instinctive solution as an ex-athlete is to run, sometimes on his own two legs, often on wheels: "Harry sits wordless staring through the windshield, rigid in body, rigid in spirit. The curving highway seems a wide straight road that has opened up in front of him. There is nothing he wants to do but go down it." Not long after the novel begins he takes to the road for the first time, impulsively, after a quarrel with his wife Janice, getting all the way to West Virginia before turning back. Soon he is living with a part-time whore, Ruth, who also becomes pregnant, but he comes back home when he learns that his wife is in labor, leaving Ruth as abruptly and unthinkingly as he had left his wife. When he runs out again on Janice, she accidentally drowns their baby, in one of the most painstakingly horrific scenes in recent fiction. After another reconciliation, and after the baby's funeral, he rejects the guilt others seem to be heaping on to him and takes off again, running for his life.

Summarized in this way the novel seems flimsy and repetitious. As a middling sensual male with a positive gift for messing up his life, Rabbit hardly seems worth the writer's loving attention. His two women are more real than their counterparts in *On the Road* but they remain essentially male projections: Janice the resistant female, the intractable wife who has lost her sexual appeal; Ruth the compliant female, the tough but tender broad who has been around, who knows the score. Sex is no hang-up for her, though she has grown cynical about the way men use her to get it. When Rabbit demands and receives oral sex — a signal moment in the sexual history of the American novel — she feels humiliated only because he is bent on humiliating her, bringing her to her knees, where she must prove herself by servicing him. (A briefer, less explicit scene of oral sex in Mailer's *The Deer Park* {1955} had caused the original publisher to drop the book.) The next morning, Rabbit's wife gives birth and he guiltily leaves Ruth behind, having in a sense gotten all he wanted from her.

As Rabbit rattles his chains, the two women remain passive objects of his need and anger. His real antagonist in the novel is another man, the Reverend Eccles, who becomes his persistent goad and confidant, working tirelessly, despite his own troubled marriage, to bring Rabbit and Janice together again. Superficially sympathetic but meddlesome, Eccles is a version of the therapeutic figure who had been reappearing in plays and films since the late forties, especially in social-problem dramas like *The Best Years of Our Lives, Home of the Brave, The Men,* and *Rebel Without a Cause.* He is Updike's mordant comment on this new authority figure of postwar culture, the doctor, minister, psychiatrist, or social worker who began offering post-theological solutions to the sense of alienation — the seismic shifts in social relationships — that had shaken American life since the war. Eccles is a vehicle for Updike's larger ambition: to make *Rabbit, Run* more than a documentary take on the miseries of married life, to turn it into a novel of ideas. Eccles stands for a therapeutic liberalism that blatantly intrudes into other people's lives; his religious skepticism deifies social and personal bonds over any higher powers. To Updike, Eccles represents the vaunted religious revival of the fifties, humanistic instead of dogmatic, this-worldly rather than otherworldly, altogether enlightened and reasonable but spiritually null. Eccles's technique for saving souls is manipulative, not authoritarian. His own soul is in a questionable state; perhaps it has been replaced by his social conscience, which Updike sees as a subtle will to power. By befriending Rabbit and bringing him back to Janice, disastrously, he bears some responsibility for the death of their child.

To Rabbit, it is his flight, his "sin," even his need for sex that must surely be to blame for his daughter's death. In relation to *On the Road,* Rabbit is at once the guilty, conflicted Sal and the amoral Dean, for Updike has taken the cry for liberation at the heart of the lyrical novel and enmeshed it in the fateful and ironic consequences of the fiction of relationships, the fiction of entrapment. "There is a case to be made for running away from your wife," Updike told an interviewer in 1969. "In the late Fifties beatniks were preaching transcontinental travelling as the answer to man's disquiet. And I was trying to say: 'Yes, there is certainly that, but then there are all these other people who seem to get hurt.' That qualification is meant to frame a moral dilemma." (In 1995, in an introduction to a one-volume edition of all four Rabbit novels, he framed the point even more moralistically. *Rabbit, Run,* he says, "was meant to be a realistic demonstration of what happens when a young American family man goes on the road: the people left behind get hurt." But he acknowledges that "arriving at so prim a moral was surely not my only intention: the book ends on an ecstatic, open note that was meant to stay open. . . . The title can be read as advice.") In *On the Road* the same moral issue, framed by women but also by Sal, only highlights Dean's terrifying spontaneity, his amoral charisma. It affirms Dean's mythic status but offers little counterweight to the lure of the road. "Funny," thinks Rabbit near the end of the novel, "how what makes you move is so simple and the field you must move in is so crowded."

If Rabbit is ambivalent like Sal, he is also a quester like Dean, a confused, propulsive id who lives in his body yet seeks something beyond, a transcendence that other people scarily discount. Here, the earthbound Eccles is his antagonist. When they play golf together *(golf!)* Rabbit, growing too articulate, feels the pull of a world behind the visible: "there's something that wants me to find it." When he lands a shot, when the ball "with a kind of visible sob takes a last bite of space before vanishing in falling," he says triumphantly: "That's *it!*" Eccles is skeptical, however. To him, "all vagrants think they're on a quest." "That was all settled centuries ago, in the heresies of the early Church," he tells Rabbit. "It's the strange thing about you mystics, how often your little ecstasies wear a skirt." Rabbit's half-articulated goal, which Eccles mocks, is what Kerouac in *Visions of Cody* calls "the Go — the summation pinnacle possible in human relationships." "I'm a mystic," Rabbit says jokingly of himself. "I give people faith." Still, his simple story resists taking on this cumbersome freight.

It is typical of the younger Updike to give a slightly allegorical cast to an essentially realistic novel, to seek God in the suburbs, to allow his characters (not wholly convincingly) to debate theological issues on the golf course, and to put someone like Rabbit at the center of such a conversation. Eccles speaks for maturity, adjustment, the sober, hard-nosed realism cherished by social thinkers of the 1950s, but Updike makes Rabbit his unlikely spokesman for a keen spiritual and sexual hunger. To Eccles, Rabbit should come to grips with life's limits, should accept the "muddle" of diminishment as other couples do. Rabbit demurs: "After you're first-rate at something, no matter what," he tells Eccles, "it kind of takes the kick out of being second-rate. And that little thing Janice and I had going, boy, it was really second-rate." Though no postwar novelist writes more lyrically about married love than Updike, *Rabbit, Run* is grounded in the male sense of enclosure, the loss of sexual freedom and variety – a sense of being weighed down by family, no matter how much loved, and having one's wings clipped. "If you're telling me I'm not mature," Rabbit tells Eccles, "that's one thing I don't cry over since as far as I can make out it's the same thing as being dead."

But by giving us a Rabbit who does not simply want to be free but has a longing for something beyond, Updike attaches the novel to the utopian discourse that emerged in the late fifties, which marked a path for the counterculture of the next decade. In its own way, *Rabbit, Run* is a Christian version of not only the violent sainthood of the Beats but also the spiritual-sexual mythology of Herbert Marcuse's *Eros and Civilization* (1955); Norman Mailer's "The White Negro"; Norman O. Brown's apocalyptic *Life Against Death* (1959), with its appeal to Christian mystics like Boehme and its radical reading of Freud; and Paul Goodman's *Growing Up Absurd,* which famously interpreted both the hell-raising of delinquent youth and the bad-boy behavior of the Beats as a cry of existential anguish, an inchoate quest for meaning. Updike connects sex to theology, physical grace to spiritual grace. *Rabbit, Run* is at once a fifties recoil from maturity, a male outcry against being domesticated, a Freudian rebuff at the instinctual sacrifices that make civilization possible, and a Christian dream of unfallen perfection. This is a terrible weight for any novel to bear, but Updike's book, with its wonderful surface realism, its plenitude of sharply observed details, carries it off from scene to scene, as if the physical world itself had great sacramental purpose.

Rabbit, Run relocates the road novel in middle America, at the heart of American marriage, far away from the voluble sophistication of Salinger's precocious young or the bohemianism of Kerouac's self-consciously marginal rebels. Unlike some of Updike's more pretentious or experimental novels, the Rabbit books are grounded in the ordinary, the concrete, whatever their spiritual or historical themes. Rabbit gets away, but Updike never lets him get off easily and he allows him moments of complex awareness beyond what the character can bear. Even before his daughter dies, Rabbit is surprised when someone "seems oblivious of the gap of guilt between Harry and humanity." He experiences the recognition of limits that Eccles has been projecting at him. "He feels the truth: the thing that had left his life had left irrevocably; no search would recover it. No flight would reach it. . . . The fullness ends when we give Nature her ransom, when we make children for her. Then she is through with us." This is Updike's thinking, not Rabbit's.

In *Rabbit Redux,* the situation of the previous novel is reversed. His wife Janice leaves him – *she* is having the affair – and we see the world at least initially from her point of view. Instead of chafing at his static surroundings, Rabbit, grown increasingly conservative, has turned pensive and downhearted as the world explodes around him. The scene is the summer of 1969, the summer of the first moon landing, Ted Kennedy's fall at Chappaquiddick, and riots in the streets of American cities. In a culture saturated with casual sex, desire has leaked out of Rabbit like the air from a balloon, or his rapidly fading memories of early success. He has grown passive, become a working stiff whose job in a print shop will soon be lost to automation. After Janice takes off, he lives at home with his teenage son, then takes in an 18-year-old runaway girl and a young black fugitive who has been to Vietnam and now dreams of becoming the black Jesus. But Rabbit's amorphous politics recoil at everything the newcomers represent: the new youth culture, the antiwar movement, and the hopped-up rhetoric of black nationalism. Though this is Updike's most topically attuned novel, trying too deliberately to take in the whole sixties scene, Rabbit seems more than ever the ordinary man: he is no longer dreaming of special ecstasies, and his stubborn, almost shell-shocked recalcitrance prefigures the sullen American backlash against the counterculture, which lies just over the horizon.

Like Philip Roth's *American Pastoral* twenty-five years later, *Rabbit Redux* relies on stereotypes to evoke the era, especially the figure of the violent, wayward, aimless child, the angry adolescent; yet it was a prophetic book, less about the sixties than about their impact on middle America. Once, Updike had found a metaphor for his own sense of restlessness in Kerouac's evocation of the road; now Rabbit's own mother, almost paralyzed by Parkinson's disease (a "movement disorder," as doctors call it), urges him to leave, to run away, but there is nowhere he wants to go; he already feels old, wasted. The road seems closed to him. Now that the moral world that once confined him has broken up, he misses its stability. The sexual freedom he coveted is everywhere, not simply among the young but in the suburbs, as Updike had already demonstrated in *Couples* (1968). Surrounded by the cacophonous bacchanal of the late sixties, Updike, still in his thirties like Rabbit, writes a precocious novel about middle-aged depression. As America grows absurdly younger, Rabbit ages prematurely.

The even more spent and tired protagonist of *Rabbit Is Rich* and *Rabbit at Rest* is a much coarser figure, reunited with his newly independent and self-sufficient wife, battling viciously with his son, even sleeping with his daughter-in-law. Like the narrators of other late novels such as *Roger's Version,* Rabbit becomes the rancorous, disappointed shadow of his increasingly distinguished author, the vehicle of Updike's pet peeves as he had once been the earthy dreamer of his visionary hopes. Retired to Florida, Rabbit observes the mores of aging Jews with distaste but feels reassured by having a Jewish surgeon tinkering with his defective heart. At the same time Updike is perfectly aware of Rabbit's limitations, and he laces *Rabbit Is Rich* with strategic references to Sinclair Lewis's *Babbitt.* The novels themselves grow longer, becoming more like reportage, an accumulation of realistic details about a changing America, with little of the allegorical cast, the young writer's wild ambition, that gave another dimension to *Rabbit, Run.* Accepting an award for *Rabbit at Rest,* Updike paid tribute to the tradition of realism descending from William Dean Howells, who had not previously been his household god.

Rabbit's inexorable decline speaks to a sense of loss at the heart of Updike's imagination, an empathy with failure at odds with his own carefully managed, beautifully evolving career, which seemed to go from strength to strength in every department of writing: novels, innumerable stories, light verse, brilliant book reviewing, art criticism, memoir, the whole terrain of the man of letters. The key lies undoubtedly in Updike's sense of the past, of life unfolding in time and inexorably running down, as indeed it must. Despite Updike's fluent ability to conceptualize a book and will it into being, the core of feeling in his work is lyrical and autobiographical, as it finally is in the works of Cheever and Nabokov as well. Nothing in Updike's work can quite match the emotional intensity of such stories as "Flight" and "The Blessed Man of Boston, My Grandmother's Thimble, and Fanning Island," both in *Pigeon Feathers* (1962) or the closely related novella *Of the Farm* (1965) and its 1990 sequel, "A Sandstone Farmhouse," collected in *The Afterlife and Other Stories* (1994). They pay a mixed tribute to his difficult mother, who believed in his future even when he was a boy, who told him thrillingly that he was "going to fly," and they evoke the final years of his maternal grandparents, whose lives open up a vista of historical time he feels he must preserve, and finally his mother's own death. At the same time that he deals with the paradoxes of growing up and growing old, Updike, like Salinger and Kerouac before him, feels an immense tenderness toward every aspect of his own experience – every tangle of relationship, every nuance of perception, every observed or imagined fact.

In *Of the Farm,* the protagonist, on a visit to his mother's farm, feels emotionally estranged from his new wife when he begins to see her through his mother's judging eyes, the eyes that first helped him see and feel. "You've taken a vulgar woman to be your wife," his mother tells him, almost mesmerizing him with her force of will – but the younger woman, like the city to which he must return, belongs to the life he has chosen, the grown-up world he loves and needs. His mother must let go, as he must let go of her and of the farm, of the whole dreamy boyhood preserved so perfectly in memories that the farm itself brings flooding back. His mother has a spell of illness that foreshadows her death and the sale of the farm. "I saw her, now, as an old woman. Always before she had appeared to me as a heavier version of the swift young mother outsprinting my father from the barn. . . . In sleep my mother had slipped from my recognition and blame and had entered, unconsciously, a far territory, the arctic of the old." As Charles Thomas Samuels remarks of the Updike paradox: "Definition requires that we keep faith with our past; freedom demands that we move beyond it."

Memory takes on an even more sublime cast in "The Blessed Man of Boston. . . ," a tryptich about all the stories he could write, the people he could recreate, the memories he could turn into words if he had world enough and time. Written in an almost magical style that brings to mind the play of memory in Wordsworth's *Prelude,* the story shows us an Updike in almost an ecstasy of involuntary recollection. Finding a silver thimble, his grandmother's wedding present, he falls down a Proustian well. With this "stemless chalice of silver" between his fingers, "the valves of time parted, and after an interval of years my grandmother was upon me again." He must "tell how once there had been a woman who now was no more, how she had been born and lived in a world that had ceased to exist, though its mementos were all about us." In the story's most ecstatic moment, he recalls lifting the sick, brittle old woman, in the full pride of his young strength, and whirling her dangerously around the room: "Had I stumbled, or dropped her, I might have broken her back, but my joy always proved a secure cradle. . . . I was carrying her who had carried me, I was giving my past a dance, I had lifted the anxious caretaker of my childhood from the floor, I was bringing her with my boldness to the edge of danger, from which she had always sought to guard me." The young man is about to step out on a date, the vibrations are intensely sexual, but the erotic anticipation of his immediate future spills out onto the vivid relics of his past, a world he hugs to his heart even as he is leaving it behind. The narrator's exhilaration comes from making the past live, from lifting aged forebears into one last dance, momentarily reversing the flow of time. Updike's sense of decline, like Wordsworth's, is grounded in the luminous plenitude but also the concreteness of the remembered past. Of "A Sandstone Farmhouse," which deals with his mother's death, Updike himself commented that "by keeping the focus on the house – its stones, its smells, its renovations – I hoped to convey the dizzying depth of life its walls have contained. . . . The story is about *things* – how they mutely witness our flitting lives, and remain when the lives are over, still mute, still witnessing."

❧

Though the later Updike would often grow cerebral, recruiting stuffy pedants, or the pedant in himself, to narrate some of his novels, his deepest affinity as a writer was not only with the gorgeous prose, the profligate imagination, of predecessors like Vladimir Nabokov, but with the sense of lost radiance that gives their narratives such a poetic charge. In the brief preface to *The Stories of John Cheever* (1978), the collection that finally gained him unassailable stature as a modern classic, Cheever remembers a "long-lost world when the city of New York was still filled with a river light, when you heard the Benny Goodman quartets from a radio in the corner stationery store, and when almost everybody wore a hat." Cheever tells us how he chanted aloud some passages in which the best stories spin off into sublimity – bursts of poetic gusto he finds as thrilling to recall as they were to indite. Cheever's higher flights, which disconcerted his editors at *The New Yorker,* were as essential to his work as were his powers of social observation. In their flow of images, occasionally in their pull toward fantasy, Cheever's stories veer from a level realism toward glimpses of paradise that break through a fog of misery or depression.

Though he is oddly known as a cheerful chronicler of suburbia, and as Updike's precursor as a keen social historian, Cheever, born in 1912, writes about the suburbs as a state of mind, almost an imaginary place, a pastoral utopia that seems as cut off from history and memory as from suffering and tragedy. Yet behind the spacious houses, well-trimmed lawns, inviting swimming pools, and perfectly groomed children, behind the façade of a community built on wealth and exclusion, behind the impeccable manners and decorum, Cheever's stories give us glimpses of alcoholism, lust, family combat, and melancholia. One character thinks wistfully, "How sad everything is!" but the line could come from almost any of the stories, with their inextricable sense of "the pain and sweetness of life."

In view of his light tone and his long connection to *The New Yorker,* which broke down as his work grew darker and less simply realistic, it is remarkable how much unhappiness we find even in Cheever's early work, how much bitterness, disappointment, and latent violence, whether he is writing about the Massachusetts in which he grew up, the New York he lived in during the late thirties and forties, or the Westchester County, New York, towns where he raised his children. This is the kind of bad news that comes in over "the enormous radio," unhinging a woman who is armored in her innocence and gentility yet, like the writer himself, obsessed with other people's secrets. Though some stories seem infused with a willful bleakness, others glow with longing, shimmer with Edenic recollections of summers past and boyhood dreams. Like Updike's Rabbit, Cheever's characters are divided souls, schooled in duty, discretion, and self-restraint, fueled by lust and passionate longing, wracked by unappeasable melancholy. Despite these conflicts, their lives are redeemed by moments of transcendence in love, in nature, in language, or in some lovely pocket of the past, miraculously unspoiled, at least in memory. Cheever's 1978 preface points to three privileged moments, composed aloud in a frenzy of inspiration, in which his own language turns poetic and incantatory: the conclusion of the fratricidal "Goodbye, My Brother," in which two women, the narrator's wife and sister, rise naked out of the sea; the opening of "The Housebreaker of Shady Hill," which begins almost with a chant; and the close of "The Country Husband," a tale of deep marital and social discord, which signs off exuberantly in the magical language of romance: "It is a night where kings in golden suits ride elephants over the mountains."

Cheever's often unconvincing endings were his way of escaping unhappiness and redeeming misery and self-division into art. The endings are foreshadowed by Cheever's deceptively bright tone, which fits in rather too well with the decorous cheeriness and the limited social spectrum of the old *New Yorker*. Acordingly, the stories were persistently undervalued; their core of darkness was scarcely taken in (though Alfred Kazin shrewdly observed that "his marvelous brightness is an effort to cheer himself up"). Such superb collections as *The Enormous Radio and Other Stories* (1953) were tarred by reviewers who disliked the self-satisfied tone of the magazine, with its focus on upper-middle-class manners. Cheever collaborated with this misunderstanding by sanitizing his family history in *The Wapshot Chronicle* (1957), though every theme of his work – including his grim sense of Puritan origins, his fierce rivalry with his brother, his parents' painful marriage, his father's feeling of being rendered superfluous, and even his own fear of turning homosexual – is tucked into the narrative with unobtrusive charm. (He was especially proud of including a four-letter word that alarmed his genteel publisher.) Scattered into storylike episodes, the book is a warm tribute to his failed father; it combines nostalgia for a lost Eden with the sense of a world gone terribly awry. The book was a great success for the wrong reasons: a wistful poetry of recollection somehow allays any temptation to despair.

The stresses that seem so attenuated in the novel are powerfully compressed and controlled in the three stories singled out in Cheever's preface. "Goodbye, My Brother," the perfect overture to the collected stories, contrasts the gloomy, puritanical brother, harsh in his judgments, morosely indifferent to his family and his past, with the life-affirming narrator who, looking out at the sea, finds beauty and rebirth where his sibling sees only death and decay. The narrator, Cheever himself in his most exalted vein, extends his tolerance to everyone except his brother, without realizing how much he resembles him in his own self-righteousness. Like many Cheever stories, it turns on an act of transgression when the narrator, exasperated by his brother's saturnine gloom, murderously strikes him from behind, in a sense expelling him from the family and subduing his own dark alter ego. For this moment at least, a violent gesture restores the family to the summer and the sea and a sense of paradise regained. The story, with its Cain-and-Abel theme, its tincture of fantasy and the breach of the social code, becomes a way of facing down the writer's own despair and recapturing an unspoiled sense of nature.

The other two stories, both among Cheever's best, are about another form of trouble in paradise: the quiet misery of suburban marriage. Losing his job, disappointed in his family, which seems impervious to his problems, the husband in "The Housebreaker of Shady Hill" takes to stealing from his neighbors. "The Country Husband" is not much more realistic in dealing with family discord. It begins with a cinematic sequence about an air crash, in which Francis, the husband, is nearly killed; but when he gets home he finds the family too preoccupied to pay any attention to what has happened to him. Feeling that he is taken for granted, that his needs do not really matter, Francis manages to be rude to the town's social arbiter, to blacken the family's standing with its conforming neighbors, and to fall in love absurdly with the baby-sitter. In both stories, the husband feels his wife, children, friends, and neighbors do not understand him, as Cheever himself repeatedly complained in his journals. In both stories, he commits a transgression that represents his very tentative bid for freedom, his attempt to regain the state of joy he once knew and still dreams about. In both, the husband and wife quarrel and almost separate but are quickly reconciled. In another story, "The Cure," the couple actually does separate, but the husband then sinks into a misery so complete that he grasps desperately at restoring his marriage. This seems to have been much the story of Cheever's own marriage, with his bisexuality left out.

In Cheever's world, freedom, including sexual freedom, is an abstract good and a pressing need but not quite as strong as the need for family bonds and social acceptance, however narrow and hollow they may sometimes seem. "The Country Husband" is full of touches that point to a larger moral and historical world, images of challenge and adventure including memories of the war, symbolized by a French maid whose head was shaved for consorting with Germans, but also suggesting romantic passion, symbolized but also mocked by the husband's infatuation with the baby-sitter. (Her father is brutal and alcoholic – she cries on Francis's shoulder when he drives her home.) The allusions to the war are unusual for Cheever, despite his years of military service, and utterly unthinkable in the sheltered world of Shady Hill. "The war seemed now so distant and the world where the cost of partisanship had been death or torture so long ago. . . . The people in the Farquarsons' living room seemed united in their tacit claim that there had been no past, no war – that there was no danger or trouble in the world." The Farquarsons' living room stands not only for Shady Hill but for postwar America, where the sense of Edenic happiness seems built on the denial of social misery and historical tragedy.

In "The Country Husband," Francis rediscovers the joys of being deliberately rude and chafes at "the strenuousness of containing his physicalness within the patterns he had chosen." Its title alludes to Wycherley's 1674 erotic farce, *The Country Wife,* in which a man feigns impotence in order to seduce unwary women. The country husband, on the other hand, really is impotent, trapped in a world of straitlaced conventions and sublimated needs. Francis rediscovers passion but is unable to act on it any more than he can talk to people about what happened after the war, since "the atmosphere of Shady Hill made the memory unseemly and impolite." They are, however, the customs *he* had chosen, as Cheever himself, on the evidence of his journals, had done as well, and in the end these rebels invariably choose to return home, even when (as in "The Swimmers") that home is now empty and deserted.

This is where Cheever, who seems to celebrate home and family, oddly fits in with the postwar direction of the road novel as well as the closely related fiction of youth and transgression shaped by the Freudian tension between civilization and its discontents. Behind the façade of manners in Cheever's world is a dream of freedom along with a steady accumulation of misery. Later recollections of Cheever, including Updike's numerous tributes, highlight his youthful energy and buoyancy, for which he never found sufficient outlet; his despondency, which made him suicidal and alcoholic; and his family feeling, which forced him to curb and contain himself.

Cheever's journals frequently explore the anarchic sexual itch, especially the homosexual feelings, that remained masked but essential in his fiction, but also the strong needs that restrained him from exposing them, even to his closest friends, or acting on them. "But then there are the spiritual facts," he writes in his journal in 1962: "my high esteem for the world, the knowledge that it is not in me to lead a double life, my love of perseverance, a passionate wish to honor the vows I've made to my wife and children. But my itchy member is unconcerned with all of this, and I am afraid that I may succumb to its itchiness." Typically, the attraction is to another man, and as time passed, Cheever succumbed more openly and frequently, all the while maintaining his tempestuous marriage, marred by his narcissistic demands for unconditional love and approval from his long-suffering wife. And the more he succumbed, the more his work changed. His stories grew more surreal and, in a more permissive cultural climate, his novels (especially *Falconer*) began exploring more dangerous terrain: homosexuality, incarceration, fratricide.

Cheever belongs with Updike not simply because he influenced him, they admired each other, and both explored the troubled suburban marriages of white Protestant males. If they seemed equally at home in lyrical and mandarin prose, in the sensuous and the Apollonian, it was because both of them were riven by the conflict between sex and marriage, between the pull toward freedom and call of home, between instinctual need and family life. Between them, they domesticated the themes of the road novel. Like the larger popular culture of the 1950s, Cheever's work is divided between a celebration of the nuclear family, however dysfunctional, and an attraction to the figure of the outlaw, the deviant, however self-destructive. "There does seem to be, in my head some country," wrote Cheever in his journals, "some infantile country of irresponsible sexual indulgence that has nothing to do with the facts of life as I know them."

Ironically, "the facts of life" refers here not to the birds and bees but the concrete facts of social and family life, the settled domestic world that keeps the road runner at home, that keeps this fiction writer wedded to the quotidian, not the apocalyptic. Once, Cheever even puts this in the form of a small parable, inspired perhaps by Kafka's retelling of Greek and Hebrew myths:

He could separate from his red-faced and drunken wife, he could conceivably make a life without his beloved children, he could get along without the companionship of his friends, but he could not bring himself to leave his lawns and gardens, he could not part from the porch screens and storm windows that he had repaired and painted, he could not divorce himself from the serpentine brick walk he had laid between the side door and the rose beds. So for him the chains of

Prometheus were forged from turf and house paint, copper screening, putty and brick, but they shackled him as sternly as iron.

All the tensions in Cheever's work come to a head in this self-conscious fragment. He sees himself with fallen grandeur as Prometheus the light bringer, the rebel, but also as the victim bound in chains of domesticity, the willingly shackled adventurer who never left home. Instead, Cheever became the bard of suburbia, the explorer of the joys and trials of middle-class marriage. His transgressive impulses he largely reserved for his tortured private life; in fiction, he became the superlative celebrant of the joys of the quotidian. An unlikely admirer, Vladimir Nabokov, was charmed by the wealth of circumstantial detail in his stories, and pointed out that "The Country Husband" was "really a miniature novel beautifully traced." Cheever in turn admired Nabokov but saw that his own style was as different as his origins: "The house I was raised in had its charms, but my father hung his underwear from a nail he had driven into the back of the bathroom door, and while I know something about the Riviera I am not a Russian aristocrat polished in Paris. My prose style will always be to a degree matter-of-fact."

❧

Nabokov, of course, was forced to leave home. He was born in Russia in 1899; his father was a distinguished liberal and reformer who was imprisoned by the czar, chased and scorned by the Bolsheviks, and finally assassinated by Fascist thugs in Berlin in 1922. For Cheever and Updike, nostalgia for lost boyhood was an aspect of temperament, a way in which they remained "open to tender invasions." For Nabokov, this remembered radiance was produced by physical exile and the dislocations of modern history. For all his privileged upbringing, which he celebrates with great sensuous immediacy, far from being "a Russian aristocrat polished in Paris," he led a penniless, hand-to-mouth existence in Berlin in the twenties and thirties, supporting himself by writing for émigré journals and for publishers with a minuscule readership.

One of the most moving of the autobiographical essays that appeared mainly in *The New Yorker* between 1948 and 1950 — collected in *Conclusive Evidence* (1951) and, in revised form, in *Speak, Memory* (1966) — is his account of how, as a Cambridge student, he went about reconstructing the Russian culture, language, and literature he had taken for granted in his cosmopolitan home: "The story of my college years in England is really the story of my trying to become a Russian writer. I had the feeling that Cambridge and all its famed features — venerable elms, blazoned windows, loquacious tower clocks — were of no consequence in themselves but existed merely to frame and support my rich nostalgia." When fully

assembled and revised in 1966, the book became an album of fifteen portraits, only very loosely chronological, richly portraying the figures and
settings of his youth: his mother, his father, his colorful tutors, his Russian
education, his English education, and an early love interest.

The loving detail of these reminiscences, the almost hallucinatory intensity with which he conjures them up, impels us to question Nabokov's cus-
tomary rejection of realism, his insistence that his art is essentially a
magician's game, a set of artful tricks. Both his early work in Russian and
English and such late, self-indulgent works as *Ada, or Ardor* (1969) are
marred by a hothouse atmosphere of strained allegory, an oppressive literariness. Nabokov himself insists on the unreality of the "real" world around
him – always very concretely described! – as compared to the superior reality of memory, fantasy, and mental invention. "'Reality,'" he says in the
afterword to *Lolita,* is "one of the few words which mean nothing without
quotes." "I open Nabokov," Cheever wrote in his journals, "and am
charmed by this spectrum of ambiguities, this marvellous atmosphere of
untruth." For Nabokov, the matter-of-fact world so beloved by Cheever, or
imposed on him by his spare origins, carried no charge of emotion except as
material for satire or invitations to murder, while the remembered world
was suffused with nostalgia and charged with psychic energy. In his 1951
album and the novels and stories that followed, however, Nabokov, perhaps
drawn by the mainstream audience of *The New Yorker,* made a pact with
common life, inspired by his new American setting as he had been by his
Russian past. Though he was the least sentimental of émigrés, he achieved
his greatest power, in *Lolita,* by fusing memory and desire, nostalgia and
impossible longing. His autobiography is a key to his published work,
inaugurating his most passionate and accessible decade as a writer. It was
followed by *Lolita* (1955), *Pnin* (1957), the short stories in *Nabokov's Dozen*
(1958), and the diabolically clever *Pale Fire* (1962).

Like many lyrical writers, including Salinger and Updike, whom he
always singled out as the current American authors he most admired,
Nabokov's work is heightened with an intense feeling that makes his style
luminous and incandescent yet utterly precise. But he was also an ironist
whose work is a hall of mirrors, a multitude of deceptive masks, tricky and
problematic, with stylized characters full of Dickensian vitality, ranging
from the harmlessly eccentric to the maniacally obsessive. His past in
Speak, Memory is the sun-dappled garden of the country estates around
Petersburg. His descriptions are full of remembered pleasure but also shot
through with darker anticipations: his father's murder, his mother's wid-
owhood and poverty, and his separation from his siblings, his social position, his beloved language, and his country.

Art is Nabokov's method for recreating a perfect, unchanging past. One of his metaphors for art – and the subject of the most charming and revealing chapter of *Speak, Memory* – is his passion for butterflies, which he began collecting and identifying at the age of seven and continued to pursue and classify for the next seven decades; this was a love affair (like Humbert Humbert's) that was also a fierce obsession. The mounted butterfly, like the book itself, is nature under glass, a timeless, flawless reality armored against contingency and disintegration. Nabokov writes of the butterfly's protective coloration as a cunning device, gratuitously "carried to a point of mimetic subtlety far in excess of a predator's power of appreciation. I discovered in nature the nonutilitarian delights that I sought in art. Both were a form of magic, both were a game of intricate enchantment and deception." Nabokov's self-image, often belied by the work itself, is that of the writer as a conjuror, not a passive recorder, using mimetic effects that are a form of enchantment rather than realistic representation.

Along with Alfred Kazin's *A Walker in the City* (1951), Mary McCarthy's *Memories of a Catholic Girlhood* (1956), and Robert Lowell's *Life Studies* – a collection of poems that includes his prose memoir "77 Revere Street" – *Speak, Memory* is one of the essential autobiographies of the 1950s, not only an album of recollections but a work like Wordsworth's *Prelude* that interrogates the nature of time and the sinuous process of remembering. One of Nabokov's favorite ideas was that time was really a form of space – what Wordsworth called a "spot of time" – part of the lush terrain of our mental life, to be revisited at will. "The act of vividly recalling a patch of the past is something that I seem to have been performing with the utmost zest all my life," he said. Nabokov recalled how his parents did it before him, repeatedly memorializing vital moments of experience almost as a hedge against future losses. Of his mother, he wrote:

As if feeling that in a few years the tangible part of her world would perish, she cultivated an extraordinary consciousness of the various time marks distributed throughout our country place. She cherished her own past with the same retrospective fervor that I now do her image and my past. Thus, in a way, I inherited an exquisite simulacrum – the beauty of intangible property, unreal estate – and this proved a splendid training for the endurance of later losses.

Just as Wordsworth constantly insisted that the fullness of memory had more than compensated him for the loss of his sensuous childhood, Nabokov endows the past with an unsentimental poignance that anticipates deprivations to come. Instead of chronology, he gives us (as his title suggests) a dialogue with memory, a series of visits to corners of the past as conserved in his own mind, rescuing characters who had already been

transformed in his fiction, shuffling different periods like a pack of scattered cards, reconstituting "things that fate one day bundled up pell-mell
and tossed into the sea, completely severing me from my boyhood."

But this loss, he insists, is a source of imaginative strength, far superior
to a banal, uneventful continuity, to whit, an American experience innocent of the tempests of history ("a smooth, safe, small-town continuity of
time, with its primitive absence of perspective"). As his lost Russian past
would remain a source of intense emotion, the vulgar American present
would become the object of frenzied, cruel, but curiously loving and
minutely attentive satire.

Nabokov had nothing but scorn for the czarist émigrés who mourned
the loss of wealth or privileges. He himself had come into an estate and
become wealthy barely a year before the revolution, but this, he insists,
meant nothing to him. *His* losses and gains, like Humbert Humbert's, are
Proustian, not material. *Speak, Memory, Lolita,* and *Pnin,* all written
between 1948 and 1955, form a trilogy on the inner life of the émigré, in
which *Lolita* is the delirious comic inferno, *Pnin* the mild and wistful purgatorio, and *Speak, Memory* the paradise of the past recaptured, pinned and
mounted under glass. We might say that what the past represents for the
nostalgic biographer as he contemplates his blissful childhood, Lolita, the
downy nymphet, incarnates for Humbert Humbert, who is Nabokov's
most ingenious mask.

Lolita is *Speak, Memory* as a hall of mirrors, an uneasy tissue of obsession
and deception that connects remarkably to the cultural themes of America
in the 1950s. Where Nabokov the autobiographer seems to have sur-
mounted his losses, imaginatively reconstructing his past within him,
Humbert's loss of his first young love (named after Poe's "Annabel Lee")
has left him tormented by predatory sexual needs, fixated on the transient
moment when childhood is turning into adulthood. Where Nabokov
could turn his harmless mania for butterflies into a mixture of aesthetic
passion, adventure, and scientific pedantry, Humbert is enslaved to the
fantasies he projects on this one specimen of America's coarse but energetic
new youth culture.

No one, however morally censorious, can fail to be moved by the
baroque language of Humbert's passionate attachment to his nymphet,
around whom he weaves a solipsistic plot as rich as any writer's imaginative flights. As in other lyrical novels (though far less colloquially),
Nabokov uses all the tricks of voice to give Humbert an overwhelming
presence – to make us complicit with his feelings and needs, even as he
himself describes them with wicked relish. But Humbert's is also a tale of
self-loathing, the fable of beauty and the beast from the beast's point of

view, as written in the archly euphemistic language of both romantic love (with Lolita as the bewitching demon child) and Victorian pornography (with Lolita as the coyly seductive victim of a besotted sexual predator).

Again and again, Humbert describes himself as a pervert, a maniac, the depraved victim of his own revolting lust, an enchanted hunter manipulating (and being manipulated by) his prey. On the very first page, he even attributed his gloriously arch European prose to his kinkiness and criminality: "You can always count on a murderer for a fancy prose style." By the end, after he loses her, he recants almost convincingly, killing a farcical rival even more sordid than he is, feeling redeemed only by the fact that he loved her: "It was love at first sight, at last sight, at ever and ever sight." "I loved you. I was a pentapod monster, but I loved you. I was despicable and brutal, and turpid, and everything, *mais je t'aimais, je t'aimais!*"

As Lolita is the product of the youth culture that gave us Holden Caulfield and James Dean, her strange admirer is the neurotic, maladjusted, but feelingful male who runs like a thread through postwar culture: the returning war veterans unable to adjust to a peacetime world; the disaffected young misfits, represented by Brando and Dean, who can find nowhere to channel their surly individuality and sexual energy; the outright madmen of Mailer's "The White Negro" and Yates's *Revolutionary Road,* whose psychopathic gaze pierces the timid rationalizations of the "normal" world. As Humbert's sexual compulsion and lack of moral inhibition distantly connect him to the priapic Dean Moriarty, so *Lolita* is a send-up of the lyrical novel that, in a sense, parodied *On the Road* even before it appeared.

Both were transgressive works that in different ways challenged moral as well as fictional norms; both were rejected repeatedly by publishers, appearing in America only years after they were written. But where *On the Road* is an Emersonian celebration of anarchic personal freedom, turning its hero into a countercultural myth, *Lolita* masquerades as a case study in deviance and abnormal psychology, satirizing the roadside America that Kerouac effusively celebrates. For Kerouac, the road is a metaphor of movement, of breakthrough; through Humbert's European eyes, it stands for aimless flight, a feigned sense of "going places," an illusory progress through a phantasmagoric landscape of cultural kitsch and inward fixation. Nabokov's book is a tissue of ironies, a modernist hall of mirrors; Kerouac's is as innocent of irony as it is of any sense of evil. The young who would adopt *On the Road* as one of their canonical books were also the young who were mercilessly lampooned as teenage cretins and stealthy masturbators in Nabokov's novel.

Kerouac's America is a cartoon seen through the eyes of a worshipful, sad, and sheltered observer; Nabokov's America is a cartoon of natural wonders, impoverished humanity, and purblind compulsion. "We had been everywhere. We had really seen nothing. And I catch myself thinking today that our long journey had only defiled with a sinuous trail of slime the lovely, trustful, dreamy, enormous country that by then, in retrospect, was no more to us than a collection of dog-eared maps, ruined tour books, old tires, and her sobs in the night – every night, every night – the moment I feigned sleep."

From *The Catcher in the Rye* to *Portnoy's Complaint,* a favorite device of the lyrical novel is the psychiatric monologue, the confession of the unhappy outsider who, after a life of conflicts and confusions, finally lands on the couch. With its clever, well-defended hero and his made-up dreams, *Lolita* mocks the therapeutic language of 1950s analysis and criminology. It begins with a Swiftian mask, a burlesque preface by "John Ray, Jr., Ph. D." whose "scientific" and moralistic language and laughable air of authority are exploded by the passionate metaphorical language of the work itself, and by Humbert's brilliant mockery of those who try to explain him. A tongue-in-cheek work from start to finish, *Lolita,* unlike many of Nabokov's other novels, breaks through to real feeling in its portrayal of the schemes and sufferings that flow from Humbert's fixation – which a later generation might describe clinically as a form of incest and child abuse, as Lolita herself (and the obtuse Dr. Ray) already do.

Nabokov always believed that fiction was neither moral, social, nor psychological but a sensuous exercise in style that (as he says in his 1958 afterword to *Lolita*) leads to a state of "aesthetic bliss." His curmudgeonly essays and interviews deride social novelists like Balzac and Stendhal and ridicule Freudians as Viennese quacks who substitute cheap formulas for experience. John Ray is one such scientific charlatan, like the mad and meddlesome editor, Kinbote, in *Pale Fire;* yet Humbert, as his assumed name indicates, is something of a humbug himself, though both speak at moments for the elusive author. Despite their modernist tricks and games, however, Nabokov's stories, memoirs, and novels from the late forties to the midfifties are also his closest encounter with realism, his most open and direct works. (Compare them to his previous novel, *Bend Sinister* [1947], a clotted *1984*-ish allegory of totalitarianism.) In *Lolita,* faced with erotic obsession on the one hand and American vulgarity on the other, the writer transcends himself, escaping the airless world of some of his other novels to achieve a burning intensity in dealing with both love and the American landscape.

Lolita is a road novel but also an antinovel, a metafictional tissue of literary allusions (besides Poe, to literally dozens of writers) and parodic names (characters like Humbert Humbert, Harold Haze, and Miss Opposite; places like Lake Climax, Insomnia Lodge, or "the township of

Soda, pop. 1001") that belong to savage farce and undercut our reference to the "real" world. Nabokov's bent for caricature reminds us of satiric writers as different as Dickens, Sinclair Lewis, and Nathanael West, as well as his friend Mary McCarthy and his student Thomas Pynchon. His mixture of cruelty, disgust, and Flaubertian sense of outrage focuses rather than blurs his attention to detail. The author's peculiar blend of empathy and disdain for Humbert, his love-hate relationship with America, enable the book to escape his control and to become a uniquely fresh comment on American life.

From the very beginning, Humbert's monologue follows directly from the nostalgia and timelessness so central to *Speak, Memory*. A nymphet, as Humbert defines her, is a creature in whom time is suspended, "an enchanted island" between the ages of nine and fourteen "surrounded by a vast, misty sea." "Ah, leave me alone in my pubescent park, in my mossy garden," he says. "Let them play around me forever. Never grow up." In this respect, nymphets resemble mounted butterflies, or chess problems, or crossword puzzles – Nabokov created the first ones in Russian – or for that matter the past itself, perfect and unchanging. But Lolita, like any particular nymphet, does not quite fit this prototype, for not only will she soon turn into an ordinary woman, a bovine adult, losing her perilous magic, but her very nature is mixed, open to the immediate and the contingent. "What drives me insane," says Humbert, "is the twofold nature of this nymphet – of every nymphet, perhaps: this mixture in my Lolita of tender dreamy childishness and a kind of eerie vulgarity." Lolita is not only immature but, unlike her mother, with her French affectations, she is the complete product of American popular culture, the teenage consumer for whom the ads were written, the movies were filmed, the candy bars confected, the roadside attractions promoted. In enslaving himself to Lolita and escorting her forcibly across the country, Humbert, like other fifties runaways, is both escaping and discovering America.

Though Humbert is a haughty, fastidious émigré exuding a Frankfurt-style disdain for American popular culture, *Lolita* is no more a version of Henry James's international theme, as some early readers saw it, than of *On the Road*. Humbert's nefarious designs upon "the child," which include the dream of killing her mother and various schemes of how to drug and deflower her, point deceptively to a contrast between European decadence and American innocence. Instead, Lolita, already deflowered by a precocious 13-year-old at camp, playfully initiates *him,* in one of the novel's most tender and troubling scenes. "In my old-fashioned, old-world way, I, Jean-Jacques Humbert, had taken for granted, when I first met her, that she was as unravished as the stereotypical notion of the 'normal child,'" he writes in his posthumous brief. Instead she instructs him in a "game she and Charlie had played." With Humbert rather than Lolita as the protagonist, the novel gives us a satiric reverse angle view of the coming-of-age materials of Vidal, Capote, Jean Stafford, and Salinger.

As Humbert sums up his mock sexual initiation, "Suffice it to say that not a trace of modesty did I perceive in this beautiful hardly formed young girl whom modern co-education, juvenile mores, the campfire racket and so forth had utterly and hopelessly depraved. She saw the stark act merely as part of a youngster's furtive world, unknown to adults." Here, Humbert the European moralist allows himself to be shocked before giving way to Humbert the lover, who allows himself to be consumed by "the perilous magic of nymphets."

Both sexually and as a consumer, Lolita reflects the directions of the postwar youth culture, which Nabokov observed as an outsider who idealized his own very different childhood. When he was young, he tells us in *Speak, Memory,* even mutual masturbation was unthinkable and "the slums of sex were unknown to us," for all sex was airy romantic fantasy. As a young émigré writer in Berlin, Nabokov, like another displaced writer, Samuel Beckett, belonged to the first generation that fully assimilated the impact of Joycean word games, Proustian recollections, and Kafkaesque themes of entrapment and paranoia, all of which figure in the shaping of his novels. Beckett's self-exile was voluntary, but he, too, achieved a breakthrough by shifting to another tongue, freeing himself from the literary associations and daunting precursors of his native language. But where Beckett's fiction and drama move relentlessly toward a pared-down, timeless space, Nabokov's American novels develop into a comic dialogue between European modernism and a New World culture of consumerism, progressive education, youthful autonomy, fussy academic careerism, and small-town provincialism.

Nowhere is Nabokov's gift for ridicule (or penchant for disgust) more sharply etched than in his account of Humbert's cross-country travels with Lolita. Nathanael West in *Miss Lonelyhearts* and *The Day of the Locust* had uncovered a pathos, almost poignant, at the heart of America's cultural wasteland, but Humbert writes about America's roadside and motel culture like the proverbial visitor from Mars, astonished at the strange enormity of it all. Roadside America becomes the incongrous backdrop for his overheated passion and the raw material for his overcharged style. Like West he is a master of the grotesque, yet his account is also punctuated by Kerouac-like paeans to the "smooth amiable roads" that radiated "across the crazy quilt of forty-eight states" and to "the lyrical, epic, tragic but never Arcadian American wilds." He finds them "beautiful, heart-rendingly beautiful," with their "quality of wide-eyed, unsung, innocent surrender" that lacquered Swiss villages and the overpraised Alps no longer possess.

Despite such moments of celebration, *Lolita*, far from being a lyrical novel, turns in upon itself like Ellison's *Invisible Man*, to disappoint all its characters' hopes – indeed, in this case, to kill off the characters themselves. In the form of a criminal's confession, a pervert's guilty plea to judge and jury, the novel is actually a network of correspondences that reveal the all-powerful control of that playful artificer, the one Humbert calls "McFate," which in turn connects destiny with the manipulations of the author, whose own hands are never too far from the puppet strings. As Humbert's aimless travels with Lolita give way to his stalking of Clare Quilty, who has lured Lolita away from him, and as Humbert tracks down and farcically murders him, *Lolita* is transformed into a mock detective story full of hunters and hunted, crime and punishment. Were it not for Peter Sellers's nimble performance as the almost unkillable Quilty in Stanley Kubrick's 1963 film version, this darker second half of the novel would be far less remembered than it is today. Yet it brings home what we should feel from the start – that Humbert is both an unreliable narrator and a moral monster; there is the devil to pay for both the pleasures he stole from his 12-year-old mistress and for the laughs we enjoyed in the great comedy of seduction and betrayal.

Along with *Invisible Man, Lolita* foreshadows both the dark, scabrous comedy of the novels of the sixties and the paranoid vision that makes them so intricate, so rich with menace. If black humor is comedy about the forbidden, comedy that negotiates moral boundaries and shatters taboos, *Lolita* epitomizes it. The work of Pynchon, Heller, Vonnegut, and Philip Roth can hardly be imagined without *Lolita*'s boldness, the uneasy mixture of comedy and horror in its perpetually unstable tone. Humbert's possessiveness and jealousy with Lolita make him her jailer as well as her adoring lover, but like so many later fictional characters – in Heller's *Something Happened* (1974), for example, another autobiography of a heel, or Pynchon's *Gravity's Rainbow* (1973) – he is also the slave of his own obscure compulsions, enjoying at best an illusory freedom.

In *Lolita* the road novel takes on an uproarious but troubling agenda and implodes. The youth culture of the fifties is at once idealized (in Humbert's infatuation with Lolita) and satirized (in the cultivated European's view of America). The lyrical novel of Emersonian self-assertion turns into the ironic novel of Kafkaesque entrapment and self-loathing confession, a transgressive work that remains genuinely shocking yet, in its playfulness, still somehow liberating. First read as a piece of sexual scandal, a glimpse of the author's own darkest impulses, the book has been transformed by academic readers into an elegant set of tricks and allusions, a postmodernist exercise in self-reflexive writing. What was lost was the novel's encounter with its own age, with an exploding popular culture, a rampant consumerism, and a rambunctious younger generation that represented both a new market and the rapidly changing sexual values of a prosperous, permissive liberal culture.

Lolita's mixture of seductive innocence and brash vulgarity was typical of the ambiguous outlook of the new culture, which would soon turn into the counterculture. American culture in the fifties was staid and repressive at the center, in its treatment of women, for example, or its range of political debate, but there was also a liberal idealism that survived from the New Deal and the war. This culture was also highly self-critical – pop sociology and psychology were virtual cottage industries – and alive with change at the margins. Not only were long-forbidden works soon to be published (*Lolita, Naked Lunch, Lady Chatterley's Lover, Tropic of Cancer, Tropic of Capricorn*) but much of the popular culture – from the seamy small-town setting of *Peyton Place* to the family melodramas of Douglas Sirk, such as *Written on the Wind* and *Imitation of Life* – took on a lurid, feverishly troubled cast. Where many today look back nostalgically at the fifties as a golden age, the filmmakers, writers, and social critics of the period saw trouble in paradise: anomie, conflict and tense uncertainty amid suburban prosperity. While some writers had used the road novel to declare their turn from the American mainstream, others invented a kind of anti–road novel to explore these tensions and uncertainties, to show how hard they might be to resolve. Two dark, ironic works, John Barth's *The End of the Road* (1958) and Richard Yates's *Revolutionary Road* (1961), offer a counterstatement to the kind of self-liberation celebrated by Kerouac, mythologized (soon afterward) by Ken Kesey, explored ambivalently by Updike and Cheever, and transformed into deviant or criminal passion by Mailer and Nabokov.

Of all the practitioners of the first-person novel in the 1950s, few have a more distinctive or more astringent voice than John Barth. Born in Cambridge, Maryland, in 1930, Barth often returned to the Maryland shore as his intricately textured local world, his native ground, as O'Hara and Updike created a social microcosm out of the small towns and cities of Pennsylvania. But Barth's interest in society was much more limited than theirs. He was the most cerebral of novelists, building his plots less out of milieu than from an interrogation of the nature of fiction. If Nabokov turned the road novel into the anti–road novel, making the road a timeless locale of forbidden passion, Barth turned it into the antinovel, an experiment in the problem of fictional representation.

Barth's fastidious manner sometimes resembles Nabokov's, especially in his habit of dealing with sex in a tone of educated circumlocution. While remaining impeccably "literary," both writers echo the elevated diction of classic pornography, skillfully deploying an arch manner that titillates the reader yet eludes the censor, including the moral censor in the individual reader. But where the scheming Humbert Humbert is helplessly dominated by his obsessions, Barth's manipulative, coldly calculating heroes are more theoretical in their motives and hence more repugnant specimens of humanity. Once upon a time, Barth's protagonists played the game of emotional entanglement, the old drama of needs and relationships; later they learned to look beyond it, to use other people for their own purposes.

In Nabokov there is a plangent emotional core behind the satiric disgust and cultured rage. Barth uses the first-person narrator for the least lyrical aims imaginable, just as he plays with the confessional mode with scarcely any tincture of Freudianism. His heroes are either the typical innocents of picaresque fiction, such as Ebenezer Cooke in *The Sot-Weed Factor,* or hardened cynics who have turned their default of feeling into a bottomless nihilism. They can manipulate and even torment people, but essentially they are indifferent to them. *The End of the Road* is Barth's best novel because it beautifully explores the personal cost of such a failure of feeling. The novel wreaks vengeance on Barth's heartless hero as he wreaks havoc on everyone around him. It gives us a brilliant anatomy of this recurrent character type, whose philosophical indifference and detached, almost inhuman intellectuality preside over Barth's whole body of work.

Barth's early books come in pairs, but whether they are seemingly realistic novels like *The Floating Opera* (1956; revised 1967) and *The End of the Road* (1958), or mock-historical novels like *The Sot-Weed Factor* (1960; revised 1967) and *Giles Goat-Boy* (1966), or sequences of metafictional texts like *Lost in the Funhouse* (1968) and *Chimera* (1972), or even an epistolary novel synthesizing (or burlesquing) all the preceding works (*Letters,* 1979), their real subject is the nature of narrative. Barth is fascinated by earlier, more naïve forms of storytelling, such as the Greek myths, the *Arabian Nights,* or the picaresque novels of the eighteenth century, which take us "back to the original springs of narrative." He idealizes the storytelling past the way Nabokov cherishes the lost world of his own past. But his nostalgia for the mesmerizing qualities of these old stories, their power to induce belief, does not prevent him from deconstructing them into postmodern narratives, laying bare their stereotypical qualities. What draws him most is not the stories themselves but the framing devices that loosely link such collections as *The Thousand and One Nights, The Canterbury Tales,* and *The Decameron,* or the direct address to the reader that punctuates the picaresque novels, always reminding us that fiction is a constructed artifact. Todd Andrews, his narrator in *The Floating Opera,* tells us from the outset that he is no novelist. He jumps backward and forward in chronology, and his cold, witty tone, his analytical precision, so typical of Barth's protagonists, can read more like legal brief or an investigative report than a personal history.

"Storytelling isn't my cup of tea," he says, not simply because he cannot resist digression but because his mind-set, along with his clinical view of character and personality, is austerely factual and skeptical. He is reporting to us, almost twenty years after the fact, about a day in 1937 when he changed his mind, when he decided not to kill himself. But he also thinks human behavior should always be logically defensible and organized around rational choice. "I tend, I'm afraid, to attribute to abstract ideas a life-or-death significance," he says. Yet life and death have repeatedly found ways of nullifying his conscious choices. He confesses that he has experienced a strong emotion only five times in his life – the specific number is typical of him – and each time he responded by completely altering his approach to the world, adopting a new "mask" and essentially becoming a different person. In each case, whether he behaves for years as a rake, an ascetic, or an utter cynic, he lives his life as a conscious project, first adopting a pose out of some unexpected burst of feeling, then rationalizing it in abstract terms like a man who pretends to know exactly why he does whatever he does.

These roles, even the role of the cynic, finally collapse for him, so he decides quite reasonably to commit suicide. But when he realizes that even suicide is a meaningless choice, that Hamlet's question has no answer, he decides (in good Dorothy Parker fashion) that he might as well live. From then on, he spends his time pursuing an elaborate *Inquiry* into his father's suicide, with little confidence that anyone can truly explain anything. Like the novel itself, this inquiry becomes a metaphor for the limits of knowledge. It thus comes to resemble David Hume's *Inquiry* in its skeptical account of causality. After years of reading and thinking, he decides that "there is no will-o'-the-wisp so elusive as the cause of any human act. . . . [A]s Hume pointed out, causation is never more than an inference."

Such an intellectualized view of behavior and motivation seems like very unpromising material for a novel; actually, it is a perfect recipe for the kind of antinovel or postmodern novel that Barth already anticipated in the 1950s, with its sense of a decentered self and its view of the world as a "mirror-maze" (as Barth would later call it in *Lost in the Funhouse*) in which everything is a representation. Like the picaresque writers of the eighteenth century, Barth gives us novels whose busy, involuted plots undermine their apparent realism, novels without any clear cause and effect: all action with little character development or psychological "depth." Barth's characters do not grow or change like those in Shakespeare's plays or in nineteenth-century novels. Instead, they simply alter their existential project, moving on to the next stage. Todd Andrews and Jacob Horner, Barth's first two heroes, are early examples of decentered selves, completely constructed personalities always defined by the masks they assume. Barth's early novels turn Sartrean existentialism into a form of intellectual play. It was Sartre who had pointed to the option of suicide as the ultimate source of man's freedom, Sartre who had insisted that existence precedes essence and people are defined by what they do, not by who they "are."

Barth turns this notion of an arbitrarily constructed, radically contingent self into a comedy of nihilism and a subversive exploration of the form of fiction. For a fabricated personality like Todd Andrews, life itself is an occasionally gorgeous but discontinuous spectacle that engages him only intermittently and ironically. His metaphor for this is the "floating opera," the showboat that moves up and down the river providing the audience on shore with no more than discontinuous glimpses of what is being performed on board. Born with the century in 1900, Todd gives us just such glimpses of his own life: his service in the trenches of World War I, his chronic heart and prostate conditions, his modest legal career, his father's suicide in 1930, his ascetic home life in a geriatric residence hotel, his long affair with the wife of a client and friend, and his efforts in court to salvage a large inheritance for his friend from the man's eccentric father. Except for his experience in the trenches, which first convinced him of the sheer animal meaninglessness of life, Todd describes every one of these experiences, especially his affair and his suicide plans, with cynical detachment, as if life itself were a game in which the actual moves mattered very little. His defective heart is a metaphor for his defective humanity, but also for the brute contingency of life itself. (He often reminds us he might die before finishing the chapter.)

Barth turns the melodramatic material of ordinary novels – paternal abandonment, wartime violence, courtroom strategy, an adulterous love triangle – into a *virtual* plot that highlights its own fictional nature. The more story we get – as in overstuffed later books such as *The Sot-Weed Factor* and *Giles Goat-Boy* – the more constructed it seems, giving substance to Todd's theory of behavior as a sequence of masks. Salinger and Kerouac were drawn to the antinomian qualities of picaresque fiction, its metaphors for escape, personal freedom, and irresponsibility, its shaggy-dog version of one man's progress. The casually constructed road novel, especially when written in the first person, establishes the claims of individual voice against the pressures of literary form as well as social convention. This sound of innocent outrage, with its wounded sincerity, is what eventually made *The Catcher in the Rye* and *On the Road* such canonical texts of sixties youth culture.

The lyrical novel turns sincerity into an instrument of social protest, but sincerity is the last thing we would expect in a Barth hero. Barth is drawn instead to the antiquarian aspects of the picaresque, its rogue hero, its sheer accumulation of detail, which takes him back to a period before romantic individualism grew dominant, and enables him to link the premodern to the postmodern. If the lyrical novel achieves authenticity by way of the personal voice, Barth parodies the first-person novel by telling his story in a voice so dry, so antiseptic in its illusionless clarity that it makes personality, psychology, and motivation seem like outworn remnants of nineteenth-century narrative.

But Barth's novels also capsize themselves and turn harshly against their protagonists. Despite his insistence that all behavior is a social mask, without a "real" self behind it, Todd Andrews finds himself periodically upstaged by his own emotions, from the wave of fear he feels in the trenches to the surge of self-disgust that finally propels him toward suicide. This is where *The End of the Road* — the "companion-piece" to *The Floating Opera* (both were written in 1955) — completes the earlier novel and gives it a tragic dimension. *The End of the Road* is an inversion of the road novel, a reversal of its kinetic energy and movement; its hero, Jacob Horner, like his proverbial counterpart, is stuck in a corner, afflicted with complete immobility. The story is framed by his treatment at something called the Remobilization Farm, a curious send-up of the whole therapeutic and progressive culture of the fifties, which put its faith in personal improvement through socialization. At this farm, with its Progress and Advice Room, Horner is treated by a brilliant quack — one of the innumerable mad doctors of fifties fiction, like Dr. Benway in Burroughs's *Naked Lunch* — whose methods flow from the theory of masks of the preceding novel.

To this doctor, life is simply performance, motion rather than emotion, the challenge of playing a part as though you believed in it. What he calls Mythotherapy is a form of dramaturgy: stereotyped role playing that at least serves to get you moving. Like so many well-rewarded vendors of positive thinking in the 1950s, the doctor urges his patients to take charge of their own story. As Dean Moriarty in *On the Road* solved all personal problems simply by moving on, leaving friends, jobs, and lovers behind, Jake Horner, paralyzed by sheer immobility, is urged to become the protagonist of his own drama, to get a life, as if he were writing a novel or casting a play.

But the life that Jake Horner simulates has a devastating effect on other people, largely because he invests so little feeling or humanity in the roles he plays. *The End of the Road* gives a deeper cast to the most frivolous and satiric of all fifties genres, the academic novel. Like Todd Andrews, Horner has an affair with a friend's wife, but this leads not to the enlightened civilities of *The Floating Opera,* where all the parties pride themselves on being tolerant and open-minded, but to her miserable death on an abortionist's table. Andrews was frank about seeking sex "without falsifying it with any romance." "The truth is," he explains, "that while I knew very well what copulation is and feels like, I'd never understood personally what love is and feels like." Todd's detachment could be interpreted as fear or despair on the few occasions when he has ever experienced a genuine emotion, but the games he plays do not have much impact on anyone's lives. Jake's manipulations, on the other hand, destroy other people's lives and cripple his own.

Jake begins his course of mayhem by callously wounding an older woman he picks up at the beach, making his contempt for her all too clear and virtually forcing her to beg for sex, which he performs with barely contained ill will, even disgust. "It was embarrassing," he says, "because she abandoned herself completely to an elaborate mood that implied her own humiliation – and because my own mood was not complementary to hers." Besides, "I was always uneasy with women who took their sexual transports too seriously." In this kind of novel, as in the road novel, the woman generally becomes the victim, whether of male lust or male indifference, of male wanderlust or male conventionality.

Jake's destructive behavior with this woman prefigures his clinical detachment during his affair with his colleague's wife. Much as he tries to avoid any messy emotional entanglement, however, this is an attitude he cannot sustain. Finally stirred to action by his pregnant mistress's suicidal anguish, Jake frantically arranges for her to have an abortion. Following her gruesome death, he collapses into a terminal apathy that puts an abrupt end to his experiment in remobilization. Like Todd Andrews in *The Floating Opera,* he has been unable to play a single "role" consistently, giving way instead to "irrational flashes of conscience and cruelty, of compassion and cynicism." Like Andrews, too, he is undermined by bursts of spontaneous humanity that his theory denies. But such moments of compunction only worsen the damage he has already done through cynicism and indifference. If the road novel uses movement as a metaphor for freedom, *The End of the Road* shows how movement alone, without a moral or emotional compass, leads to a dead end, to paralysis, to Jake Horner's dark corner. By the end he is a full-time patient, like Holden Caulfield, with nothing to do but tell his story. As he takes leave of that story, his final word to the cab driver, "Terminal," nicely catches the ambiguity of his fate. He can go to the station to catch the train, even rejoin his mad doctor, but he has nowhere to go. His case is terminal.

The paradoxes of identity and movement also provided the material for Barth's experimental short fiction in the 1960s. The stories in *Lost in the Funhouse* are all comic turns on going nowhere, on being caught between an unmediated "reality" that is no longer available, at least to this writer, and various forms of role playing or fictional representation that will be quickly paralyzed by self-consciousness. The title story, "Lost in the Funhouse," is one of several that never quite gets told; it is interwoven with a pedantic handbook on fictional technique. Ambrose and his family are off on an excursion to "the funhouse," the hall of mirrors of all representation. But the narrator's infernal dithering, his fondness for cliché, and his acute awareness of narrative choice constantly retard the narration, preventing any suspension of disbelief and reducing the story to mere words. This was a game Laurence Sterne played long ago in *The Life and Opinions of Tristram Shandy,* backtracking and digressing to make us wonder whether his hero would ever manage to get born.

Barth's often cogent comments on fictional technique point up the fact that he was one of our first writers to study in a creative writing program – there were only two in the United States when he enrolled at Johns Hopkins University in 1947 – and one of the first to make his living as a full-time professor of creative writing, initially at Pennsylvania State University, where he taught English from 1953 to 1965, then in Buffalo, New York, until 1973, when he finally went back to Johns Hopkins. His excess of concern about fictional form, his nostalgia for a period when storytelling was a simpler matter, bespeak a certain professorial relation to the study of fiction. "Plot and theme: notions vitiated by this hour of the world but as yet not successfully succeeded" ("Title"). But the influence of Beckett has overlaid the example of Sterne: "The final question is, Can nothing be made meaningful. . . . And I think. What now. Everything's been said already, over and over; I'm as sick of this as you are; there's nothing to say. Say nothing." (Think of Beckett's "you must go on, I can't go on, I'll go on.") In *Lost in the Funhouse* and *Chimera* Barth's genial narrators soon grow as heartily sick of this self-consciousness as we do. He even tells us that his wife and adolescent daughters "preferred life to literature and read fiction when at all for entertainment. Their kind of story (his too, really) would begin if not once upon a time at least with arresting circumstance, bold character, trenchant action."

In these short texts, the problems posed by fictional technique lead to the same paralysis that beset the heroes of his first two "realistic" novels; there, too, self-consciousness and emotional distance had entrapped his characters and kept them from really living their lives. Barth's nostalgia for storytelling is a nostalgia for more spontaneous living, and his obsession with fictional technique becomes a metaphor for an arrested emotional life, for a shyness or coldness that inhibits his characters from making real contact with other people. "I was cursed," Jake Horner said, "with an imagination too fertile to be of any use in predicting my fellow human beings: no matter how intimate my knowledge of them, I was always able to imagine and justify contradictory reactions from them to almost anything." Horner's problem in writing the script of his life becomes Barth's problem in writing a story while feeling swamped by an excess of possibility. At one point in *The Floating Opera* Barth's hero, methodical as ever, perfectly in character, actually advances the plot by drawing up a two-page list of all the ways the action might develop.

Barth's protagonist is a figure who recurs in postwar fiction: the intellectual whose springs of feeling have dried up, whose whole existence is a simulation of living, a series of abstract choices. In this social masquerade, reminiscent of Melville's *Confidence-Man* or Gaddis's *The Recognitions* (one of the secretly influential texts of postwar fiction), Barth's writing becomes "Another story about a writer writing a story! Another regressus in infinitum!" – which seems to weary him as much as the reader. Barth is a forerunner of postmodernism, not simply in his formal experiments but in portraying an inevitable loss of affect within a culture in which all the stories have already been told, the plot gambits tried, the forms exhausted from repeated use. His longer books are as removed from spontaneous storytelling as his characters are cut off from spontaneous interaction. They become no more than "novels imitating the form of the Novel, by a writer who impersonates the role of the Author." Barth thus anticipates the French theorists for whom the so-called author became simply a formal construct, the "author function," a convenience of literary discussion.

❧

There could hardly be a writer more different from Barth than Richard Yates. At a time when the realist aesthetic was waning, or simply migrating from literature into film and television, Yates emerged as one of the last of the scrupulous social realists. As other members of the World War II generation – Mailer, Styron, Heller, even James Jones – shifted toward history, apocalyptic fantasy, myth, and black humor, Yates emerged as the faithful chronicler of the lives of his contemporaries. His characters were men who fought in the war but were not war heroes, who married too young, had children too young, and were swallowed up by the suburbs and the large corporations. Born in 1926, Yates was a prep-school boy who saw infantry service in World War II; he was the archetype of the aspiring writer who spent the postwar years in journalism or on Madison Avenue dreaming of writing the great American novel. Remarkably, he came close to doing it. His finely crafted stories, eventually collected in *Eleven Kinds of Loneliness* (1962), drew critical admiration all through the fifties, but with *Revolutionary Road* in 1961, Yates wrote the definitive history of a part of his generation.

The popular version of Yates's story had already been told by William H. Whyte in *The Organization Man* (1956) and in novels like Sloan Wilson's best-selling *Man in the Gray Flannel Suit* (1955). *Revolutionary Road* rewrites Sloan Wilson's novel as tragedy, as it also gives us a perfect mirror image of *On the Road*. In Yates's novel the title is wholly ironic: the road that beckons becomes the road not taken. The book tells the story of the would-be rebel, the imagined free spirit, who never leaves home, never quits his job – the man who, more typically than Sal Paradise, seeks his pastoral utopia not in the American West but in the suburban towns of Connecticut. Like *The End of the Road,* it ends catastrophically with a botched abortion – this one is self-inflicted – and it leaves the novel's male protagonist, Frank Wheeler, as little more than a ghost of himself.

The young suburban couple we meet at the beginning of the novel, Frank and April Wheeler, despite the buoyant lilt of their names, are already people with diminished expectations. After rebelling against his virile, defeated father, Frank had eventually joined the same IBM-like corporation. He had lived most intensely as a soldier, as an undergraduate intellectual at Columbia University, and as a Greenwich Village bohemian after the war. There his affair with April had first begun. Now he feels the smoldering discontent of many prematurely sober young professionals of the 1950s. April, once a drama student, now a mother of two – Revolutionary Road is their suburban address – remains the keeper of what is left of Frank's artistic hopes, which soon crystallize in a quixotic plan to sell the house, leave the job, and move the family to France, where he can fulfill his youthful dream of becoming an artist. (Her own talents, of course, have long since been subsumed in his, almost as an extension of her motherhood.)

As this possibility arises, Frank, for one brief moment, is exhilarated, but unconsciously he is appalled. He has no real desire to live out his old fantasy, or to take up the freedom to be poor and creative (rather than comfortable and stultified). Soon April is pregnant again and he manipulates her into carrying the child while he himself carries on a little affair in the city. "Paris" is Frank's road, his dream of escape, but this is a road novel in reverse, with the hero secretly unwilling to go anywhere, except to the next rung of the corporate ladder. For Frank, bohemianism is the pipe dream still cherished by his wife, since it made him the man who first attracted her; she is the keeper of his earlier self, with which he has secretly lost faith. Unable to be frank with anyone, not even himself, Frank mouths glib clichés attacking conformity, adjustment, security, and togetherness, those familiar staples of fifties social criticism. Meanwhile, he maneuvers his wife into a suburban domesticity that shields him from his own sense of diminished horizons.

In *The Man in the Gray Flannel Suit,* Sloan Wilson finesses these conflicts and lets his hero, Tom Rath, have it both ways. He is a war hero with few regrets about the blood he spilled; indeed, the war and the romance that came with it provided the only real excitement of his life. He discovers that he has an understanding wife who encourages him to support the child he had by his Italian mistress. Soon it turns out that he even has a sympathetic corporate mentor who treats him as a surrogate son and allows him to turn down the rat-race job he himself had once pressed on him. Tom is also helped by a benign Jewish judge who enables him to inherit his grandmother's property and turn it into suburban housing. In short, the novel takes up the problem of the organization man and resolves it through wish fulfillment. "I don't think I'm the kind of guy who should try to be a big executive," he tells his boss, who has damaged his own life by choosing the same options. "I'll say it frankly: I don't think I have the willingness to make the sacrifices." Tom can have it all: can take responsibility for his wartime past, support his mistress but also rekindle his marriage. By just saying no, he can keep his job yet preserve his integrity and his family life – all by an act of personal choice. With a timely theme yet also a happy ending, the novel – and the film version starring Gregory Peck – became immensely popular.

Connecticut real estate also figures significantly in *Revolutionary Road,* beginning with the title, but it offers no easy solution to Frank Wheeler's problems. Like Tom Rath, he is nostalgic for the desperate excitement, fear, and romance of the war years, which his wife imagines they can recapture as twenties-style expatriates in Paris. During the war, he tells her, "I just felt this terrific sense of life. I felt full of blood." Now he wants to recapture that feeling, to break out of the cellophane bag that envelops his life. This could have been anyone's story in the 1950s: suburbia, family life, the corporate ladder, the loss of brave possibility once glimpsed in the war. It is too archetypal, too fraught with generational significance. But Yates adds a daring touch that transforms the novel. Through their real estate agent, Helen Givings, the town busybody, the Wheelers are exposed to a schizophrenic young man, her son, who eventually strips away their lies and self-deceptions and triggers the disaster that befalls them.

If *Revolutionary Road* impresses us with its verisimilitude and social realism, John Givings seems like a mutant, a strange interloper from a novel by Céline, Burroughs, or Kerouac. He is brilliantly mad: grievously damaged but lucid, dysfunctional but clairvoyant. A one-time mathematician whose face and memory have been scarred by too many electroshock treatments, he is the tragic demon the suburbs are designed to repress, the bad news no one welcomes in this pastoral utopia. His chirrupy mother, a master of denial, is adept at papering over cracks, looking at the bright side of everything; his stolid, impassive father deals with her by turning off his hearing aid. Mrs. Givings, who sells the Wheelers their house and then sells it again after April's death, is the very spirit of the suburbs in her obtuse and meddlesome cheerfulness, like a character from one of John Cheever's more sardonic stories:

The Revolutionary Hill Estates had not been designed to accommodate a tragedy. Even at night, as if on purpose, the development had no looming shadows and no gaunt silhouettes. It was invincibly cheerful.

After the Wheelers have departed, she is indignant that they failed to keep the house up, and prefers the "*really* congenial people" who have taken their place.

But while they were there, she sensed their difference — their tolerance and vulnerability — and so guessed that she could take the risk of initiating them into her private tragedy: the institutionalized son whose condition, we soon understand, reflects strains in the "normal" family that produced him. The young man first adopts Frank and April as surrogate parents, identifies with their planned escape to Europe, but turns on them brutally when they back out. As he sees it, April's new pregnancy, which binds them to Connecticut, can only spawn an unloved, unhappy child like himself. He alone in the novel sees through Frank's cowardice and manipulation, but he makes Frank's wife see through him as well. "You got cold feet, or what?" he says to Frank. "I wouldn't be surprised if you knocked her up on purpose, just so you could spend the rest of your life hiding behind that maternity dress." To April he says, "you must give him a pretty bad time, if making babies is the only way he can prove he's got a pair of balls."

Givings's role as madman and truth teller is so audacious that it ought to shatter the economy of the novel. Instead it shows us how much even realist fiction has changed since the start of the decade. The mad seer is really a figure from the Laingian counterculture of the sixties — who belongs to novels like Ken Kesey's *One Flew Over the Cuckoo's Nest* (1962) – not someone from the sober and sensible 1950s. Yet Salinger, Nabokov, Barth, and even Cheever had focused on characters who break down out of emotional turmoil, and Kerouac had portrayed Neal Cassady as an inspired madman, a kind of saint or "Holy Goof" who, like the egregious Randall McMurphy in Kesey's book, helps liberate his more timid friends. So Yates prophetically imports Givings into the Wheelers' life as a return of the repressed, a perverse product of suburban optimism, and a distorting mirror that reflects back the compromises and denials that enabled the Wheelers to construct their little world.

Givings has had shock treatments to short-circuit his emotional conflicts, but the therapy also obliterated his mathematical gift. "It's awful for anybody to forget something they want to remember," April tells him. But her husband, by his dishonesty, has also muffled his feelings and talents, emptying himself out all on his own. From the beginning she had collaborated "by telling easy, agreeable lies of her own, until each was saying what the other most wanted to hear." The truth was that at bottom, behind the self-deceptions, he was simply ordinary, not the stifled artist he imagined. Her self-induced abortion is a gesture of harsh honesty that she turns on herself.

In the end Yates's message was not very different from Salinger's or Kerouac's. The world of Revolutionary Road, like Cheever's Shady Hill, stands for the life Holden Caulfield mocks for its phoniness, the world the Beats left behind, the premature home-and-family trap Updike's Rabbit tries hard to escape. Frank and April Wheeler are another version of the bright, well-meaning young liberal couple whose good intentions get rough treatment in so many postwar fictions, from Trilling's *Middle of the Journey* to Barth's novels, from Cheever's stories to the cycle of marriage stories Updike collected in *Too Far to Go*. But with John Givings, *Revolutionary Road* crosses the WASP novel of manners and personal relationships with the Beat novel of spiritual accusation and salvation, to frame perhaps the most comprehensive indictment of the whole decade. For Yates, the corporate jobs and garden suburbs that crystallize the American dream are also the bland settings in which America has lost its memory and misplaced its adventurous, risk-taking soul.

To many historians, the fifties were an era of prosperity and tranquility – an island of stability in a century of violent change – but the novelists, filmmakers, and social critics of the period saw it differently. They looked at youthful rebellion and dysfunctional marriage as evidence of deep social malaise. With the spread of xenophobia and McCarthyism, the pervasive anxieties connected with the Cold War and atomic weapons, such fears were very close to the surface. Critics also saw a timid conformity, even a spiritual poverty, at the heart of America's prosperous economy and spectacular growth, with its emphasis on home and family and its conservative view of women's roles. When Frank Wheeler tries to convince his wife that she is emotionally disturbed, even unnatural, for not wanting to bear his next child, he is substituting a kitsch Freudian language of mental health for the patriarchal authority he resented in his father; the effect is the same. At the end he is merely an empty shell, like Barth's and Nabokov's hero-villains.

From Salinger and Ellison to Yates, the best writers of the fifties identified with the outsider, not with a dominant culture they found hollow and oppressive. They saw rebellion, neurosis, and madness as forms of lucidity, and portrayed adjustment and sanity as symptoms of deadly compromise. In her great story "A Good Man Is Hard to Find," Flannery O'Connor could even identify with the Misfit, an escaped and demented criminal, as a violent bearer of unpleasant truths to foolish people. Where O'Connor traffics comically in mass murder, other writers use failed abortion, tormented youth, or the death of children (as in *Rabbit, Run* or Joseph Heller's *Something Happened*) as an indication of social failure and loss of humanity.

Never did so triumphant a period produce such a mass of angry criticism, which accelerated toward the end of the decade with Beat writers like Kerouac and Ginsberg; mordant novelists such as Nabokov, Barth, and Yates; and the trenchant social commentary in C. Wright Mills's *The Power Elite* (1956), Galbraith's *The Affluent Society* (1958), Mailer's *Advertisements for Myself* (1959), and Paul Goodman's *Growing Up Absurd* (1960), which was itself a critical synthesis of the new youth culture. Even in the political realm, the winds of change were finally stirring. The end of the Korean War and the death of Stalin in 1953 led to the first of a series of thaws and détentes with the Soviet Union that softened the atmosphere of intolerance at home. With such works as Arthur Miller's *The Crucible* (1953) and Don Siegel's *Invasion of the Body Snatchers* (1956), liberals struck back at McCarthyism, and McCarthy himself was censured and effectively destroyed by his fellow senators in 1954. He died in an alcoholic haze in 1957, an embarrassment even to his diehard supporters.

Soon cracks began appearing in the blacklist, but also in the moral blacklist that barred any frank treatment of sexuality in books and films. Nabokov, D. H. Lawrence, Burroughs, and Henry Miller became hot new authors, though their books had been written, suppressed, and published elsewhere years earlier. The Supreme Court's unanimous 1954 decision in *Brown v. Board of Education of Topeka* took the nation on its first halting steps toward desegregation and racial equality, and in the late 1950s, the young civil rights movement under Martin Luther King, Jr., turned to direct action with bus boycotts and lunch-counter sit-ins in Southern towns and cities.

In the 1958 midterm elections, an eager class of young liberals was elected to Congress, where the Democrats controlled both houses by almost two-to-one margins. By 1960, John F. Kennedy could mobilize the widespread discontent of the late fifties into a political campaign that stressed youth, energy, change, and, in its final moments, social justice for black Americans. A child of privilege, the son of a political fixer, and raised in an increasingly right-wing Catholic family, the young candidate ironically inherited the mantle of expectations created by Brando and Mailer, James Dean and Jack Kerouac – in short, by all the angry, wounded, mysterious, and sexually charged young men of the 1950s. Soon, by the narrowest of margins, the political outsider was president and a new era would begin, burnished by a stirring rhetoric of social responsibility, a turbulent decade of confrontation and social change for which the critical culture of the fifties had helped pave the way.

5

❦

APOCALYPSE NOW: A LITERATURE
OF EXTREMES

ISTORIAN E. J. Hobsbawm has described the twentieth century
as the age of extremes. In a strange way, no quarter of the century
had to grapple with extremity, or its terrible aftermath, more
than the seemingly tranquil decades after the Second World War, which
some Americans still look back on as a golden age. Though the war had
spared the North American continent, its effects were brought home as
Americans emerged from their traditional isolation. Besides coming to
terms with the general carnage on an unheard of scale, and moving rapidly
toward the reconstruction of Europe and Asia, the postwar world had to
assimilate the most shocking news of the war, perhaps of the century as a
whole: the details of Holocaust and the effects of the atomic bomb. The
Holocaust and the bomb do not often explicitly appear in the literature of
the forties and fifties, perhaps because writers found them too large to
encompass and too remote from their direct experience. Despite this eerie
silence, they contributed to an undercurrent of anxiety that was freely
reflected not only in poems and novels but in the popular culture, including horror films, science fiction, and the new vogue of ghoulish comic
books that alarmed the moralists and psychologists of the period. Along
with peace and prosperity came a heightening of anxiety and insecurity.

Ordinary Americans, insulated from immediate knowledge of the worst
horrors of the war, recoiled after 1945 into an island of normalcy, a world
of getting and spending, as they had done after the First World War.
There was an emphasis on family and domesticity, on traditional gender
roles, and on a new culture of consumption made possible by rapid economic growth. The war industries retooled to produce consumer goods,
beginning with new homes and cars. But the impact of the bomb, the
Holocaust, and the mass destruction caused by the war was widely felt,
along with other changes that were transforming the world at midcentury:
the spread of Communism to eastern Europe and China and its strong
influence in western Europe, the rise of other forms of totalitarian and military dictatorship, the new bipolar world created by the Cold War and the
fear of nuclear annihilation, the elaboration of the welfare state, the con-

stantly increasing effects of technology on daily life – from new weapons systems and new domestic appliances to new forms of instant communication – the dismantling of outright colonialism and its replacement by subtler forms of economic and cultural domination, the major upheavals in race relations – first in America, then in western Europe – and a gradual resurgence of nationalism and religious conflict in areas previously attached to the former empires.

It is perhaps too easy to see the arc of the century, from 1914 to the 1990s, beginning and ending in Sarajevo, a city of varied inhabitants – Serbs, Moslems, Jews – that would come to symbolize the murderous ferocity of ethnic hatreds. The "ethnic cleansing" of the former Yugoslavia was part of a vicious process of fratricide and displacement that ran through much of the century. It is certainly no exaggeration to take the religious violence and the uprooting of whole populations on the Indian subcontinent in the late forties as a prologue to the second half of the century, which would be marked by lethal struggles between Jews and Arabs, Greeks and Turks, Asians and Americans, Irish Catholics and protestants, Bosnian Christians and Moslems, Hutus and Tutsis, black and white Americans.

Though writers must stay close to what they know, the American novel at its best reflected the pressure of these fears, hatreds, and passions. The neglected American masterpieces rediscovered and reinterpreted at midcentury – the works of Melville, Hawthorne, Whitman, Emerson, Thoreau, and Emily Dickinson – themselves compose a literature of extremes, as do the modern classics that gained a wider readership in the postwar years: the dark fables of Kafka and Beckett, the encyclopedic social canvases of Joyce and Proust, the inquiries into the heart of darkness in Conrad and Thomas Mann, or into the mainsprings of sexuality in Lawrence and Freud. The influence of existentialism and crisis theology worked against earlier traditions of American optimism. Emerson, Whitman, and the pragmatists looked dated and naïve to many American intellectuals after the war; the tragic vision of Melville and Hawthorne, Kafka and Dostoyevsky seemed more in tune with a world gone amok.

Very few American writers were equal to these challenges, but even fewer remained wholly unmoved by them. The travail of uprooted people in their futile attempt to find a place for themselves can be traced in stories as different as Nabokov's "Signs and Symbols" (1948), about an old émigré couple whose misery is reflected in their brilliant and demented son; Flannery O'Connor's "The Displaced Person" (1954), which savagely portrays the insularity of a Southern community through the fate of one refugee family; and Bernard Malamud's "The German Refugee" (1963), a story of maladjustment that ends in suicide. Modernist writers like Joyce made exile a

metaphor for their sense of estrangment from ordinary life; later writers like
Vladimir Nabokov and I. B. Singer dealt with the literal effects of exile and
dislocation. By the end of the century, the upsurge in immigration would
lead to a large hyphenated literature of cultural displacement.

It would be easy to put too much emphasis on the obvious fault lines
within postwar American literature: between the cautious small-scale novelists and poets of the fifties and the more apocalyptic writers of the sixties;
between the writers who applied a Jamesian irony to social issues and those
who took on more metaphysical themes with an Emersonian expansiveness;
between WASP authors who wrote about America in homogeneous or
regional terms and the new ethnic and homosexual writers who helped
decenter American literature in line with a shifting population and changing social values. In the long run, the more complacent and conservative
writers of the period have been forgotten; they were looking back nostalgically to a vanishing way of life. It would be futile to resurrect the legion of
genteel *New Yorker* fiction writers and humorists of the forties and fifties
except as documents of their class and times. Those who are still read, like
John Cheever, S. J. Perelman, or Jean Stafford, make deeper claims. By the
sixties, the well-made story or poem, the well-bred novel of manners, came
to seem irretrievably dated. What survived best from the fifties had an
undertone of hysteria, as in the desperate pathos, the sense of entrapment in
Saul Bellow's *Seize the Day,* the fecundity of imagination in Ellison's *Invisible
Man,* the mournful sense of fear or loss in Malamud's *The Assistant* and *The
Magic Barrel,* a riveting confessional authenticity of the kind that burns in
James Baldwin's early essays, or the exaggerated, often futile assertion of
freedom, as in the road novels discussed in the previous chapter.

It is hardly an accident that many of these writers were black or Jewish,
for race and ethnicity had situated them on painful ground, the point of
contact between the social marginality of the group and the psychological
stress of constructing one's identity as an individual. ("It was enough to
make a man pray to God to remove his great bone-breaking burden of selfhood," thinks Bellow's Herzog.) At a time when more Americans then ever
were becoming middle class, the humble, even despised origins of these
writers gave them a classic American story to tell: the tale of the outsider
straining to get in, the divided soul struggling to come together, but
someone who has a privileged view of the society not as a seamless whole
but as an arena of conflict and difference. For the ethnic writer this was
best expressed not by an omniscient narrator and a smooth linear fiction
but by explosive parables (as in Malamud and Baldwin), constantly shifting styles (in the work of Mailer and Ellison), and emotional extremes
reflected in unstable characters and equally unstable mixtures of comedy,

tragedy, and pathos (see Bellow's *Herzog,* for example, or virtually any of the sixties black humorists). Unless these writers were eaten up by their anger, as Baldwin was in his later work, it mattered little whether they were creatively inspired by the eruptions of the sixties, as were Philip Roth, Norman Mailer, and even John Updike, or condemned them root and branch, as did Saul Bellow in *Mr. Sammler's Planet* (1970). Bellow's sweeping moral censure was as apocalyptic as Mailer's ambivalent celebrations of sexual and political excess.

Because of the underlying continuity of postwar culture, it no longer feels useful to contrast the best writers of the fifties with those who flourished in the sixties. Often they were the same people, moving restlessly from one style to another. Despite some striking changes after the mid-fifties, the quarter of a century after the war seems more like a single sweep of time. Beneath the surface calm of the fifties we can now feel the seismic rumblings of discontent; it was the cosseted children of the fifties, the children of social mobility, suburban affluence, progressive education, and Cold War anxiety, who became the shock troops of the civil rights movement, the antiwar protests, the campus uprisings, and the sexual revolution. Some, like Philip Roth, would later recall the postwar years as a time of innocence, Edenic and uncorrupted, but this was not how the best writers experienced them at the time. The sense of metaphysical irony in a work like *Invisible Man* foreshadows the apocalyptic mood of the fiction of the 1960s. There is a despairing innocence about Salinger's *Catcher in the Rye* that feels very different from Philip Roth's deliberate, even cartoonish outrageousness in *Portnoy's Complaint.* Yet both are therapeutic monologues, wounded confessions full of anguished protest; both are good-boy's books, fundamentally moral, at bottom rather childlike, as eager to please and ingratiate as to complain. Many of the lesser writers of the fifties were abnormally mature, cautious in their limited goals, grown up before their time, and they were heavily criticized even then for their timidity. Among the writers whose work still matters, the quest for a presocial innocence, the quest for absolution, unites writers of the fifties and sixties in their focus on harsh subjects and extreme states of mind.

Other links emerge clearly as we look at the whole period between 1945 and 1970, as the preceding pages show. The reliance on realistic technique connects most of the war novelists of the forties to the naturalists of the thirties. But there are also moments of riveting absurdity or keen political insight in *The Naked and the Dead* or *From Here to Eternity* that looked forward to the war novels of the sixties. Mailer's dark revolutionary novel, *Barbary Shore* (1951), and his fascinating Hollywood novel, *The Deer Park* (1955), develop connections between politics and sexuality that are obscure but remarkably prescient, anticipating the Nietzschean or apocalyptic turn of sixties culture. The gay and bisexual writers of the late forties, such as Tennessee Williams and Paul Bowles, seem especially prophetic of the transgressive literature that began with Burroughs and the Beats and became a major element of the literary culture of the sixties. Ellison's *Invisible Man* not only anticipated the black humor and black nationalism of the sixties but developed notions of cultural identity that would make a new impact in the debates over diversity and multicultural-ism in the 1980s and 1990s. Even aside from traditional literary forms, the fifties and early sixties saw a major boom in social criticism as the widely read work of David Riesman, Hannah Arendt, Vance Packard, John Kenneth Galbraith, William H. Whyte, and Betty Friedan gave way to the psychosexual speculations of Herbert Marcuse, Norman O. Brown, and Paul Goodman. Relentless self-criticism, not complacency, was the real key to postwar culture.

MAILER: THE FIFTIES AND AFTER

Among the literary figures who gained fame before the fifties ended, the most prophetic, most attuned to the cultural eruptions soon to come was Norman Mailer, followed closely by Ellison, Baldwin, Bellow, Nabokov, Roth, and Updike. If the postwar literature of extremity can be said to have crystallized in a single work, it would be Mailer's feverish essay "The White Negro" (1957), with strong competition from Allen Ginsberg's dithyrambic manifesto *Howl,* published the previous year. As *Howl* focuses on the madness that was an undercurrent of the enforced sanity of the fifties – the same demon that haunts works as different as *The Catcher in the Rye* and Robert Lowell's *Life Studies* (1959) – "The White Negro" explores the sources of that insanity through the figure of the hipster – the cool, murderous misfit who incarnates it. Like Ellison and Baldwin before him, Mailer understood that race, not class, would become a major metaphor of social identity in the postwar years. By turning the Negro into a psycho-sexual metaphor for the hipster, however, Mailer ran the risk of distorting the actuality of race in America, which was already fraught with half-acknowledged sexual myths and fantasies.

Among the sources of Mailer's existential portrait, he insists, were the pervasive threat of the bomb and the unbearable knowledge of the death camps, which nearly all American writers, even the Jews, had managed to avoid confronting. What the war in Europe and Asia had revealed about human nature, the more bland American culture of the fifties had some-how managed to suppress. The hipster had taken this knowledge upon himself, not suicidally, not as illness (like Carl Solomon, the subject of *Howl*), but as a Nietzschean challenge to live dangerously. The hipster, by his example – and Mailer, by his writing – tempts us to go beyond the strict limits of middle-class life, to explore the existential risk of sex and violence as both our damnation and our salvation.

Where other writers saw the genocidal cruelties of the war as a blinding revelation of the human potentiality for evil, a confirmation of original sin, Mailer saw them as a leap into the irrational, a challenge to the bland lies of civilization, the compromises and adjustments of middle-class life in the 1950s. For him the Holocaust and the bomb are not pointers toward the moral abyss so much as they are prototypes of the modern form of collective death, death by technology, that robbed death of all personal meaning or heroism. Mailer himself, like Philip Roth, grew up as the beloved young prince of a middle-class Jewish family. He had an incubus of respectability that he needed to shake off. Though he got his literary education at Harvard, not in prison, "The White Negro" was his manifesto as a moral explorer in the tradition of outlaw writers like de Sade and Genet, or writer-adventurers like Hemingway and Malraux.

Mailer's first three books had been written when "the novel" still existed in its traditional form, as an arena of huge ambition for young writers. The passion for film that developed in the sixties and seventies was still fixed upon prose fiction in the years after the war. Despite its absurdist touches, *The Naked and the Dead* had essentially been a conventional novel, grounded in the prewar naturalism of Farrell and Dos Passos. Mailer had planned the novel as a student at Harvard; its literariness clashed with its vivid sensory intelligence. But no American writer since Melville had made such a sharp turn away from his initial success. *Barbary Shore*, Mailer's Marxist political allegory, and *The Deer Park*, his brilliantly sordid Hollywood novel, pleased neither the critics nor the public, though they were important steps in his gradual transformation from a writer concerned with social themes to a cultural radical exploring a new psychosexual terrain.

The Deer Park begins as a novel in the prewar tradition of Hollywood gothic – the mode of Nathanael West and Fitzgerald; it portrays Hollywood as a swamp of moral corruption dominated by tyrannical studio chiefs, personified by the egregious Herman Teppis, a Louis B. Mayer–like figure, and his son-in-law Collie Munshin. Before long, the blacklist becomes a key theme. Mailer's protagonist, a longtime director named Charles Eitel (pronounced "I tell"), at first refuses to cooperate with the congressional committee, but then makes his peace and returns to work, only to find that his talent has been dissipated in moral compromise. If this were all that happened in *The Deer Park*, Mailer would have remained true to the thirties-style anti-Fascism of *The Naked and the Dead* and the book would resemble other novels and plays of the fifties attacking the blacklist. As it proceeds, however, and as Mailer revised it from its original conception, it focuses much more on the sexual complications of its characters than on their political wrongdoing. Eitel's reluctant decision to name names and his consequent return to work at the studio not only undermine him morally and politically but damage him as a lover and an artist – Mailer insists on these parallels.

Eitel's love affair with Elena Esposito (a character loosely based on Mailer's wife at the time, Adele Morales) had enabled him to retreat from politics, to give up the world and concentrate on his creative work. When he falls into the smooth professionalism of the studio hack, he becomes as coolly calculating in love as in his writing. This is not only Mailer's verdict on Hollywood, it is his view of the compromises of the 1950s, the morally fatal concessions of middle age, and the sinister ease of the well-oiled literary career, the safe commercial path Mailer himself had been unable or unwilling to follow.

But Mailer's novel is not content with telling the story of Eitel and Elena. In the final version of *The Deer Park,* two other figures struggle to emerge: a Nick Carraway–like narrator, Sergius O'Shaugnessy, who served as Mailer's surrogate in several works in the 1950s, and Marion Faye, Mailer's first portrait of the hipster, a psychopathic moral adventurer who tests the limits of experience by killing all compassion in himself. A study in sexual ambiguity, a pimp who, much like the studio bosses, crystallizes the stew of corruption that intrigues Mailer in Hollywood – a world in which sex, work, and people themselves are constantly bought and sold – Marion signals Mailer's own shifting interest from a politics of altruism and compassion to a psychopathology of human nature. "The White Negro" would become Mailer's hypnotic commentary on his portrait of Marion Faye, the remarkable creature whom he had introduced but not really integrated into *The Deer Park.* (Later, he would try again by adapting the novel into a play.)

In his conception of Sergius O'Shaugnessy, the other character grafted onto *The Deer Park,* Mailer tried to create another kind of moral outlaw, the handsome, swaggering fake Irishman who is the author's inverted tribute to his own Jewish origins. At one time, Mailer projected Sergius as the hero of a huge eight-part novel, a modern *comédie humaine,* but *The Deer Park* and a few pieces of fiction in *Advertisements for Myself,* including Mailer's two best stories, "The Man Who Studied Yoga" and "The Time of Her Time," are all that remain from this grandiose plan. Sergius is an off-stage presence in "The Man Who Studied Yoga," which Mailer intended as the prologue to the eight novels. He figures as Cassius O'Shaugnessy, psychopath and sinner, political adventurer and avant-garde writer between the wars, who later enters a monastery.

"The Man Who Studied Yoga," like *The Deer Park,* is about the compromises of middle age, the onset of tepid sex, tepid politics, and tepid art which Mailer identifies with the gray atmosphere of the early 1950s. Sam Slovoda, the protagonist, is Mailer's Rabbit, his version of what he himself might have become had he settled unprotestingly into the groove of middle-class marriage and routine work. But a Dr. Sergius also is mentioned as Sam's shrink, the very oracle of the kind of psychic adjustment Mailer detests about the liberal, therapeutic culture of the period.

Written in 1952, the story is unlike any other fiction Mailer published. In its deliberately flat, musing manner, it reads like the solemn, half-satirical fables about intellectuals that we find in Delmore Schwartz's best book, *The World Is a Wedding* (1948), or the fiction Saul Bellow began writing with his first novel, *Dangling Man* (1944). What distinguishes Sam from Mailer's other protagonists is his lack of distinction, the matter-of-factness of his whole being. He is neither ordinary nor extraordinary, young nor old, tall nor short. Once he dreamed of becoming a great novelist, but now he's writing continuity for comic strips. Once he belonged to the Party, dreamed of redeeming suffering humanity, but that too is little more than a memory. He has some sense of himself as a great lover, but in the story this devolves into an evening with old friends watching a crudely made porno film, then making love to his wife after the friends depart. In his passivity, Sam even feels he is psychically a Jew, though he is only one-quarter Jewish. In short, Sam is everything the Mailer of the fifties is trying to escape yet fears he essentially *is.* As Mailer later described it in *The Armies of the Night,* among his many selves was "a fatal taint" of "the one personality he found absolutely insupportable – the nice Jewish boy from Brooklyn. Something in his adenoids gave it away – he had the softness of a man early accustomed to mother-love."

To Mailer during this period, psychoanalysis was simply another version of the dance of adjustment that had long enabled Jews to survive but had become for him an unbearable form of capitulation. It reeks of the caution that had destroyed the previous literary generation. "Defeated by war, prosperity, and conformity," he wrote in *Advertisements for Myself,* "the best of our elders are deadened into thinking machines, and the worst are broken scolds who parrot a plain housewife's practical sense of the mediocre – worn-out middle-class bores of the psychoanalytical persuasion who worship the cheats of moderation, compromise, committee and indecision, or even worse, turn to respect the past." He says of his own World War II generation, on the other hand: "The past did not exist for us. We had to write our way out into the unspoken territories of sex — there was so much there, it was new, and the life of our talent depended upon going into the borderland."

The same animus against psychoanalysis colors "The White Negro." Mailer writes of his hipster hero: "The psychopath is ordinately ambitious, too ambitious ever to trade his warped brilliant conception of his possible victories in life for the grim if peaceful attrition of the analyst's couch." A few lines later, in the essay's most notorious passage, Mailer eulogizes the courage, if not the therapeutic value, of two 18-year-old hoodlums who murder a candy-store owner. He does not mention that the storekeeper, like the psychoanalyst, is likely to be Jewish, representing a rejected part of his own identity. (Mailer's maternal grandfather kept a grocery in Long Branch, New Jersey, besides being the town's unofficial rabbi. The writer himself was born there in 1923.)

This was hardly the first time Mailer identified with the perpetrators rather than the victims of violence. His secret fascination with sex, power, violence, and irrationality was an undercurrent in his first three novels, beginning with the characters of Croft and Cummings in *The Naked and the Dead,* but with "The White Negro" it emerged in a wholly new style as the major direction of his work. The essay, which makes painful reading today, followed the critical and commercial failure of *Barbary Shore* and his long effort to complete and publish *The Deer Park,* but it also came out of other stresses: his struggles with pot and Seconal, with the new Beat phenomenon that changed the course of his work, with his own Jewishness, with writer's block, with the exigencies of conventional literary form, and with the gray cultural climate of the 1950s. For too many reasons this period was not a happy one for Mailer; his obsession with violence became his way of defying and exorcising it.

The famous *Partisan Review* symposium on "Our Country and Our Culture" in 1952 has often been seen as a turning point, marking the postwar reconciliation between the once-alienated writer and American society. Mailer's contribution, however, was an angry, dissenting one:

This period smacks of healthy manifestoes. Everywhere the American writer is being dunned to become healthy, to grow up, to accept the American reality, to integrate himself, to eschew disease, to revalue institutions. Is there nothing to remind us that the writer does not need to be integrated into his society, and often works best in opposition to it?

Between 1952 and 1957, Mailer turned from this stereotyped rhetoric of alienation to a more radical resistance that synthesized all the countercultural themes of the 1950s. He evolved the self-promoting, self-lacerating confessional stance that would carry him through the next decade and a half. In place of the "healthy manifestoes" that accepted the American reality, "The White Negro" is a deliberately *un*healthy manifesto in the surrealist tradition, a feverish text that sings the praises of criminality as an antidote to totalitarianism and (like the surrealist manifestoes) rarely bothers to distinguish lurid metaphor from literal prescription. Mailer's proclaimed goal is "to encourage the psychopath in oneself," "to try to live the infantile fantasy," and always to seek "an orgasm more apocalyptic than the one which preceded it."

Some of the essay is simply Reichian boilerplate. As the outlaw analyst expelled by Freud, who put so much stock in the healthy release of sexual energy, and who finally died in a federal prison, Wilhelm Reich was a major influence on dissident writers in the fifties and sixties. Some of Mailer's language is recycled from the antinomian tradition that runs through Blake, Nietzsche, D. H. Lawrence, and the Beats, a language of energy against reason, movement over stasis, physical intensity over civilized reflection, self-expression over repression. Some of it — the portrait of the Negro as the violent, jazz-soaked primitive, the fumbling vocabulary of Hip — is simply embarrassing, a primitivist myth left over from prewar modernism. Yet for all its overheated rhetoric and dubious moral outlook, it marks not only a new phase of Mailer's career but also a momentous shift in American literary culture, a turn toward the dark side, the rebellious and the demonic. Renouncing the Apollonian program of postwar society, Mailer also turns away from conventional literary form, toward a prose that mingles fact and fiction, social criticism and confession, cultural prophecy and personal therapy.

❦

Already in *The Deer Park,* Mailer seemed at odds with fiction as a literary medium. Though the minor characters (Teppis, Munshin) and the Palm Springs setting come through wonderfully, all the major male characters — Eitel, Faye, O'Shaugnessy — were projections of Mailer himself or his developing ideas; the pimp Marion Faye, the book's devil figure, animates two or three scenes brilliantly, but only Eitel and Esposito are fully realized characters. (The second half of the novel breaks down under the weight of Mailer's ideas, anticipating his search for greater immediacy in discursive writing.) Mailer's next book would not be a novel but a collage assembled out of the blockage of his career as a novelist. The sinews of *Advertisements for Myself* — the confessional prose that knits the book together — came from "The White Negro," which had been published separately two years earlier. The remarkable persona that Mailer shaped for this book, the figure of the risk-taking yet disaster-prone moral adventurer, the maladroit, ambivalent existential hero, dominates his next novel, *An American Dream* (1965), as well as the great participatory journalism that would soon make him one of America's most influential writers. The sixties would redeem for Mailer what the previous decade had nearly destroyed.

After turning away from early success as a conventional novelist, Mailer found that he worked best in a jam: when he was feeling pressed for money, in despair about his reputation, blocked as a writer, or out of touch with his audience and his times. *Advertisements* was the prototype for how he turned his losses into strengths, his sense of failure, neglect, or misunderstanding into cultural meaning. One model for the book was undoubtedly "The Crack-Up," Fitzgerald's three *Esquire* essays of 1936 around which Edmund Wilson had built a posthumous collection in 1945. The thirties had been a bad decade for Fitzgerald in much the same way the fifties were for Mailer; Fitzgerald too had tried to recoup his losses by way of confession, which appalled many of his friends, including Hemingway. "I'd started off with the idea of a collection of stories and articles," Mailer recalled in 1985, "but discovered that my collection would have no meaning unless I threw in a lot of the worst pieces. Because where I had failed often offered the most interesting revelations." Subtly, apology gave way to self-projection. "Unconsciously I was trying to take inventory. I was trying also to end a certain part of my literary life and begin anew. I wanted to declare myself, put myself on stage firmly and forever."

Mailer had long been searching for a hero, dogged by the Hemingway view that heroism was at best elusive in the modern world, that heroes were now the sum of their damages. In *Advertisements,* amid the wreckage of his hopes, he found himself as his own flawed but exemplary protagonist. Mailer was scarcely the only one to look to the self in search of cultural meaning. James Baldwin had already probed his own experience in his deeply introspective reports on race in America, which marked a major shift from the naturalistic approach of many earlier black writers. His essays, first collected in *Notes of a Native Son* (1955), had staked out new territory for the fiction writer. Robert Lowell, partly inspired (like Mailer) by the Beats, made a parallel turn toward the confessional in the poetry and prose brought together in *Life Studies* (1959). This shift was not well grasped by their many imitators, since both Lowell and Mailer had an almost Augustan sense of decorum, a high degree of self-consciousness, and a mordant, civilized wit that were hardly duplicated by those who followed them along the confessional path. Mary McCarthy was another novelist who had strayed into autobiography and published essays and memoirs almost indistinguishable from her fiction. Together, McCarthy,

Baldwin, and Mailer did much to erode the lines dividing the novel from the essay. Together they helped make the essay a major literary form, first by importing fictional techniques, then by rescuing the essay from the whimsical voice of the eccentric gentleman – the wayward musings of an E. B. White still writing in the tone of Charles Lamb – and infusing it with a sense of personal immediacy and social crisis. Out of this was born the New Journalism, the quintessential literary form of the eruptive 1960s.

Mailer's gift was to match his own problems with his intuitive sense of the moment. *Advertisements* was put together at a time when the sexual discretions of the fifties were breaking up; the book's most celebrated and reviled story, "The Time of Her Time," was one of the most daring pieces of erotic writing of the decade. Sergius O'Shaugnessy would personify Mailer's role-playing in the fifties, much as the character called Mailer (in *The Armies of the Night* [1968]) or Aquarius (in *Of a Fire on the Moon* [1971]) would personify it in the sixties. In "The Time of Her Time," the shy narrator of *The Deer Park*, traumatized by war and (also in the Hemingway mold) wounded in his sexuality, would be transfigured into the Irish stud who would wield his "avenger" to ignite the sexuality of Denise Gondelman, a bohemian Jewish princess.

Nothing brought Mailer more grief from later feminists like Kate Millett than this curious story of sexual conquest. Like Stephen Rojack subduing his late wife's German maid in *An American Dream,* Sergius humbles and excites Denise by attacking her from behind. Yet he sees himself as an infinitely generous lover, determined to give pleasure – and to reap the psychological rewards of that pleasure – even by way of pain and humiliation. He has the vanity as well as generosity of the saint, he tells us. "I was the messiah of the one-night stand, and so I rarely acted like a pig in bed, I wasn't greedy." Though he is fired by his "rage to achieve" and his need to "lay waste to her little independence," he is less a sexist than a sexual utopian, eager to lead a recalcitrant, domineering woman to the promised land of orgasm, eager for "those telepathic waves of longing" that would surely accrue to him over the years "because I had been her psychic bridegroom."

Where Denise's Jewish analyst and passive Jewish boyfriend have failed, Sergius will succeed, pushing her excitement over the edge at the crucial moment by calling her a "dirty little Jew." His only fear was that "some bearded Negro cat" would get there before him, "would score where I had missed and thus cuckold me in spirit." At the end, Mailer, at least as giving as his hero, allows Denise to turn the tables on Sergius by calling him a "phallic narcissist" and repressed homosexual. But this neat reversal hardly diminishes the author's identification with his character. Coming together in this story are Mailer the fantasy fascist – the scourge of milk-fed Jews, assertive women, and intellectuals who chat about T. S. Eliot – and Mailer the sexual metaphysician, who evolves an exquisitely complex style to gauge the most minute vibrations of sexual power and energy that pass between people. This emphasis on sex as an arena of power eventually earned Mailer the hatred of many feminists, yet it also became an ax they would wield in their own analysis of the relations between the sexes.

Advertisements for Myself salvaged Mailer's career by turning him into a cultural figure, another prophet of the orgasm, substituting the author and his Napoleonic ambitions for the conventional novels he could not write, novels that were no longer anyone's royal route to fame. The winds had shifted from a literary culture to a media culture, a celebrity culture in which Mailer would thrive as much as Byron or Hemingway did in their own time. Mailer's career as a New Journalist appropriately began with a landmark report on the 1960 convention that nominated John F. Kennedy, the essay in which Mailer surprisingly turned the telegenic young senator into the hipster hero whose advent was announced in "The White Negro." Mailer might not have known of Kennedy's sexual adventures, but he was drawn to the candidate's youth, vitality, and energy, his seeming emancipation from the liberal catchphrases Mailer had often mocked. He saw the sentimental candidacy of Adlai Stevenson, ignited by Eugene McCarthy's eloquent nominating speech, as the last gasp of the old, tired, puritanical liberalism. Kennedy's, on the other hand, was a liberalism of power and realism, an image-oriented liberalism that played into Mailer's Carlylean quest for heroes, his great-man theory of history.

Writing about the public world for *Esquire,* Mailer had a new career before him, a wider field for his personal metaphysics. With Kennedy, Mailer sensed that the drab political atmosphere of the fifties was a thing of the past, that the dynamics of the Democratic and Republican parties could become as interesting as the dynamics of the sexual underground. Mailer picked up where another keen observer of political conventions, H. L. Mencken, one of the granddaddies of the New Journalism, had left off. It turned out to be a very close election; Mailer was both pleased and shocked by the influence of his piece, which "had more effect than any other single work of mine," or so he wrote in his second collection of essays, *The Presidential Papers* (1963), published just weeks before the assassination. He discovered a new power in writing a kind of fiction about real people, something not to be found in fiction as he had known it. "I was bending reality like a field of space to curve the time I wished to create."

Kennedy was elected, and Mailer enrolled (in his own mind, at least) as court wit, jester, and advisor to the new president, determined to save him from "intellectual malnutrition." But the self-destructive furies of the

1950s caught up with Mailer, and almost terminated his new career before it began. Soon after Kennedy was elected, Mailer stabbed and nearly killed his second wife, Adele Morales, after a disastrous party meant to launch his candidacy for mayor of New York. "My pride is that I can explore areas of experience that other men are afraid of," he told the court. "Your recent history indicates that you cannot distinguish fiction from reality," responded the judge, who committed him to Bellevue for psychiatric observation.

The stabbing, which seemed like a page out of "The White Negro," proved to be an exorcism that marked the end of a bad period for Mailer. Though he continued to explore the dark side of the psyche in his next major piece of journalism, "Ten Thousand Words a Minute" (1962), an *Esquire* account of the first Sonny Liston–Floyd Patterson boxing match, and especially in *An American Dream,* he soon emerged less as the scrapper than as the distinguished gentleman of American letters, a writer who would carve his own niche by sheer intelligence and self-projection, outside accepted literary categories. Above all, through his uncanny instinct for the Zeitgeist, he would be able to connect with the turmoil of the sixties as he had not been in tune with America since the years right after the war. The existential self-creation he had projected onto Sergius and admired in Kennedy would flourish in a period of personal and political theater, which looked to the self as an Emersonian field of creative possibility.

Mailer's first boxing piece set the pattern of his work of the next decade, which would prove to be the peak of his career. In *Advertisements* he had written freely of himself for the first time, shaping a personal legend out of the loose ends of his occasional writing. In "Ten Thousand Words a Minute" he becomes a novelistic character, the protagonist of a larger public story. When the bad boy of boxing, Sonny Liston, knocked out Floyd Patterson in the first round of their title bout, reporters were left with a nonevent as unpalatable as it was insubstantial. Mailer shapes his immensely long piece as an attack on journalism, with its "excessive respect for power" and its failure to find the truth amid "a veritable factology of detail." He shifts the dramatic center of the piece from the Liston–Patterson match, which ended almost before it began, to a stunning account of an earlier bout in which welterweight Emile Griffith killed Benny Paret in one of the most horrific displays of ferocity in boxing history:

Paret died on his feet. As he took those eighteen punches something happened to everyone who was in psychic range of the event. Some part of his death reached out to us. One felt it hover in the air. . . . He went down more slowly than any fighter had ever gone down, he went down like a large ship which turns on end and slides second by second into its grave. As he went down, the sound of Griffith's punches echoed in the mind like a heavy ax in the distance chopping into a wet log.

There is an almost unbearable dream logic to these slow-motion images, which interpret the event even as they visualize it; there is an almost feral intelligence on display here. Mailer's subject is never simply the event itself but its psychic resonance, brought home to us through arresting, indelible metaphor. This account leads Mailer into a defense of boxing as a reflection of some primitive "religion of blood, a murderous and sensitive religion which mocks the effort of the understanding to approach it." Nowhere is Mailer closer to Ernest Hemingway and D. H. Lawrence than in his portrayal of boxing as an existential encounter with violence and death; nowhere do bad ideas inspire such electric writing.

For the Liston–Patterson match itself, however, Mailer takes a different literary tack. He concentrates on his own antics as he tried to give a press conference afterward, then offered to promote a rematch, and even tried to pick a fight with Sonny Liston. This is the reader's first encounter with Mailer as inept scene stealer, the buffoon with grandiose ideas who tries to project himself into the center of the event. This is the Mailer of infinite bravado and questionable judgment, who achieves in his prose what he could not bring off in real life. The Hemingway–Lawrence Mailer would shortly write *An American Dream* in eight monthly installments for *Esquire.* But the buffoonish Mailer would soon reappear, with spectacular effect, when, after many setbacks, he would find a way to step back from his own legend. He would create himself in the third person as a comic character swept up by history in *The Armies of the Night,* his best book, and in *Miami and the Siege of Chicago,* his best piece of convention reportage, both published in 1968 as the conflicts of the sixties came to a boil.

Just as "The White Negro" and *Advertisements* developed out of *The Deer Park, An American Dream* is closely linked to *The Presidential Papers,* and especially the Kennedy essays. In Mailer's view, the writer, the politician, the hipster, and the boxer are all (at their best) adventurers, self makers on a quest into the unknown. Unlike the reporter, who is "close to the action" but "not *of* the action," who is inhibited "by a hundred censors, most of them inside himself," and "learns to write what he does not naturally believe," the real writer "discovers something he did not know he knew in the act itself of writing." In line with this faith in self-discovery, Mailer evolved a prose of Carlylean complexity, a cumulative, periodic style designed to convey a sense of risk, the sense of a mind in motion as it examines the world from every angle. The serial composition of *An American Dream* added another element of contingency to the book's Dostoyevskyan pretensions. Stephen Rojack is fictionally tied to Jack Kennedy – they were both war heroes and entered Congress together – but where Rojack turned to explore the dark side, to pursue his "secret frightened romance with the phases of the moon," Kennedy remained the kind of rational liberal Mailer himself had once been, the political actor whose personality is built over a void. Rojack and *An American Dream* become bold (or foolhardy) vehicles for Mailer's pulp fantasies about murder, espionage, and the spidery tentacles of wealth and power in America.

No book of Mailer's divided critics as violently as *An American Dream*. Those who expected a realistic novel with credible, rounded characters and a well-structured plot were angry and disappointed. Mailer had stabbed his own wife only a few years earlier, and now he was indulging himself in a shapeless tale of "crime without punishment" that begins with a man strangling his wife. But *An American Dream* was written under the influence of Burroughs and Céline, not Farrell and Dos Passos. (Mailer was testifying for Burroughs in an obscenity trial over *Naked Lunch* as he was writing his book.) *An American Dream* is more a nightmare, a hallucination, than a realistic novel. It projects the mood of Mailer's "mad" period of the late fifties onto the public hubris of the Kennedy era, when America pumped up its imperial pretensions and, in a high-stakes confrontation over Soviet missiles in Cuba, came chillingly close to nuclear war. *An American Dream* is the nightmarish underside of Camelot, a twilight zone girded by Mafia connections and CIA plots, by a paranoia that sees a web of evil behind every event.

In personal terms *An American Dream* is also a book about the sour feelings of middle age; Mailer had just turned forty when he began writing it. Like Sergius in "The Time of Her Time," Rojack is haunted by the men he killed during the war, by the darker side of his own heroism. He is lacerated by a core of violence in his soul, which he exorcises in the course of the book, and he passes through murder, sexual aggression, megalomania, and madness to emerge "something like sane again" in the final lines.

Ever since the heyday of gothic novelists and Romantic poets, the emblematic image of the dark side, of what we sometimes call lunacy, has always been the moon. Behind *An American Dream* is a residue of the Greek myth of Endymion, the shepherd who falls in love with the moon. Rojack kills a wife who represents every kind of human rot; he is drawn instead to the moon in constant suicidal tests of irrational male daring. But by challenging himself, by walking close to the edge in every way, by walking a parapet thirty floors above a city street, he expels his demons and becomes a new man, or so at least we are meant to believe. This theme of personal transformation is exactly what Mailer would pursue again in *The Armies of the Night*, but as comedy and history rather than pulp fantasy. The Mailer of *An American Dream* plots out a Dostoyevskyan idea of spiritual renewal using the noir techniques of Jim Thompson, James M. Cain, and Mickey

Spillane. *Armies* would transfer the same idea into a larger public arena, linking the 1960s, with comic-epic extravagance, to the figure of a recalcitrant, unheroic, middle-aged Mailer.

❦

We would have to look back to Byron to find a precedent for the comic turn Mailer takes with his own long-cultivated legend in *The Armies of the Night*. Like Byron when he wrote *Don Juan,* Mailer was already a known quantity, not entirely respectable, a "semi-distinguished and semi-notorious author," as renowned for his disorderly life, truculent temper, and naked ambition as for his literary achievements. A sense of scandal attached to both men, who had pursued fame, as Hemingway did, by nurturing a personal myth and becoming a public character. Now, however, like Byron in *Don Juan,* Mailer steps back from the ego and its metaphysics, examining his own legend with a poised urbanity that freshens and restores it. Byron's *Don Juan* is perfectly modern in being a poem largely about itself: its structural principle is digression; its form allows the writer to include anything that crosses his mind. This is true for *Armies* as well, but with a difference: here the antihero, the old lion who has already fought his battles, who is long beyond his angry radicalism and grown attached to his comfortable life, must answer the call of the historical moment, the 1967 Pentagon march protesting the Vietnam War. *Armies* is not just about Mailer but about the sixties with "Mailer" as protagonist. Written in the third person, like *The Education of Henry Adams, Armies* is also a very American book, steeped in millennial patriotism but also in the self's hunger to kidnap history and become its agent.

As in the Liston essay, Mailer begins by attacking conventional journalism – in this case, *Time* magazine's account of his loutish behavior – for exploiting his notoriety while distorting what really happened. As Lowell had done in his latest poetry, Mailer sounds the confessional note, full of small, seemingly trivial details, making the reader his intimate collaborator, almost his co-conspirator. He fabricates personal drama out of his unwillingness to get involved at all, and makes gossip of his jealousy of other writers at the march, including Lowell and Paul Goodman. This is Mailer's old self-indulgence in its most relaxed, conversational form. Situating himself at some distance from the event, he stresses his distaste for both the middle-aged radicals who have organized it and the young rebels and hippies, so different from him, whose spirit shapes it; they somehow seem to be carrying history in their bones. Mailer had been an ideologue of sex, a theorist of Hip, but these are kids who "conceived of lust as no more than the gymnasium of love." As far as the older radicals, the pacifists, "Mailer could feel no sense of belonging to any of these people. They were much too nice and much too principled for him." To Mailer, "the modest everyday fellow of his daily round was servant to a wild man in himself," an exigent brute perhaps responsible for the worst and best in his work, the Mr. Hyde he had no wish to kill off.

If "The White Negro" and *An American Dream* give us the psychopathology of the brute, *The Armies of the Night* and the last forty pages of *Miami and the Siege of Chicago* celebrate the emergence of a more Apollonian Mailer, reasonable but newly courageous, dignified yet as protean as ever. The middle-aged Mailer, now more Burkean than Marxist, a "left conservative" who holds onto his sense of sin, is redeemed from inertia by the younger generation he had scorned at the end of his report on the 1960 convention, the Puritans and defeated idealists who made a last stand for Adlai Stevenson. In both the Pentagon and Chicago pieces, the old war novelist inspects his ragged troops and, to his own satisfaction at least, leads them into battle.

With *In Cold Blood* (1966), Truman Capote had made much of writing a "nonfiction novel," but he had kept himself out of the picture and confined his story to a single crime. It was the ultimate *New Yorker* article, vivid yet coolly detached, exquisitely calibrated in tone and detail. Tom Wolfe and other magazine journalists had been using fictional techniques to great effect in evoking the carnivalesque uproar of sixties culture. But only Mailer, conflating fiction, journalism, and autobiography, had made himself the protagonist of the story, filtering history through the prism of his own ambivalence and harnessing the whole decade to his own comically refurbished legend. By stepping back from "Mailer," setting him in a larger public world, the author, like Henry Adams, projected his personal quirks into a dialogue with America at one of its defining moments.

In the journalistic works that followed *Armies,* including *Miami and the Siege of Chicago, Of a Fire on the Moon* (on the astronauts and their moon landings), and *The Prisoner of Sex* (on the new feminism), Mailer tried time and again to renew this exchange between the perceiving self and the national destiny, with gradually diminishing results. His prose sang, but beginning with the moon book, his real involvement waned. Mailer's persona, with his Emersonian ambitions – the initial hesitations, unflagging intelligence, and predictable heroism – began to grow tired, predictable, like a trick worked up once too often. With *The Fight* (1975), a pedestrian account of the George Foreman – Muhammad Ali match in Zaire, the personal anchor faltered definitively, though Mailer could still summon up sharp memories of the fight for a documentary film twenty years later. By the midseventies, though, American culture itself had grown less interesting. Its public life offered no characters of the size of the Kennedys, King, or Malcolm X, the martyred figures of the sixties. Instead Mailer, always drawn to personal myth and mystery, began to channel much of his energy from journalism into biography – first with such literary predecessors as D. H. Lawrence and Henry Miller in *The Prisoner of Sex,* then with full-scale portraits of Marilyn Monroe (1973), Gary Gilmore (1979), Lee Harvey Oswald (1994), Pablo Picasso (1995), and, most surprisingly, Jesus Christ (1997). By and large, these books were more workmanlike than inspired, the product of Mailer the professional writer rather than the driven artist. The first three used materials assembled by an entrepreneurial researcher, Lawrence Schiller; the Monroe and Picasso books were criticized for their undue reliance on the work of other biographers. All were highly readable, ambitiously explanatory, but in some degree derivative, written to make money yet elaborating at too great a length on old Mailer obsessions, which sometimes obstructed our view of the subject.

The great exception was the longest of them all, the Gilmore book, *The Executioner's Song,* the most untypical of Mailer's masterpieces, a book that meets *In Cold Blood* on its own flat Midwestern ground. Where Capote's book was limited by its *New Yorker*-ish detachment, its blandly even tone, which belied Capote's almost excessive involvement with his subjects, Mailer's book was clearly saturated with Mailer's own themes, though they never break into the narrative. Mailer had been fascinated by men like Gary Gilmore from the beginning, psychopathic killers who are not Hip but who *are* unstable containers of a violence that could erupt at any moment. On the surface, *The Executioner's Song* is as objective and impersonal as Mailer's previous books had been steeped in ego, or scored with pet ideas coming down from "The White Negro." Described as a "true life novel," the book pursues the greatest challenge of any novel: the writer's empathetic identification with people very different from himself. With his silly accents and strange fictional masks, Mailer had always tried to be everything but what he was. "Mailer" the literary character and Sergius the fake Irishman were the opposite of "the nice Jewish boy from Brooklyn," yet they let loose a torrent of Jewish introspection and ambivalence, a riot of self-analysis that enabled him to recoup in prose what had eluded him in dealing with people. But in the Gilmore book Mailer really sets himself aside, not by assuming a mask but by feeling his way into the mind of this character, the other, as he had rarely done since *The Naked and the Dead.* "I'm not as interesting to myself as I used to be," he told an interviewer in 1981.

To do this he develops yet another style: quick declarative sentences, short paragraphs, the prose equivalent of documentary filmmaking yet free of the careless megalomania that ruins the films he actually made. Mailer's closest approach to Gary Gilmore had come, oddly, in his book on the astronauts, for there too he was extending himself to take in another America, the middle American world of the Faustian WASP, untouched by inwardness and self-doubt, insulated by scientific know-how and emotional cliché – the square, patriotic, ramrod American that Tom Wolfe would capture very well in *The Right Stuff* (1978). Gary Gilmore had anything but the astronauts' commanding confidence, but he was the ominous underside of the same flat Midwestern landscape, the misfit and loser who eventually fired back the violence that had been pounded into him as a child.

Whatever fantasies Mailer had once spun around the violent criminal as existential hero are redeemed by this harrowing account of the nine months between Gilmore's release from prison in April 1976 and his execution for murder – the act that restored capital punishment in the United States – in January 1977. During this time he became an unguided missile seeking out a target, a lethal weapon simply bound to explode. Mailer creates Gilmore, his girlfriend Nicole Baker, and dozens of other characters by immersing us in a steady accumulation of details as he had submerged himself in thousands of pages of interviews, letters, and court documents. "I came to know him better than almost anyone in my life," Mailer later told an interviewer. "I began to see that he was a man easily as complex as myself."

The book is a collage of viewpoints told from within, that Mailer carefully shapes without intruding himself. With a colorless prose accented by an occasional touch of slang, Mailer looks for clues to how these people think, how they look at the world. Perhaps there is something mannered about the way the story is told from inside the minds of people below the literary horizon, free of the authorial commentary that might dispel their mystery. Despite its thousand-page length, the book has an affinity with the spare blue-collar minimalism of such lockjawed writers as Raymond Carver and Joan Didion; their work, like Mailer's earliest fiction, is ultimately rooted in the stark, unpolished writing and broad social sympathy typical of the Depression years.

Like those Depression writers, Mailer sees Gilmore as the product and victim of all the forces that created him. Mailer's old belief in personal freedom gives way here to a brooding sense of how the unvaried landscape, Mormon culture, and dysfunctional families resonate in people's lives without fully explaining their behavior. The book reverts to a less formulaic version of the determinism that shaped the characters in *The Naked and the Dead,* where each of them was simply emblematic of his background, and the whole mix was America. Some of the life goes out of the book halfway through when Gilmore has been captured, tried, and sentenced, but until then Mailer recreates a real piece of American life, frightening in its blind unreasoning force, prophetic of the explosive white violence and frustration that would later haunt the nation. This white male anger would show itself in the renewed popularity of capital punishment, the bitter battles over gun control, and the festering growth of right-wing militias that culminated in the bloody bombing of the Alfred P. Murrah Federal Building in Oklahoma City in 1995.

MALAMUD AND BELLOW: THE JEW AS PARIAH

Mailer's brief foray into environmental determinism, his exploration of a grim Utah landscape of gas stations and convenience stores and ex-cons, makes *The Executioner's Song* one of his most "American" books, even more than *An American Dream* and *The Armies of the Night*. With its impressive qualities of realistic observation, the book shows that Mailer might have become our Zola rather than a restless reincarnation of Hemingway. But it also links Mailer to such Jewish writers as Malamud and Bellow, who have very little of his belief in personal freedom, who pride themselves in being moralists and humanists and dark ironists of the human condition. For Mailer the Holocaust and the bomb were horrors because they nullified personal heroism and individual destiny. For Malamud and Bellow the Holocaust is an extreme example of mankind's inhumanity, confirming the sense of entrapment that Jews had always understood and tried to evade.

After 1945, very few American writers thought they could make much sense of history. They focused instead on small epiphanies in private lives; this was the only reality they felt they knew. But from his portrayal of Cummings and Croft in 1948 to his work as a participatory journalist of the late 1960s, Mailer, the Orson Welles of American literature, creates hugely egocentric characters who try to meet history on their own terms. Malamud's work is exactly the opposite. His "hero" is an Americanized version of the schlemiel figure out of Yiddish literature and Jewish humor, darkened by an implicit knowledge of how the Jews were uprooted, tormented, and murdered during the war. Malamud's subject is the ironies of character and fate, which few can evade, and the occasionally redemptive nature of suffering, which sometimes allows us moral victories in spite of worldly defeats. If Mailer was the lyrical writer who emerges defiantly from the repressive culture of the 1950s, Malamud was the doleful, ironic writer who retrieved some dark humor out of two thousand years of Jewish persecution.

Born in Brooklyn in 1914, almost a decade earlier than Mailer, Malamud was shaped by the economic struggle of the Depression rather than by Harvard and the war. The small shopkeeper's world of *The Assistant* (1957), his best novel, was a poetic transposition of where he grew up; it turns his father's store into a harsh, isolated dramatic setting for the whole human condition. For Malamud, people are locked in by the unalterable past, by economic necessity, by the jocular ironies of fate, and by the inexorable weight of their own character. The fate of Morris Bober in *The Assistant* is to suffer, as the fate of his young helper, Frank Alpine, is to assume gradually the moral burden of that suffering, to redeem himself from a life of drifting and petty crime by becoming a Jew. To Frank, Jews are "born prisoners," people who shut themselves up "in an overgrown coffin" of self-denial. But the novel centers on Frank's redemption, the apprenticeship in suffering through which he discovers his own moral nature, "the self he had secretly considered valuable."

Mailer too was a Jewish moralist, in the same way a Satanist is an inverted Christian. "I don't consider myself moral at all," he once told an interviewer. "I see myself as a man who lives in an embattled relation to morality." The expansive form and loose texture of his books convey his sense of unlimited human possibility, his need to defy received conventions of form and behavior. He is interested in how people shape – or fail to shape – their own destiny. Malamud's form, on the other hand, is always more closely knit, more constricted. Like Flannery O'Connor, he uses symbols, images, and recurring plot motifs to load his stories with significance but also to convey the burden of necessity that weighs on his characters. His belief in craft and form reflects his severe morality.

The Assistant is as tightly written as a prose poem. In Malamud's early books and stories, no writer is farther from the picaresque – the form whose fluidity and mobility proclaim a typically American assertion of freedom. Unlike Mailer, Malamud prefers not the grandiose personal history or the Napoleonic biography but the Kafkaesque short story, with its knifelike ironic twists and turns, its pinched scope, which so well suits a writer whose imagination insistently humbles all personal pride. (Even his more picaresque heroes, such as Levin in *A New Life* [1961] and Fidelman in *Pictures of Fidelman* [1969], looking for satisfaction far from home, must go through endlessly humbling experiences.) *The Assistant* is an extended short story, more realistic in texture but similar in outlook to the wonderful stories collected in *The Magic Barrel* (1958). At the end of his career, he turned, like Mailer, to biography, and even wrote a long novel about a biographer, *Dubin's Lives* (1979), but his late stories about Virginia Woolf and Alma Mahler, though carefully researched, are scarcely half a dozen pages long, and are written in a staccato mode from which all expansiveness and flow have been harshly expunged.

Malamud's stories, even such novels as *The Assistant* and *The Tenants,* are two-character pieces, densely written chamber compositions rather than orchestral works. Where Mailer, who once described himself as a "Nijinsky of ambivalence," puts all his dialectics into the individual ego, Malamud focuses on the interplay of self and other, now literal, now symbolic, to bring his characters toward some kind of self-understanding. His stories begin with swift, hard strokes, like rap sheets on people whose lives can be reduced to a few phrases attached to their names. Always they seem pinned to the destiny that has already overtaken them, or to one they are desperate to evade:

Feld, the shoemaker, was annoyed that his helper, Sobel, was so insensitive to his reverie that he wouldn't for a minute cease his fanatic pounding at the other bench [from "The First Seven Years"].

Manischevitz, a tailor, in his fifty-first year suffered many reverses and indignities. Previously a man of comfortable means, he overnight lost all he had, when his establishment caught fire and, after a metal container of cleaning fluid exploded, burned to the ground [from "Angel Levine"].

Henry Levin, an ambitious, handsome thirty, who walked the floors in Macy's book department wearing a white flower in his lapel, having recently come into a small inheritance, quit, and went abroad seeking romance [from "The Lady of the Lake"].

Fidelman, a self-confessed failure as a painter, came to Italy to prepare a critical study of Giotto, the opening chapter of which he had carried across the ocean in a new pigskin leather brief case, now gripped in his perspiring hand [from "The Last Mohican"].

Even if "The First Seven Years" were not loosely based on the story of Jacob and Laban, there would still be something biblical about these sharply condensed openings, which have the generalized quality of fairy tales ("he overnight lost all he had"). We feel the heavy clang of fate in such terse accounts of the bare details of these lives. Malamud's hapless protagonists are either older men, already ground down by the unforgiving hardness of their immigrant lives, the reverses or illnesses that have hemmed them in, or else younger men of the next generation, Malamud's own, who still dream of a new life in which early failures can be avoided or undone. The old men tend to be cranky, bitter, rigid, and blind to their own shortcomings, but the younger men are even more cold-hearted in their dreams of love and fame. In the stories, they invariably encounter their opposite – their demon and alter ego – often a slightly magical figure as mercurial as they are unbending, as emotionally labile as they are walled up in themselves, who exposes their limitations but also gives them a glimpse of their own stifled humanity.

Some of these "others" are simply people in need – the love-smitten helper in "The First Seven Years," the evicted tenant in "The Mourners" – whose humanity must be recognized before their tormentors can gain access to their own. Others are the fixers, con men, and ghetto operators who fascinate Malamud – Salzman, the marriage broker in "The Magic Barrel"; the slightly sinister, endlessly intrusive Susskind in "The Last Mohican," who finally destroys Fidelman's Giotto manuscript ("the words were there but the spirit was missing"); the shadowy real estate agent Bevilacqua in "Behold the Key"; the black guardian angel out of Frank Capra in "Angel Levine." These men are almost a mirror of the protagonists' deeply repressed needs and wishes. Where the heroes are stiffly "American" – pale intellectual products of the second generation, with its never-ending ordeal of civility – their alter egos are colorful ethnics, black, Italian, ghetto Jewish, like a reflux of some disreputable vitality the Americanized characters have suppressed in themselves.

Bellow too is fascinated by the unruly vitality of small-time crooks, con men, and wheeler-dealers, the dense underbrush of urban life. But Malamud's nimble tricksters, like Ellison's Rinehart, also have a good deal of the fantastic about them. They materialize unexpectedly but are hard to find when you look for them. Their office is "in the air"; they work out of their own socks. Behind them is the tradition of the wonder rabbi but also the black market: Jewish survival in the cracks of a civil society that scorned them. In this encounter between the famished heart and its repressed double, Malamud takes the material of Depression literature and Yiddish fiction – the cost of living, the brutal lot of the tradesman, the apprentice, the greenhorn, the refugee – and gives it a touch of magic realism, turning away from the economics of poverty toward the metaphysics of human loneliness and longing.

For all their realistic detail, their poetic authenticity of speech and feeling, Malamud's best novels and stories are parables rather than documents of immigrant life. Their abrupt poetry and folkloric characters give free play to Malamud's superb sense of comic incongruity. Often the time and setting are dreamlike and unspecific. *The Assistant* seems be set in Brooklyn during the Depression, but its world is a handful of houses, stores, and families that reflect the constricted lives and limited horizons of the people caught in it. Even this bleak world has room for a wraithlike figure who offers to burn down the wretched store for the "insurinks." "I make a living," he says. "I make fires." The world of Malamud's novel has no mayor, no governor, no president – and no respite from its own moral intensity. The life that persists in it is a burden, and its people are honored bitterly for bearing that burden. "He was, through the years, a hard man to move," Morris Bober's wife feels. "In the past she could sometimes resist him, but the weight of his endurance was too much for her now." The grocery store to which Bober is chained is metaphorically, almost literally, a prison, as are nearly all of Malamud's settings right up through *The Fixer* (1966), which is actually set in a prison, and in a Russia that is simply a much larger prison, at least for poor Jews.

But alongside this parable of suffering is a parable of redemption. Morris Bober dies, but not before finding a surrogate son to make up for the son he lost long ago, someone to whom he can pass on his strenuous moral example. The rabbinical student in "The Magic Barrel" will face up to his scarcely acknowledged sexual need, the longing that bedevils his failed spiritual vocation, in the fallen daughter of the marriage broker. ("This is my baby, my Stella, she should burn in hell," says Salzman in tears.) Thus the marriage broker becomes the instrument of Leo Finkle's fall as well as his redemption. By facing up to the "evil" in his own nature, the lure of the forbidden, Leo may overcome the coldness and emptiness at the heart of his own stunted humanity.

But Salzman is also the ghetto Jew whom the rabbinical student has subdued in himself, the past he is so eager to overcome. In a more schematic story, "The Lady of the Lake," Henry Levin has even changed his name to Henry Freeman as a way of asserting his freedom from the burdens of Jewish identity. He imagines that "a man's past was, it could be safely said, expendable." Being Jewish? "What had it brought him but headaches, inferiorities, unhappy memories?" Abroad, he finds love and beauty in a mysterious Italian woman, almost an apparition, but she turns out to be Jewish herself, a survivor of Buchenwald. "I can't marry you," she says to him, not quite credibly, before he can undo the erasure of his own identity. "We are Jews," she adds, before flitting away. "My past is meaningful to me. I treasure what I suffered for." Like Fidelman in "The Last Mohican" and Carl Schneider, the primly moralistic graduate student in "Behold the Key," Freeman has turned himself into a brittle construct, a hollow self-made man who can neither find himself nor find his way in a society in which the past still matters.

In "The Silver Crown," the best of Malamud's later stories, Albert Gans seeks out a wonder rabbi to heal his desperately ill father. As a rational man, however, he is also dogged by his inability to trust anyone, his fear of being taken in, which also betrays the limits of his love for his father, whom he secretly detests. When he ceases to put any faith in the miracle cure, when his suspicions take over, his father expires, done in by his son's failure of imagination and failure of feeling. If the older generation, in its struggle to survive, is shady, colorful, devious, and cunning, the younger generation's advanced worldly wisdom has made it spiritually sterile.

Like "The Magic Barrel," "The Silver Crown" shows Malamud's close kinship with the work of I. B. Singer, who also found imaginative truth in fantasy, superstition, and rabbinical lore. The well-received publication of *A Treasury of Yiddish Stories* (1953), edited by Irving Howe and Eliezer Greenberg, and Singer's *Gimpel the Fool and Other Stories* (1955) helped create a market for stories more closely rooted in Jewish magic and folklore than the naturalistic fiction produced by such American Jewish writers as Abraham Cahan, Anzia Yezierska, Ludwig Lewisohn, Michael Gold, and Meyer Levin before the war. This was part of the postwar shift from Marx to Freud, from the mechanics of society to the dynamics of the unconscious. Malamud's work shows how much the fiction of the fifties was internalized into myth and psychological fable. But because of the unforgettable facts of persecution and discrimination, ethnic writing also maintained an important social base. It was impossible for a black or Jewish writer to focus on the self without also writing about the social conditions that assaulted and helped define it. Such black writers as Ralph Ellison and James Baldwin would turn away from the naturalism of Richard Wright while remaining grounded in the problems of the community, which were reflected in their own search for identity. Purely personal writing was a luxury the ethnic author could scarcely afford. As long as social acceptance remained problematic, as long as people could be hated or excluded because of the color of their skin or the shape of their nose, an "American" identity could never fully substitute for ethnic and communal roots. However much they might try to escape it, Jews and blacks were indelibly marked by their own history, which had been imprinted on them from the beginning of their lives.

❧

Saul Bellow's career was more varied and expansive than was Malamud's; his books were longer, more American, often less emphatically Jewish. But his most deliberately American work, *The Adventures of Augie March* (1953), was his most confected and least authentic, though its picaresque form and nimble, vernacular prose were a major breakthrough for Bellow. *Henderson the Rain King* (1959) was a more unified and ingenious picaresque fantasy, a high intellectual comedy set in an Africa that derives from the movies and from Bellow's anthropological reading, but it was also infused with his meditations on the modern self and its destiny. Both these upbeat books proved to be dead ends for Bellow. Between them, astonishingly, he wrote a great novella, *Seize the Day,* a classic of Jewish American writing, a failure story very close in spirit to Malamud's or Singer's work.

Like Henry Freeman (né Levin) in Malamud's "The Lady of the Lake," Bellow's Tommy Wilhelm, formerly Wilhelm Adler, has tried to alter his destiny by changing his name. Instead of going to Europe like Freeman, he had gone to Hollywood, the dream factory that embodies the American idea of an infinitely malleable identity, the belief in new beginnings. "Tommy Wilhelm" was his bid for freedom, which failed in Hollywood and fails definitively in the day-long course of the story. To his cold, dignified, censorious father, Dr. Adler, who lives in the same residence hotel on Manhattan's Upper West Side, he remains Wilky, the inarticulate son who embarrasses him, whom he refuses to "carry." "He had cast off his father's name, and with it his father's opinion of him." His father tells him, "I want nobody on my back. Get off! And I give you the same advice, Wilky. Carry nobody on your back." But hapless Wilky carries the weight of the world on his back.

Since the Jewish novel is almost synonymous with the family novel, and since he himself is being squeezed for alimony payments by his estranged wife, Wilhelm's rejection by his selfish father is perhaps the worst blow he receives in the course of the day, though not the final one. It is comparable to the concluding scene of Kafka's story "The Judgment," in which Georg Bendemann's enfeebled father rises titanically from his bed and condemns him to death by drowning, a sentence he quickly executes on himself. Rather than drowning, Tommy Wilhelm is suffocating. He is clogged with feeling, congested with a sense of inarticulate desperation as his life comes apart. Just as the tragic quality of *The Assistant* is grounded in Morris Bober's bad luck – and the good luck of insensitive neighbors like Karp, the liquor store owner, who thrives wherever Morris stumbles – *Seize the Day* is about the "flavor of fatality" that draws Wilhelm unerringly toward disaster. *Seize the Day* is a Jewish joke turned dead serious, a schlemiel fable about real people. More obliquely than *The Assistant,* it is also about the redemptive power of suffering.

"Maybe the making of mistakes expressed the very purpose of his life and the essence of his being here," Wilhelm thinks. Perhaps, he wonders, his suffering has more meaning than the prosperity of those around him. The instruments of Wilhelm's downfall are not simply his pitiless wife and father but also his surrogate father, a trickster figure named Dr. Tamkin. The con man as Emersonian philosopher, Tamkin convinces Wilhelm to "seize the day" and venture everything on the commodities exchange (which he scarcely understands) in one last bid for freedom. When he hits bottom and loses his last $700 on a wild investment, Wilhelm is reduced to that bedrock of humanity, the tormented heart, that remains Bellow's ultimate ground of value. In the story's famous ending, he wanders into the funeral of someone he does not know and begins weeping:

Soon he was past words, past reason, coherence. He could not stop. The source of all tears had suddenly sprung up within him, black, deep, and hot, and they were pouring out and convulsed his body, bending his stubborn head, bowing his shoulders, twisting his face, crippling the very hands with which he held the handkerchief. His efforts to collect himself were useless. The great knot of ill and grief in his throat swelled upward and he gave in utterly and held his face and wept. He cried with all his heart.

At this impersonal, wholly unexpected moment, the emotional block within him finally gives way. The other mourners, awed by this show of grief, take him to be a close relation. As a fellow human being, in a sense he is. Swept away by a flood of feeling he grieves for himself, for everyone, or for no one in particular, yet moves "through torn sobs and cries toward the consummation of his heart's ultimate need."

Critics have questioned whether the clumsy, ill-fated Wilhelm is enti- tled to the author's sympathy or to his final moments of ecstatic transcen- dence. Like Malamud in *The Assistant,* Bellow sees his protagonist's worldly failure as some kind of spiritual triumph, especially as compared to his father's self-love, professional success, and bitter resentment that his less worthy son will survive him. Tamkin, on the other hand, one of those fantastic eccentrics who play bit parts in all of Bellow's novels, is a grand burlesque of the sympathetic figure Wilhelm vainly seeks in his own father. Bellow stacks the deck against Tommy Wilhelm, shows him suffer- ing blow after blow, many of them self-inflicted. Criticizing Bellow's book in *Advertisements for Myself,* Mailer complained that "it is not demanding to write about characters considerably more defeated than oneself," but he praised the ending as an indication "that Bellow is not altogether hopeless on the highest level." Certainly, the ending foreshadows the spiritual themes that emerge in Bellow's later fiction, including the speculations about "the future of the moon" in *Mr. Sammler's Planet* (1970), the streak of mysticism and the meditations on death in *Humboldt's Gift* (1975), and the concluding pages of *The Dean's December* (1982), where the hero, climbing up into the unearthly interior of the great telescope on Mt. Palomar, feels in touch with the icy spirit of the cosmos, with "its power to cancel every- thing merely human."

Perhaps it was Mailer's criticism, along with developments in his own life, that fostered Bellow's great shift in the 1960s toward a more autobio- graphical protagonist. More than most novelists, Bellow had always been an intellectual as well as a fiction writer. His first novel, *Dangling Man,* was an almost plotless novel of ideas, the musing of a wartime intellectual in the spirit of Dostoyevsky's *Notes from Underground.* In *Herzog* (1964) Bellow tackled the subject of the Jewish intellectual much more directly, using the clever device of Herzog's unsent letters to convey the comic extravagance of his breakdown and to expand upon his own vision of the larger breakdown of the modern world. Though *Seize the Day* was Bellow's most controlled and perfectly executed piece of fiction, the core of his nature work can be found in *Herzog, Mr. Sammler's Planet,* and *Humboldt's Gift,* which could be described as the *Purgatorio,* the *Inferno,* and the *Paradiso* of his modern *commedia. Seize the Day* and *Henderson the Rain King* were the last books in which Bellow was not essentially his own protagonist, as Mailer would become in much of his later work.

Tommy Wilhelm and Moses Herzog are two of Bellow's exemplary sufferers, though Herzog's disintegration is florid and operatic where Wilhelm's is choked with feelings he can scarcely express (not choked enough for his father, who tells him, "There's no need to carry on like an opera, Wilky.") "Well, when you suffer, you really suffer," Herzog's friend and lawyer Sandor Himmelstein says to *him.* "You're a real, genuine old Jewish type that digs the emotions." *Herzog,* awash in Herzog's tempest of feeling, his sea of grievance, has perhaps the thinnest plot of any major postwar novel. Herzog has been betrayed by his wife, Madeleine, with his best friend, Valentine Gersbach – the most trite story imaginable. (It seems clear, though, that the worshipful Gersbach wants little more than to be like Herzog, to *be* Herzog.) By filtering this old triangle through Herzog's tormented memories, his endless self-analysis, his grandiose intellectual constructions, however, Bellow creates a different kind of novel, formally in the third person yet subjective, rueful, hyberbolic, unstable – shifting constantly between past and present, theories and feelings, internal monologues and actual events.

Herzog is not a novel of action but a state of mind. As a desperately personal work, it seems grounded in two motives generally fatal to fiction: self-pity and the desire for revenge. Bellow's friends could recognize every character and detail, could see exactly where he distorted and fantasticated, but *Herzog* is much more than a roman à clef, for Bellow's animus sharpens his powers of observation. The novel is fired by indignation yet transcends mere retaliation. In a passage that echoes a celebrated image from Kafka, Bellow writes:

It's fascinating that hatred should be so personal as to be almost loving. The knife and the wound aching for each other. . . . Some cry out, and some swallow the thrust in silence. About the latter you could write the inner history of mankind.

Thanks to this luminous hatred, everything in *Herzog* – the characters, the settings, the feelings – glows with preternatural intensity. Herzog feels used and abused, deceived by trusted friends, passive and helpless before the women who fatally attract him, whose love is indispensable to his male pride. Like Wilhelm, Herzog is said to have a "talent for making a fatal choice," but this is simply Bellow's way of deflecting responsibility – giving him a subtler sense of victimization. The emphasis on Herzog's foolishness and depth of feeling is meant to mitigate his self-absorption. He is "foolish, feeling, suffering Herzog," an "eager, hasty, self-intense, and comical person." He is weak, good-hearted, a co-conspirator with those who take advantage of him. Everything here suggests that Bellow is writing about himself, taking stock of his own life but also transforming it in the telling. *Herzog* is one long Hamlet-like soliloquy, antic, tormented, and highly self-conscious.

Like Mailer and other novelists in the early sixties, Bellow turned from distanced, ironic, carefully structured fictions toward mercurial self-portraits, using himself as a prism through which the cultural moment could be refracted. Much of what Bellow says about Herzog's character reads like oblique self-description. Herzog's taste for paradox has been honed by Kafka and seasoned by Dostoyevsky. "He dreaded the depths of feeling he would eventually have to face, when he could no longer call upon his eccentricities for relief." When Bellow analyzes Herzog's "feminine" passivity, his "psychic offer" of "meekness in exchange for preferential treatment," it makes sense only as self-analysis, at once a display of injured innocence and an apology for becoming more aggressive and self-protective. Only his bruised vulnerability makes this egotism bearable. Beginning with *Herzog,* Bellow, like some latter-day Montaigne, would never tire of exploring the complications of his own nature. In later novels like *The Dean's December* and *More Die of Heartbreak* (1987), this inner portraiture leaves fiction behind, focusing entirely (and almost plotlessly) on the author's increasingly cranky life and opinions. But in the richly developed *commedia* of the sixties and seventies, before he received the Nobel Prize in 1976, Bellow maintains a lively balance between the self absorbed hero and the actual world.

There is a broad streak of misogyny and paranoia in Bellow, as in Norman Mailer and Philip Roth, a fierce resentment of the power women have over him. An injured male narcissism gives his work its tremendous emotional energy. The actual murder of Rojack's wife in *An American Dream* is only a more literal version of the murderous feelings of Roth's alter ego in *My Life as a Man* (1974) or the lethal characterization of Madeleine in *Herzog.* But where Roth's book, obsessed with blaming the other, remains caught up in his sense of victimization, his need for self-vindication, Bellow turns the raw material of autobiography into cultural diagnosis. The affair between Madeleine and Gersbach comes to represent a larger breakdown of decency and civility, just as Herzog himself embodies the ineffectuality of the intellectual: humane yet deeply vulnerable, brilliant but pretentious and confused, exploring with his talented mistress the same sexual freedoms he roundly condemns in his wife.

Herzog is an apocalyptic novel that disdains apocalypse, a novel of ideas that mocks intellectuals. Herzog sees the sixties, then still just beginning, as a season of moral anarchy, animated by a dream of erotic salvation of which his mistress Ramona is an early prophet. Later, the much more exaggerated forms of this new freedom would become the sour subject of *Mr. Sammler's Planet*. "She has read Marcuse, N. O. Brown, all those neo-Freudians," says Herzog of Ramona. "She wants me to believe the body is a spiritual fact, the sinstrument of the soul." He sees Ramona as "a sort of sexual professional," full of knowledge that could be learned only through experience, as well as theories from which his patriarchal Jewish being recoils. Being an incorrigible theorist himself, he turns his attraction to her into an ironic dialogue between Jewish suffering, morality, and discipline and the immediate promise of an erotic utopia. An evening with Ramona becomes an escape from the burden of history, the constraints of tradition, the inhibitions of character.

As a figure in a novel, Herzog is saved by his contradictions. "He might think himself a moralist but the shape of a woman's breasts mattered greatly. . . . When he jeered in private at the Dionysiac revival it was himself he made fun of. Herzog! A prince of the erotic Renaissance." The novel ends wishfully in Ramona's love nest, where good food, good sex, and good conversation – and perhaps the writing of this novel – have begun to heal Herzog's wounded narcissism, his damaged male pride.

Much of the strength of *Herzog* can be found in the vividness of the minor characters and the spiritedness of the book's zany intellectual comedy: Madeleine with the medieval Russian tomes she lugs to bed with her, the guilt she feels about her aborted conversion to Catholicism; Gersbach as a "second Herzog," a cheap, fawning imitation of the genius himself, with his crude, proletarian Yiddish, his easy male swagger, and ultimately his saving tenderness toward Herzog's young daughter as he gives her a bath, which prevents the crazed father from shooting him; Mady's divorced bohemian parents, themselves a small chapter of American cultural history; Herzog's assorted friends and academic colleagues in Chicago, including a professor who gives mouth-to-mouth resuscitation to a tubercular monkey. All are drawn with Bellow's sure feeling for the low-down and the eccentric.

Yet Herzog-Bellow's strength of observation is surpassed by his power of memory, the sentimental pull of Napoleon Street in Montreal, where he grew up. Long after the Bellow persona, the Bellow outlook, had overwhelmed every other element in his work, he could still write remarkable stories – "The Old System" (in *Mosby's Memoirs and Other Stories,* 1968), "The Silver Dish" and "Cousins" (in *Him with His Foot in His Mouth and Other Stories,* 1984) – exploring the tangled web of Jewish family relationships. In *Herzog* this pull of memory is the core of the book, the cultural memory expressed in Herzog's letters, family memory in his childhood recollections. Just as Herzog cannot fathom how three thousand years of discipline, suffering, and sacrifice have led him to Ramona'a bed, he cannot imagine how the kid from Napoleon Street, the "bookish, callow boy" who could not see that his own mother was dying, became the grown man who married Madeleine and was betrayed by Gersbach. His whole life feels like a falling away from some authentic point of origin, which is identified with being Jewish and being his parents' son.

Like Kerouac in *On the Road* and Roth in *Portnoy's Complaint,* who are also consumed by the contrast between where they came from and what they became, Bellow sees his identity as a novelist as bound up with the power of remembering, the curse of not forgetting, which seems like an obsession to ordinary people. When a childhood friend, now an early hippie, avoids him on the street, he thinks the man is running away from "the power of his old friend's memory." "All the dead and the mad are in my custody," he imagines, "and I am the nemesis of the would-be forgotten." To his memories of Napoleon Street ("rotten, toylike, crazy and filthy, flogged with harsh weather") Herzog's mind is still "attached with great power. Here was a wider range of human feelings than he had ever again been able to find." "What was wrong with Napoleon Street?" he wonders. "All he ever wanted was there." Herzog recognizes something unhealthy about this plangent longing, which was so common to Jewish writers as they endlessly relived their warm and crazy childhoods. "To haunt the past like this – to love the dead! Moses warned himself not to yield so greatly to this temptation, this peculiar weakness of his character. He was a depressive. Depressives cannot surrender childhood – not even the pains of childhood."

Herzog's brilliant, often incoherent letters are an equally neurotic and yet necessary way of not surrendering his intellectual past. They convey Bellow's brief against the apocalyptic temper of the times, the reign of Romanticism and individualism, the emphasis on self-development at all cost, the rise of "plebeian envy and ambition," the glorification of the erotic, the "confusion between aesthetic and moral judgments," the expansion of violence on a mass scale, and most of all the doctrinaire pessimism in the wake of European existentialism – "the commonplaces of the Wasteland outlook, the cheap mental stimulants of Alienation, the cant and rant of pipsqueaks about Inauthenticity and Forlornness."

Herzog's recoil from the modern world would only sharpen in Bellow's later work, when Bellow grew close to the jaundiced outlook of such Straussian friends at the University of Chicago as Allan Bloom. Yet Bellow's rejection of modernism, partly grounded in the feeling that his generation of writers had been unfairly overshadowed by their predecessors, was itself a modernist gesture, a fierce declaration of independence. Despite his piety toward the past and his own reserved temperament, Bellow felt a deep affinity for such wild, confused, out-of-control personalities as Von Humboldt Fleisher, modeled on his friend, the doomed poet Delmore Schwartz. Like the critic Lionel Trilling, Bellow, despite (or because of) his own quiet life and muted personality, was attracted to charismatic and crazy geniuses who spoke to his buried self, from which his imagination drew surprising energy.

Bellow's work falters when the superego in him, the hateful moral censor, gets out of hand. *Herzog's* hero is a divided soul, deeply implicated in all he condemns; the novel is powered by its ambivalence. In *Mr. Sammler's Planet* Bellow writes from the more lofty perch of the sage. Herzog's hatred is sharp and specific, laced with self-irony. Mr. Sammler's loathing is vague and sweeping, constantly in search of emblems to objectify it, like the exposed penis of a lordly black pickpocket or the sexual habits of Sammler's daughter Shula and niece Angela. As in *Herzog,* not much happens in *Mr. Sammler's Planet.* While his nephew lies dying in a hospital, an old man travels up and down Manhattan's West Side, still brooding about his own freakish survival in a Polish forest during war. His outlook is European: he is "an Anglophile intellectual Polish Jew and person of culture," once an acquaintance of H. G. Wells, that apostle of human progress.

In a tone of detached hauteur, Sammler takes the long view of the rebelliousness of the young and the anarchy he feels in the streets of New York, where at moments he sees a collapse of civilization comparable to the barbarism of the Nazis. At the end his nephew dies and he eulogizes him, despite his flaws, as a man who "did meet the terms of his contract. The terms which, in his inmost heart, each man knows." Much more than *Herzog, Mr. Sammler's Planet* is a jeremiad, a sharp rhetorical rather than fictional performance, a hyperbolic vision of the 1960s through the lens of Western culture under siege – in other words, yet another extreme attack on extremist thinking.

One difference between the two novels can be seen in the treatment of women. Madeleine is a man-eating monster but her opposite number,

Herzog's mistress Ramona, is a nurturing tutor in the new dispensation of erotic freedom. Both characters are male fantasies – woman as gorgon, woman as love goddess – but Herzog sees the high comedy of being drawn to what his nature regards with deep suspicion. In the higher synthesis of *Mr. Sammler's Planet,* sex belongs only to a constellation of moral degeneracy that centers on women, blacks, and young people in general. Sammler constantly thinks of women in terms of their foul odors, their corrupt natures, their unclean organs, "the female generative slime." There is no indication of what personal crisis may lie behind this insistence, but no writer since Swift has built his work on such a fascinated repugnance toward female odors and female organs, or expected them to bear the onus of representing a whole culture in decline. In an astonishing summary of the sixties as seen by a cultivated émigré, Bellow links the sexuality of women with the criminality of the black pickpocket as well as the anti-authoritarianism of the young, the neoprimitivism of the intellectuals, and the antinomianism of advanced art:

From the black side, strong currents were sweeping over everyone. Child, black, redskin – the unspoiled Seminole against the horrible Whiteman. Millions of civilized people wanted oceanic, boundless, primitive, neckfree nobility, experienced a strange release of galloping impulses, and acquired the peculiar aim of sexual niggerhood for everyone. Humankind had lost its old patience. It demanded accelerated exaltation, accepted no instant without pregnant meanings as in epic, tragedy, comedy, or films.

Bellow, who once edited a magazine called *The Noble Savage,* includes even Native Americans (or white myths about them) in his heinous catalog, though they were hardly part of the sixties cultural revolution. Since women are thought to embody nature rather than culture, they stand with young people, blacks, redskins, and artists in the vanguard of the new erotic utopia. With this "sexual niggerhood" as its subject, *Mr. Sammler's Planet* can be read as an inversion of "The White Negro," inspired by the same fantasies and imagery. But Sammler gives Norman Mailer's argument (and William Blake's language) a racist spin: "The labor of Puritanism now was ending. The dark satanic mills changing into light satanic mills. The reprobates converted into children of joy, the sexual ways of the seraglio and of the Congo bush adopted by the emancipated masses of New York, Amsterdam, London."

Like Trilling, who gave a more modulated account of the "adversary culture" in his late essays and interviews, Bellow saw the sixties as a literal fulfilment of the modernist vision: "The dreams of nineteenth-century poets polluted the psychic atmosphere of the great boroughs and suburbs

of New York." Most at fault for undermining civilization were "its petted
intellectuals who attacked it at its weakest moments – attacked it in the
name of proletarian revolution, in the name of reason, and in the name of
irrationality, in the name of visceral depth, in the name of sex, in the name
of perfect instantaneous freedom." Bellow connected the morality of the
young with their politics of protest. "For what it amounted to was limit-
less demand, refusal of the doomed creature (death being sure and final) to
go away from the earth unsatisfied. A full bill of demand and complaint
was therefore presented by each individual. Non-negotiable. Recognizing
no scarcity of supply in any human department." This is what Irving
Howe had called the "psychology of unobstructed need," an infantile need
for self-gratification. By portraying the new erotic utopia as an offshoot of
the culture of modernism, Bellow ignores a much more immediate source,
the consumer culture of the postwar years – and even the dreams and aspirations of the immigrant parents, who looked to a better life, unhampered
by grim necessity, for their "American" children.

For all the crisp intensity of Bellow's writing, *Mr. Sammler's Planet* often
reads more like a polemic than a novel, for it is punctuated by little discursive volleys, puritanical, patriarchal, and intolerant, delivered by Bellow
through the figure of the aged intellectual who has seen everything. Yet
Bellow's genius in his late work, beginning with *Herzog* and especially
with his great 1967 story "The Old System," was precisely to take the long
view, to step back and see the whole cycle of birth, nurture, passion, and
death through the eye of eternity yet fully grounded in human detail and
razor-sharp prose. "The Old System" sets the pattern for Bellow's later
work by giving us simply a man remembering – the author's surrogate, a
distinguished geneticist, thinking back with pleasure about some recently
deceased relatives whose unquiet lives suddenly matter to him, whose
deaths seemed to resonate with unspeakable poignance. But the almost scientific detachment that works so well in "The Old System," that lends
universality to ordinary family history, feels duplicitous in *Mr. Sammler's
Planet,* where an aura of olympian neutrality scarcely masks a mood of bottomless revulsion. Bellow shrouds his anger in the measured cadences of
the European sage, the cold, world-weary wisdom of the elderly survivor.
Surrounding Sammler with caricatures rather than characters, Bellow's
harsh indictment brooks no viewpoint different from his own.

❦

Ironically, Bellow well understood the utopianism of the young, the apocalyptic temperament of artists and intellectuals. He had been there. Along
with other *Partisan Review* writers who came of age between the two world

wars, he had cut his teeth on modernism and revolutionary socialism. He was also typical of his generation in rediscovering his suppressed Jewish identity in middle age. Donning the mantle of a scornful Hebrew prophet, Bellow sees the sixties as a revival of paganism, a return to the worship of nature, exactly what the original prophets denounced among the ancient Hebrews. But the other half of the prophetic message is missing: the appeal for social justice, the denunciation of merchants and princes, the identification with the poor and despised (as echoed by the Jesus of the Gospels). As Bellow had named Moses Herzog after the biblical lawgiver rather than the liberator, he has Sammler question "whether release from long Jewish mental discipline, hereditary training in lawful control, was obtainable upon individual application."

Beginning with *Dangling Man,* Bellow always had shown a weakness for lofty judgments and sententious pronouncements, but this was always offset by his feeling for the manic energy of characters coming apart, like Herzog and Humboldt. This balance is lost in *Mr. Sammler's Planet,* beautifully regained in *Humboldt's Gift,* then lost definitively in the discursive ramblings of *The Dean's December* and *More Die of Heartbreak,* both written after the author was crowned with the Nobel prize in 1976.

Mr. Sammler's censoriousness has been compared with the cold disdain of Dr. Adler, Tommy Wilhelm's unbending father. For all his show of detachment, his Oxonian airs, however, Mr. Sammler is deeply fascinated with the whole scene he condemns, beginning with the sex organs of the black pickpocket ("great oval testicles, a large tan-and-purple uncircumcised thing – a tube, a snake") and the lordly expression of his face ("not directly menacing but oddly, serenely masterful"). In its own way, which can be seen as racist and misogynistic, Bellow's synthesis of the sixties is both astute and covertly sympathetic. The period both inspires and unhinges him. The bemused erotic experiments of Herzog lead directly to the excesses that outrage Mr. Sammler. But even Sammler objects helplessly when his brutal son-in-law smashes the black pickpocket, whose wordless eloquence had deeply impressed him.

The cultural turbulence of the 1960s inspired little first-rate fiction but much attitudinizing. Updike's *Rabbit Redux* and Malamud's *The Tenants* ran aground in their portrayal of young people and blacks, much as Updike's *Couples* grew mechanical in depicting suburban adultery, that other half of the sexual revolution. Two strong generational novels anchored in an earlier period, Joyce Carol Oates's *them* (1969) and E. L. Doctorow's *The Book of Daniel* (1971), conclude with emblematic events of the 1960s – the urban riots in Detroit in 1967, the student uprising at Columbia University in 1968. Much later in *American Pastoral* (1997),

Philip Roth would portray the young radicals of the sixties as simply ranting, obnoxious, and demented in their hatred of grown-ups, indifferent to
human life, and quite damaged by their permissive liberal upbringing.
Bellow does better than this. Paradoxically, his apocalyptic view sharpens
his picture and makes *Mr. Sammler* one of the few reactions to the era that
matches it in intensity. Though Sammler reflects that "New York makes
one think about the collapse of civilization, about Sodom and Gomorrah,
about the end of the world," Bellow's portrait of the city itself, his sense of
the streets, is even more vital than in *Seize the Day*. This is New York as
many experienced it, as a scarily exciting jungle.

The self-righteousness of *Sammler* borders on moral cant, but Bellow's
hunger for significance is deeply felt. In his greed for meaning, Bellow
made Sammler both a survivor of the Holocaust and a witness to Israel's
Six-Day War. He should certainly not have compared the moral liberties of
the sixties to the Holocaust or implied that the Jews' trauma as fugitives
and partisans in the Polish forests had earned them the right to be pitiless
toward the next generations, which had not been tested in the same way.
Bellow used the war years as a club to beat the callow young. But only
Mailer in *The Armies of the Night* – and perhaps Thomas Pynchon in *The
Crying of Lot 49* – managed to put the sixties together as powerfully as
Bellow did in the embittered pages of this novel.

Bellow's rancor made the benign turn he took in his next novel,
Humboldt's Gift, all the more impressive. The story is virtually a memoir of
Bellow's friendship with Delmore Schwartz, compatible in almost every
detail with James Atlas's biography of the poet. Schwartz's golden promise
in his early years, his later descent into paranoia and madness, his quarrels
with virtually all his friends, and finally his miserable, anonymous death in
a cheap midtown hotel in 1966 – his body lay unclaimed for several days –
must have triggered Bellow's sense of mortality. This feeling was already
on view in "The Old System" and *Sammler,* since the first was a set of post-
mortem reflections, and the latter was framed by a death watch of an old
man who has himself passed through death and lived, yet himself feels
long dead.

Deeply touched by Delmore Schwartz's death, Bellow in *Humboldt's Gift*
is nostalgic and self-critical rather than reproachful. Instead of seeing the
world through a single lens, he splits his protagonist into the self-destructive poet Humboldt and the self-serving, successful playwright, Charlie
Citrine, the Bellow surrogate who is not all-knowing, and feels a weight of
guilt toward his troubled friend. After Citrine had had a great success on
Broadway in the early fifties – around the time Bellow himself had a major
breakthrough with *Augie March* – Humboldt had accused him of plagiariz-

ing his personality, even threatening to picket the play if he did not receive a share of the royalties. A few weeks before Humboldt died, Citrine had spotted his estranged friend on the street and avoided speaking to him, as Bellow himself had done with Delmore. Far better than *Sammler,* the novel deals with both the meaning of death and the complicated feelings of the survivor.

Despite Humboldt's zaniness and paranoia, there may have been something to the charges he levels, as Citrine acknowledges. Bellow *did* make a breakthrough in *Augie* around a character of manic energy very different from himself, to which he would return repeatedly with figures like Herzog and Humboldt. Delmore Schwartz had even acclaimed the novel in *Partisan Review.* It is not far-fetched to give some credit to him for what was best in Bellow's later fiction. Where would the self-accusing survivor, Citrine, be without Humboldt, his wild, undisciplined Other, the *poète maudit* who galvanized his imagination? Citrine himself describes this as a kind of authorial cannibalism, combining fierce admiration and envy with the novelist's gift for absorbing other people:

I did incorporate other people into myself and consume them. When they died I passionately mourned. I said I would continue their work and their lives. But wasn't it a fact that I added their strength to mine? Didn't I have an eye on them in their days of vigor and glory?

Some of Bellow's most heartfelt writing can be found in terse obituary pieces for such writer friends as Isaac Rosenfeld and John Berryman. In these essays, collected in *It All Adds Up* (1994), the sense of loss is always inflected with the inner satisfaction and guilt of the survivor. *Humboldt's Gift* is an immense version of such a fond farewell, a reckoning that is also an assertion of life, an appropriation, an ingestion.

Citrine shares many qualities with Bellow's earlier protagonists. He gets involved with petty gangsters. He is hounded by his ex-wife and put upon by an assortment of other women. He has a mistress, Renata, who is a reincarnation of Herzog's Ramona. But unlike Joseph (in *Dangling Man*) or Herzog or Sammler, he does not let himself off easy. He is a sellout who is redeemed in the course of the book, but also a spiritualist deeply involved with the ideas of Rudolf Steiner — as benign toward the world's frailties as Sammler was judgmental. For once Bellow gives the Deep Thinker a rest. The book is rueful, exuberant, and playful; it can be read as an apology for Bellow's recent political furies, especially in *Mr. Sammler's Planet.* Citrine endorses Tolstoy's admonition "to cease the false and unnecessary comedy of history and begin simply to live." His regret for the angry mood in which Bellow wrote *Sammler* is unmistakable. Citrine has experienced "the light," some access of spiritual wisdom, and this has given him "an alto-gether unreasonable kind of joy. Furthermore, the hysterical, the grotesque about me, the abusive, the unjust, that madness in which I had often been a willing and active participant, the grieving, now had found a contrast."

Besides this new tolerance and spiritual joy, the other element of Citrine's redemption is Humboldt himself, the gift of the title, the legacy of a jointly conceived story that now becomes a successful film. Implicitly, this stands for Delmore's legacy to this novel, the gift of his own character to a work that lifts Bellow out of his misanthropic slough of the late 1960s. Humboldt helps restore Bellow to the busy life of the particular that he had slighted in *Sammler,* including the "noisy bumptious types" like Ricardo Cantabile, a Chicago hoodlum who (like Humboldt) repre-sents Bellow's "weakness" for characters who are "demonstrative exuber-ant impulsive destructive and wrong-headed." Humboldt allows Bellow to reclaim his own boisterous fictional territory after the scorched earth of *Mr. Sammler's Planet.* Even the few familiar jibes at advanced sex or the advanced intellectuals ("the educated nits, mental bores of the heaviest caliber") are remarkably good-humored. *Humboldt's Gift* lacks the disci-pline and intensity of *Seize the Day, Herzog,* or *Mr. Sammler's Planet,* but it is Bellow's most purely enjoyable book, tolerant, self-critical, and humane. In this vein of mellow reminiscence Bellow finds a respite from his personal furies, as he would again in the ruminative mood of some of his later stories and his tribute to Allen Bloom in *Ravelstein* (2000).

NATIVE SONS: JAMES BALDWIN AND RALPH ELLISON

The fallout from World War II had created a rough parallel between Jews and blacks. Western shame over the Holocaust dealt a serious blow to long-standing American patterns of genteel anti-Semitism, including social discrimination against Jews, quotas in higher education, and exclu-sionary barriers in the major professions. Similarly, blacks at home com-plained and even rioted over the treatment of their soldiers in the segregated armed forces, where they were assigned to menial duties, barred from combat, harassed in and around Southern bases, and humbled when they returned to civilian life. But black soldiers, like so many other Americans, were also introduced by the war to a wider world. Fighting against racial hatred abroad, they became more conscious of their second-class status at home. "I went into the Army a nigger; I'm coming out a *man,*" said a black corporal from Alabama in 1945.

As prejudice against blacks and Jews came unstuck in the late forties, ethnic writers found a wider audience and an opportunity to influence the nation's changing attitudes. If Malamud and Bellow presented Jews as exemplary sufferers, emblems of both their people's history and of humanity as a whole, Ralph Ellison and James Baldwin were determined to avoid portraying blacks mainly as society's victims. All four writers were alike in giving their characters and stories a symbolic more than a sociological cast.

Both Ellison and Baldwin had begun as protégés of Richard Wright — Ellison in the 1930s when Wright, who was then a Communist, encouraged him to write first for his own short-lived Harlem magazine, *New Challenge,* then for the Communist *New Masses*; Baldwin in the 1940s when the older man, then at the peak of his fame, took him under his wing shortly before departing for Paris, where his rebellious disciple soon followed. At his best in *Native Son* (1940), *Black Boy* (1945), and the posthumous *American Hunger* (1977), Wright was no mere naturalist or protest writer. Ellison was drawn to him because of their mutual interest in modernist writing, and he vividly recalled Wright's frequent battles with his Party comrades and patrons who resented his independence. Wright's memories of growing up in the Jim Crow South and his feeling for life in the Chicago ghetto had almost a hallucinatory intensity, but his connection to his material diminished abroad while younger black writers opened themselves to new influences. Acclaimed by French intellectuals as an avatar of existentialism, cut off from the scenes that had nurtured his work, Wright's fiction grew abstract as he emerged as a lonely but influential public figure.

Baldwin's damaging depiction of *Native Son* in his own manifesto, "Everybody's Protest Novel" (1949), and again in "Many Thousands Gone" (1951), dealt a major blow to Wright's reputation. It cleared the ground for writing that was far more personal than Wright's, more metaphysical, more concerned with individual identity, including sexual identity. This was in line with the inward turn of other postwar writers, and it connected Baldwin especially to the Jewish writers and editors who admired his work and first published it in *Commentary, Partisan Review,* and *The New Leader.* But neither Baldwin nor Ellison ever challenged one essential tenet of Wright's — that the experience of African Americans was deeply conditioned by the traumatic facts of racial separation and discrimination. However, they insisted that this alone was insufficient to account for the varied ways that blacks had accommodated to their treatment and the complex lives they had shaped for themselves despite the humiliating often degrading conditions to which they were subjected.

Born out of wedlock in 1924, Baldwin was the son of an adoring mother who bore eight more children after she married a fiery preacher. But his harsh stepfather, whose name he bore, could barely support the family, and he grew increasingly demented and suspicious of white people before he died in 1943. One of Baldwin's most extraordinary essays, "Notes of a Native Son" (1955), interweaves his stepfather's death with the Harlem riots that just preceded it; the debris of this conflagration still littered the streets through which the funeral procession passed. The great revelation of *Native Son* had been the rage and despair that festered in the black urban ghetto, sometimes concealed behind the smile of acquiescence, friendship, or humility. Baldwin's rancorous father wore no such ingratiating mask, though his fear of whites suffused and poisoned his life. "He could be chilling in the pulpit and indescribably cruel in his personal life and he was certainly the most bitter man I have ever met," Baldwin recalls. "He had lived and died in an intolerable bitterness of spirit and it frightened me, as we drove him to the graveyard through those unquiet, ruined streets, to see how powerful and overflowing this bitterness could be and to realize that this bitterness now was mine."

Baldwin, just turning nineteen, had been away from home for a year when his father died, and in that time he had "discovered the weight of white people in the world." Working in New Jersey, he behaved almost suicidally in his encounters with Jim Crow racism on the job and in public places. In restaurants he is repeatedly told that "we don't serve Negroes here," and when he finally explodes, bringing the frustrations of the whole year to a head, he barely escapes with his skin. The next day he returns home to face his dying father ("lying there, all shriveled and still, like a little black monkey"), with whom he had always quarreled, and sees the Harlem neighborhood ignite like a vast projection of his father's (and his own) bitterness and rage.

Just as Baldwin's essays on *Native Son* helped create an opening for his own more inward kind of writing, his "Notes of a Native Son" and his largely autobiographical first novel, *Go Tell It on the Mountain* (1953), showed that writing at its best. As he explains in *The Fire Next Time* and enacts in the novel, Baldwin at fourteen had undergone a religious conversion and become an impassioned storefront preacher, which shielded him from the temptations of the Harlem streets, from his father's cruelty and power, and from his own strange new sexual feelings. At almost the same time, however, he entered an elite white high school, where he was surrounded by skeptical Jews "who laughed at the tracts and leaflets I brought to school." Reading those religious tracts himself, he too began to find them "impossible to believe."

Baldwin's fictional version of this conflict between faith and doubt comes in the wonderful opening pages of the last section of *Go Tell It on the Mountain* when the young protagonist, John Grimes, falls to the floor in an ecstatic trance, overwhelmed as if by some gigantic physical force. Yet even as those around him – his loving mother, his seething father, his dying aunt, and the young sexton, Elisha, who physically attracts him – are helping him through and seeing to his salvation, a "malicious, ironic voice" in his head keeps telling him to rise from the filthy floor, to get up from this "heart of darkness," which is reflected in his father's coal-black face, and "to leave this temple and go out into the world." This is just what Baldwin himself would eventually do.

It is hard not to see this as a parable of the contradictions of Baldwin's whole writing life, caught between the prophetic impulse, expressed in the cadences of the born preacher, and the ironic outlook, a kind of second sight, that enabled him to step outside his own feelings and analyze them with astonishing precision and eloquence. (Ellison remarked that like himself, Baldwin was "not the product of the Negro store-front church but of the library.") For fifteen years, from the time he wrote his report "The Harlem Ghetto" for the Jewish editors of *Commentary* in 1948 to the near-apocalyptic *The Fire Next Time* in 1963 (which caused a sensation when it first appeared in *The New Yorker*), Baldwin was both a first-rate novelist and a native informant, an interpreter of the black psyche for white America.

During this period Baldwin was living primarily among whites yet reporting in depth from regions of his mind. Whether he was returning to Harlem, venturing into the Deep South, living among the French in an interracial Paris, or finishing his novel in a Swiss village that had never seen a black person before, the passion he brought to racial issues was tempered by the detachment of the reporter and the introspection of the fiction writer. Never for a moment forgetting that he was black – an amnesia, he felt, that had befallen the expatriate Wright – Baldwin brought to his own life a sense of inner mystery, as well as a capacity for irony, that was perfectly in tune with the postwar scene.

His message was anything but reassuring. Like W. E. B. Du Bois and Richard Wright before him, he was an anatomist of black rage – the toxic effects of racism – and the "double consciousness" through which blacks adapted to it. He found in himself – and in virtually every black person he knew – a lacerating, soul-destroying anger scarcely visible to whites, and he understood how it could overwhelm him, as it had already poisoned his father's life. A cutting irony was Baldwin's rhetorical weapon of choice; his seeming detachment had a sardonic edge:

It is hard . . . to blame the policeman, blank, good-natured, thoughtless, and insuperably innocent, for being such a perfect representative of the people he serves. He, too, believes in good intentions, and is astounded and offended when they are not taken for the deed. . . .

Negroes want to be treated like men: a perfectly straightforward statement, containing only seven words. People who have mastered Kant, Hegel, Shakespeare,
Marx, Freud, and the Bible find this statement utterly impenetrable.

These excerpts are from "Fifth Avenue, Uptown" (collected in *Nobody
Knows My Name,* 1961), a valuable sequel to his 1948 report from the
Harlem ghetto. They show how the sardonic mode enabled Baldwin to
sidestep the sentimental pitfalls of social protest. Irony sharpened
Baldwin's message and directed it to a literate public — neither rednecks
nor homeboys but enlightened liberals who might have mastered
Shakespeare, Marx, and Freud but understood next to nothing about race.
It was a universal human message, not that Negroes want to be loved as
Negroes or as neighbors but simply that they "want to be treated like
men." The best response to color is to be color-blind, to grant blacks a full
measure of humanity. This was a simple message, but eventually Baldwin
would find it almost impossible to sustain.

Even before Baldwin published his first novel, his liberal outlook could
be gauged from an odd bit of ventriloquy we find in some early essays. In
"Many Thousands Gone," for example, he freely borrowed the first-person
plural from Lionel Trilling's essays to speak for the sentiments of the *white*
world, often with surreal results: "Our dehumanization of the Negro," he
writes, "is indivisible from our dehumanization of ourselves: the loss of our
own identity is the price we pay for our annulment of his." Or "Time has
made some changes in the Negro face. Nothing has succeeded in making
it exactly like our own." This is not Baldwin trying to pass — he was
already becoming known as a young black writer of promise — but a white-
identified Baldwin speaking hopefully as the voice of the larger society in
the act of questioning itself. It shows the awkwardness of a man eager to
belong, to make a difference, someone writing in the acceptable voice, anxious to speak from the center yet deeply uncertain about where he stands.

By the early 1960s, however, in the long novel *Another Country* (1962)
and in *The Fire Next Time,* this liberal message began to be crowded out by
another view, more strident in its rhetoric yet also prophetic of the stresses
of the coming decade. Even before a resurgent black nationalism used the
slogans of black pride and Black Power to challenge the integrationist
faith of the civil rights movement, Baldwin himself was changing. As long
as he kept the ironic and prophetic voices in balance, his inner conflicts
lent drama to his fiction and dialectical strength to his remarkable essays.
But as his anger took hold, exactly as he predicted, as success and acclaim
freed him to vent his bitterness, his prose turned preachy, his characters
became ciphers of his argument. Rufus, the self-destructive jazz musician
in *Another Country,* and Ida, his even angrier sister, become vehicles for the

writer's denunciation of white people. Even as the novel preaches a gospel of love, Baldwin uses Ida to express a bitter contempt:

They keep you here because you're black, the filthy, white cock suckers, while they go around jerking themselves off with all that jazz about the land of the free and the home of the brave. . . . Some days, honey, I wish I could turn myself into one big fist and grind this miserable country to powder. Some days, I don't believe it has a right to exist. . . .

I used to see the way white men watched me, like dogs. And I thought about what I could do to them. How I hated them, the way they looked, and the things they'd say, all dressed up in their damn white skin, and their clothes just so, and their little weak, white pricks jumping in their drawers. . . . I used to wonder what in the world they did in bed, white people I mean, between themselves, to get them so sick.

It would be too much to say that this highly sexualized hatred speaks unequivocally for the later Baldwin, who began to warn of an impending racial apocalypse in *The Fire Next Time.* Still, Rufus and Ida's all-consuming anger showed the direction their author was taking. In *The Fire Next Time* he was able to sustain a complicated mixture of feelings for perhaps the last time, at once mocking and applauding the separatist demonology of the Nation of Islam.

Like Ralph Ellison in his portrayal of the Marcus Garveyite figure of Ras the Exhorter in *Invisible Man,* Baldwin had often shown how seemingly extreme and irrational views within the black community spoke to something every black person had experienced in a life of second-class citizenship and demeaning discrimination. Baldwin was brave in trying to enlighten white readers about those prejudices and where they came from. Even in 1948, publishing his first lengthy essay in *Commentary,* Baldwin had been candid about black anti-Semitism. Glimpses of Baldwin's growing interest in black nationalism could be seen in a 1961 essay, "East River, Downtown," where he first develops his sympathetic but critical treatment of the Black Muslims. Although he rejects the Muslim faith in black supremacy as no more sensible than white supremacy, he notes that "it is quite impossible to argue with a Muslim concerning the actual state of Negroes in this country – the truth, after all, is the truth. This is the great power a Muslim speaker has over his audience. His audience has not heard this truth – the truth about their daily lives – honored by anyone else."

From his years as a preacher, Baldwin was adept at holding an audience. And because of his homosexuality, he felt as much a sexual as a racial pariah, especially in the uncertainty of early manhood. He explored these feelings separately in *Go Tell It on the Mountain* and *Giovanni's Room* (1956) before blending them in the heated atmosphere of *Another Country,* his last genuinely effective novel. Together they cover the three phases of his life up through the early sixties – the uptown life of his boyhood in Harlem, the expatriate life of his Paris years after 1948, and his downtown life in Greenwich Village in the late fifties. All three are novels of conversion and personal transformation: John Grimes in the throes of adolescence, at the threshold of maturity; David in *Giovanni's Room* resisting and finally acknowledging his own homosexuality; and, finally, all the characters in *Another Country,* black and white, gay and straight, finding ways to love and forgive each other after the suicide of Rufus, their troubled friend, brother, and lover.

With many postwar writers, Baldwin always believed, as he said in 1959, that "the private life, his own and that of others, is the writer's subject – his key and ours to his achievement." Like Bellow, Malamud, and Ellison, he rejected the documentary realism prized by the thirties generation. As Renoir said he painted with his prick, Baldwin wrote with his emotions even if they were raw and confusing. He never truly took possession of the form of the novel, never reshaped it to a vision of his own, as Wright and Ellison did. He depended too heavily on flashbacks and on melodrama to plumb what he took to be the mystery of all human relationships, "the dreadful human tangle, occurring everywhere, without end, forever," as he described it in *Giovanni's Room.* The solid world of *Go Tell It on the Mountain* – the Harlem streets, the great migration that brought its people there – was something he would rarely recapture in his fiction, though it remained part of the social fabric of his essays for another decade. The descriptive and visual sense of Paris in *Giovanni's Room* is strong, but the anguished flow of introspection is really the author's own, for it goes beyond the characters as we know them. In *Another Country* the loss of control is even greater, for the novel's plot, involving five or six major characters, never fully objectifies the tangled mass of feelings the writer brings to it.

By contrast, there is an almost mechanical element of form in *Go Tell* and *Giovanni's Room* that keeps these stories *too* tightly structured. The former takes place on a single day in 1935, John Grimes's birthday, the day he receives the Lord's call. Enclosed between the two steps of his conversion are three novellas centering on his aunt, his stepfather, and his mother. Each of them migrated to Harlem from the South; all three made terrible choices that pinched and choked off their lives; all three made a life for themselves not much better than what they left behind. Baldwin's prose does little to suggest the different contours of their minds, the personal imprint of each of their recollections.

As Eliot and Joyce shaped their stories around ancient myths and literary allusions, Baldwin reworks his own family history around biblical motifs. Thus John Grimes becomes Ham, "the accursed son of Noah," father of the Negro race, who fell into sin and shame when he looked on his father's nakedness, and also Ishmael, despised son of the bondswoman Hagar, rejected by the patriarchal father. This Oedipal struggle with the violent, paranoid father may remind the reader of Henry Roth's *Call It Sleep*: both are growing-up stories about boys who are detested by their fathers and feel like outsiders in their own home. In Roth's story, too, the father rejects a son he sees not as his own but as a child of sin; there too the boy, much younger but also troubled by new sexual feelings, undergoes a spiritual conversion that breaks his father's terrifying grip on him.

John Grimes's fate is left open at the end, but there is hope he can evade the disasters that befell the family members who have witnessed his transformation. All of them grew up in oppressive surroundings, battered by poverty or constrained by a frigid respectability, deprived of a beloved parent or hemmed in by their own bad choices. Each of them reached for freedom and love; none succeeded except for heartbreakingly brief periods. His aunt, now gravely ill, had abandoned her mother, loathed her brother, and driven her free-spirited husband away; John's stiff-necked father, torn between carnal feelings and moral inhibitions, had turned his back on the woman carrying his child, whom he never acknowledged, and then married another woman out of self-mortification rather than love; John's mother had seen her young lover destroyed by despair and anguish, then had married mainly to give her son a name. None of them remained true to their feelings; none could hold on to the kind of love that, to Baldwin, was the only salvation that mattered.

Baldwin's strength in *Go Tell,* as in his essays, comes from his emotional intelligence, which outweighs the novel's structural flaws and literariness. When Baldwin writes about his characters' hopes and disappointments, especially in love, or about the weight of the past in their lives, he can be piercingly eloquent. Elizabeth's vividly remembered feelings about the mother who dies on her; the father who abandons her; the cold, unfeeling aunt who takes her in; the lover, Richard, who sweeps her off her feet but cannot stand on his own; the harsh man she marries; and finally the son she hopes to shield – these empathetic details have precisely the strength of Baldwin's essays at their best. But the story does not unfold in an emotional vacuum. Because of who these people are, the rough and painful world they live in, the way race has affected all their lives, the novel also has an encompassing social framework. Young Richard, for example, loses his moorings after he has been unfairly imprisoned, abused, and grudgingly released. His suicide, like Rufus's in *Another Country,* is the act of a man at the end of his rope, a victim of both society and his own corrosive despair.

Unfortunately, the lessons in love we get in Baldwin's next two novels, *Giovanni's Room* and *Another Country,* really do take place in a world void of nearly everything but personal feeling. *Giovanni's Room* was partly inspired by the famous Beat murder case in the early forties in New York, in which Lucien Carr, a friend of Jack Kerouac's, was jailed for killing an unwanted homosexual suitor. (Kerouac himself was imprisoned briefly as an accessory after the fact.) Baldwin's plot, centering on Americans in Europe, is a sexualized version of Henry James's international fables, such as *The Ambassadors,* with added touches of the expatriate world of *The Sun Also Rises* and the sexual self-discovery of *The City and the Pillar,* but without Hemingway's chic despair or Vidal's earnest didacticism.

The bisexual Giovanni, an Italian peasant turned Paris bartender, stands for the kind of guilt-free Mediterranean sensuality that the American protagonist, David, can neither resist nor accept. David's fiancée Hella, though patient and understanding, stands plainly for the dull satisfactions of conventional marriage. Almost against his will, David falls into a passionate love affair with Giovanni, but he is tormented by guilt feelings and eventually pulls away, as he had once done in a youthful escapade with another young man. Torn apart by ambivalence and fear, he finds it impossible to be honest with himself or with his lovers of either sex. When he finally comes to terms with his feelings, it is far too late. After David's retreat, Giovanni falls into a sordid world of predatory old queens, which propels him, all too melodramatically, to murder, and then to execution on the guillotine. So David loses both his lover and, in due course, his fiancée, without quite rising, like Lambert Strether in *The Ambassadors* or Isabel Archer in *The Portrait of a Lady,* to the misguided dignity of a Jamesian act of renunciation.

Besides the contrast between European worldliness and American inhibition, *Giovanni's Room* has another Jamesian quality characteristic of postwar fiction: not much longer than a novella, the book is tightly coiled around a single metaphor, Giovanni's room. The room stands for Paris itself, where an American far from home can find or lose himself; small and squalid, it also represents the perilous appeal of forbidden love. For David it threatens to become a prison of sexual difference, a trap that will separate him from normal life forever, like the cell in which Giovanni awaits execution. David finds the room's clutter and disorder frightening. "I was trembling. I thought, if I do not open the door at once and get out of here, I am lost." Writing about love, Baldwin falls readily into the clichés of romance fiction: "But I knew I could not open the door, I knew it was too late. Soon it was too late to do anything but moan. . . . With everything in me screaming *No!* yet the sum of me sighed *Yes.*"

For Baldwin himself the room stands for the irresistible pull of the private life, the risky search for identity, which strikes fear into David but offers Baldwin an escape from the racial climate in America. But the room also is the void into which Baldwin's fiction could fall in the quest for love apart from a wider sphere to give it meaning. *Giovanni's Room* can be evocative – a love letter to the streets of Paris, where Baldwin felt he could breathe free air – but expatriate Paris is a small world grafted onto the life of a great city; the tumultuous ongoing life of the French capital barely appears in the book. The streets contain little but cafés, bars, and rented rooms. They do not resonate like the hieroglyphic streets of Harlem that he was leaving behind. Like Richard Wright, Baldwin seriously risked losing touch with his American material during his Paris exile.

Yet *Giovanni's Room* is a brave portrayal of the confusions of sexual identity. It is a book about self-discovery, like *Go Tell It on the Mountain* and *Another Country,* but this is thwarted by David's emotional knot, his conflicts over his own desires. Feeling like an outcast, David despises himself, but his homosexuality washes over him like the religious conversion in the previous novel (which also had a sexual subtext). *Giovanni's Room* is less a defense of homosexuality, like *The City and the Pillar,* than a brief for honesty, for attending to intimations of love wherever they appear. *Another Country* develops this theme on a much larger scale, interweaving the racial and sexual motifs that had been kept apart in the first two novels.

The main characters in *Another Country* include Rufus Scott, a jazz musician who vents his growing fury first on his white Southern girlfriend, then on himself; Ida, his tempestuous sister, who takes on his sulfurous anger after he kills himself; Vivaldo Moore, an aspiring white novelist, first Rufus's friend, then Ida's often frustrated lover; Cass Silenski, wife of a glibly successful novelist; and finally Eric Jones, an actor, also white and Southern, who is returning from some contented years in France, where he lived with a man he loved, to take a part in a Broadway play. In the course of the novel, these characters sleep with each other and deceive each other in various combinations, black and white, gay and straight, almost never for kicks but as a way of breaking the ice floe that blocks them from living happy lives.

This search for self-fulfilment makes the novel something of a high-toned soap opera. Despite its considerable daring and racy Greenwich Village setting, the novel's round-robin of relationships follows the pattern of popular bestsellers of the 1950s – it is a *Peyton Place* of interracial bohemia instead of small-town New England. Rufus's story, added by Baldwin in his final draft, is almost a free-standing novella that serves as the book's prologue. The other lives are acted out over his corpse: his friends feel they have somehow failed him, and his sister feels an inchoate need to avenge him, to take up where he left off. The other bookend is Eric, the expatriate actor, who enters the novel when it is almost half over. His early life is yet another fable about growing up gay in America, coming to terms with being different, seeing yourself as others see you. Eric's French life reflects the quest for happiness of Baldwin's own expatriate years. His return to America galvanizes his friends to connect with each other and with their own feelings. If Rufus represents the self-destructive rage they must get beyond, Eric stands for the love and release they must somehow find. Eric is a salvific figure who puts them all on a path to self-forgiveness.

Unfortunately, Eric is more a figment of fantasy, even self-idealization, than a credible character. He is not only a great lover, generous to both men and women, but a model of emotional honesty, the very quality his friends need to sort out their lives and break through in their work. We first see Eric sitting naked in an Edenic garden overlooking the Mediterranean together, with his young French lover, Yves (Eve?). Their hard-won serenity is threatened, for Eric is about to leave for Paris and New York, where he will have to deal with a world he fled years earlier. Once there, this is exactly what he does. Sleeping with Cass, he will enable her to stand up to her insensitive husband and put her marriage on a more honest footing. Sleeping with Vivaldo, he will somehow empower him to reach out to Ida with a new depth of feeling. Thus, Eric is not only a mechanism to resolve the novel's plot but also a vehicle of the author's evangelical belief in salvation through love, especially homosexual love. (To Eric, man-woman love is only a form of "superior calisthenics.") Both Cass and Vivaldo are white and heterosexual and therefore, according to the novel, uptight, uneasy in their bodies, and out of touch with their feelings. The bisexual Eric is their liberator, their bountiful instructor, like Ramona in *Herzog*. In the process Eric also saves himself. When Yves finally joins him in New York, they will find that the hothouse bloom of their love can flower in the real world.

This belief in redemption through love, and especially through a polymorphous sexuality, situates *Another Country* firmly in the period that produced Mailer's *The Deer Park* and "The White Negro" and Norman O. Brown's *Life Against Death,* that saw the first American publication of D. H. Lawrence's *Lady Chatterley's Lover,* Henry Miller's *Tropic* novels, Vladimir Nabokov's *Lolita,* and William S. Burroughs's *Naked Lunch.* As a Jamesian who at bottom was aesthetically and morally conservative, Baldwin officially disapproved of these books, as he made clear in his essay on Mailer in *Nobody Knows My Name.* Yet *Another Country* is itself a product of the existential 1950s, with its quest for personal authenticity, its fascination with the hipster, and its effort to break down rigid barriers between races, genders, and sexual identities. This utopian strand comes through most clearly in passages of unfortunate sexual description, invariably between men: "Eric felt beneath his fingers Yves' slowly stirring, stiffening sex. This sex dominated the long landscape of his life as the cathedral towers dominated the plains." When Vivaldo, feeling strange yet comfortable with another man's body, suddenly turns passive, and allows himself to be taken by Eric, Baldwin's run-on prose turns purple and utopian: "Vivaldo seemed to have fallen through a great hole in time, back to his innocence, he felt clear, washed, and empty, waiting to be filled." As if trembling on the brink of a religious revelation, he becomes as a child again, an empty vessel "waiting to be filled." A moment later he feels "fantastically protected, liberated. . . . All of his hope, which had grown so pale, flushed into life again."

Baldwin makes up for passages of dreadful writing about sex with lightning shafts of perception about people and their behavior: Cass's dawning realization of the emptiness of her marriage, Vivaldo's insight into the block that keeps him from giving life to his fictional characters, young Eric's gradual recognition of his sexual difference, which is confusing to him yet clear to everyone around him. Significantly, these are all interior changes, like the famous chapter in *The Portrait of a Lady* in which Isabel Archer, in one long fireside reverie, understands her marriage from just a glimpse of her husband with another woman. Baldwin was a lifelong Jamesian. But where James could lend drama to a character who is simply thinking, Baldwin invests himself almost too copiously in his people, reducing them to aspects of himself. "The sharp outlines of character are dissolved by waves of uncontrolled emotion," complained critic Robert Bone. "The author does not know where his own psychic life leaves off and his characters' begins."

Another Country proved to be a turning point in Baldwin's inexorable shift from the ironic to the prophetic voice. Much more than *Giovanni's Room*, it showed the intrusion of Baldwin the essayist into the work of the novelist, with every major character at some point speaking for him, either as an artist, a black man, or a homosexual who had loved both men and women. Rufus's anger and frustration, Ida's bitterness, her sense that white people do not actually *see* her, Vivaldo's conflicts over his writing, and Eric's feelings about being an expatriate, coming to terms with being gay, and finding meaning through love — all these (except the homosexuality) are autobiographical motifs better developed in Baldwin's essays. The greatest overlap is with *The Fire Next Time*, Baldwin's last major essay, the one that reads most like an inspired sermon, apocalyptic yet highly personal.

If Baldwin's best work reflects his ambivalence, the Jamesian complexity of his inner life, this essay was the last time he could keep the interior dialogue in balance. It is a rhetorical masterpiece, mesmerizing in its prose though often contradictory in its point of view. Telling the story of his religious conversion at fourteen, Baldwin takes us back to the setting of *Go Tell It on the Mountain,* but the essay itself belongs to the new racial landscape of the 1960s, which Baldwin was the first to explore. In one passage describing the music of the church, for example, Baldwin reaches back to the rhythms of the pulpit to convey a sense of unearthly beauty invisible to the white world:

It took a long time for me to disengage myself from this excitement, and on the blindest, most visceral level, I never really have, and never will. There is no music like that music, no drama like the drama of the saints rejoicing, the sinners moaning, the tambourines racing, and all those voices coming together and crying holy unto the Lord. There is still, for me, no pathos quite like the pathos of those multicolored, worn, somehow triumphant and transfigured faces, speaking from the depths of a visible, tangible, continuing despair of the goodness of the Lord.

This is warmly nostalgic, with Baldwin the preacher lending eloquence to Baldwin the writer, yet it also foreshadows the new sixties discourse of pride in the black experience. Once Baldwin had fled Harlem and the church for the freedom he could find only downtown; now he transfigures their pathos and despair into beauty, agency, and communal emotion. The world Baldwin tried to escape had also marked him for life. Just a few pages earlier, Baldwin had written about the church as his "gimmick" for transcending the ghetto, and later he describes the hypocrisy of the church, the lack of any real love in it: "It was a mask for hatred and self-hatred and despair." But here, recalling the emotions, the drama, the spectacle, the language, he lets his ambivalence shade off into incantation, even sentimentality. For the moment at least, the church takes possession of him.

The Fire Next Time, like the great March on Washington of August 1963, commemorated the anniversary of Lincoln's Emancipation Proclamation in 1863, which was also, understandably, the historical reference point in Ellison's *Invisible Man.* Thanks to the nonviolent protests organized by such civil rights organizations as Martin Luther King, Jr.'s Southern Christian Leadership Conference (SCLC), the Student Nonviolent Coordinating Committee (SNCC), and the Congress of Racial Equality (CORE), as well as the court actions brought by the Legal Defense Fund of the National Association for the Advancement of Colored People (NAACP), the racial situation in the South was beginning to change. The burning of churches, attacks on civil rights workers, and heavy-handed resistance by white Southerners were drawing national attention. In June 1963 President Kennedy, appalled by televised scenes of the police in Birmingham, Alabama, assaulting black women and schoolgirls with attack dogs and water hoses, came out strongly in support of new civil rights legislation, which his successor would shepherd through Congress after his assassination.

Baldwin's text straddles the line between the integrationist views of civil rights leaders and the angry militance soon to come. He connects his own experience in the church with the separatist teachings of the Black Muslims; in an uncanny way, they anticipate themes of black pride, black rage, black separatism, and black power that were shortly to dominate the race issue. At the end, Baldwin turns against Muslim notions of racial superiority, arguing that "the value placed on the color of the skin is always and everywhere and forever a delusion," but it is too late, for the whole thrust of the essay has been to explore the anger and pain, the history of mistreatment and dehumanization that make the appeal beyond color, an appeal to universal human standards, seem beside the point.

Earlier in the essay, Baldwin had caricatured whites for being "terrified of sensuality," for imitating jazz singing so badly "that one dare not speculate on the temperature of the deep freeze from which issue their brave and sexless little voices," and even (the low point of the essay) for "the blasphemous and tasteless foam rubber" they call white bread. In both *Another Country* and *The Fire Next Time,* Baldwin follows Mailer in upending racist clichés about black sensuality by turning them into hip virtues. In the years to come, these inverted stereotypes would become a staple of black nationalist rhetoric, along with a rhetoric of violence, of African origins, of separatism, and of communal pride, themes pushed hard by the puritanical Muslims.

In his earlier discussion of the Black Muslims in "East River, Downtown," he had quoted a "prominent Negro" saying, "I am not at all sure that I *want* to be integrated into a burning house." In *The Fire Next Time* he repeats this question in his own voice, with less qualification, and makes it his central theme: "Do I really *want* to be integrated into a burning house?" Yes, answered one critic, if it is the only house you have. Baldwin anticipates this reply by saying that "the Negro has been formed by this nation, for better or for worse, and does not belong to any other – not to Africa, and certainly not to Islam." On claims of black superiority, he writes, in the spirit of his earlier work: "The glorification of one race and the consequent debasement of another – or others – always has been and always will be a recipe for murder." Such sensible second thoughts carry little weight, however, beside the book's apocalyptic warnings. In a sentence that foreshadows the urban race riots of the 1960s, Baldwin writes: "The Negroes of this country may never be able to rise to power, but they are very well placed indeed to precipitate chaos and bring down the curtain on the American dream."

Baldwin's vision of a bloody racial conflagration combines biblical imagery ("the fire next time") with repeated references to the Holocaust. His life till then had been bound up with Jewish teachers, Jewish friends, Jewish editors, Jewish magazines. He had grown up in a literary scene in which Jews played a pivotal role. He had alluded to the Holocaust in previous essays as evidence of what an advanced Christian civilization could perpetrate on its designated scapegoats. Like the Jews of Europe, a Negro initially "just cannot *believe* that white people are treating him as they do," for it "has nothing to do with anything he has done," simply with what he is. Now Baldwin feels for the first time that whites actually intended to destroy black people, that the ghettos of our great cities may be little different from the European ghettos in which Jews were rounded up for slaughter. In the opening essay he writes to his nephew that "this innocent country set you down in a ghetto in which, in fact, it intended that you should perish." He qualifies this, however, as being "the root of my dispute with my country," that is, a family quarrel.

The Fire Next Time oscillates unsteadily between such dire predictions and less eloquent qualifications. Describing the world's passivity before the murder of the Jews, he imagines the same indifference "on the day that the United States decided to murder its Negroes systematically instead of little by little and catch-as-catch-can." Baldwin bolsters his fears with evidence from his own encounters with racism and from recent history, especially the mistreatment of colored soldiers during and after World War II. Spiraling downward into self-destructive rage, caught in the powerful whirl of his own style, he projects a vision of the coming doom of American and Christian civilization: "Time catches up with kingdoms and crushes them, gets its teeth into doctrines and rends them; time reveals the foundations on which any kingdom rests, and eats at those foundations, and it destroys doctrines by proving them to be untrue." In such passages of empty eloquence, Baldwin put his mind to rest and allowed his prophetic cadence to take over.

❦

Baldwin's newfound militance, his conversion to protest and anger, was lauded by Irving Howe in his controversial 1963 essay "Black Boys and Native Sons," which harshly criticized Baldwin's earlier attacks on Richard Wright. But it did little to endear Baldwin to the young black militants of the sixties, who attacked or dimissed him, and it seriously damaged his work, which at its best was grounded in introspection, not angry rhetoric. Baldwin's latest conversion was also mocked by Ralph Ellison in his celebrated reply to Howe, "The World and the Jug," his best-known essay, in which he wittily disparaged Baldwin for "out-Wrighting Richard" and minimized his own Oedipal relationship to the author of *Native Son.* "Wright was no spiritual father of mine," he wrote. "I rejected Bigger Thomas as any *final* image of Negro personality." Ellison explored the relationship much more affectionately in a lecture about Wright a few years later, revealing how close he was to his mentor at least until 1940. "I read most of *Native Son* as it came off the typewriter, and I didn't know what to think of it except that it was wonderful. I was not responding critically."

In this tribute, Ellison mobilizes Wright to make his own case against "the mystifications of racism," black and white. He emphasizes Wright's conflicts with his fellow Communists, who had no respect for the autonomy of art and little understanding of the actualities of black life. But he also shows how Marxism, and Wright's own confidence as an artist, enabled Wright to escape the poverty of merely racial analysis. He admired Wright as a combative figure, fearless in his integrity: "In him we had for the first time a Negro American writer as randy, as courageous, and as irrepressible as Jack Johnson."

In such essays as "The World and the Jug" and "Remembering Richard Wright," Ellison picks up where Baldwin faltered, insisting on the variety and complexity of black life and the range of influences, from Ernest Hemingway and T. S. Eliot to jazz, that can be enriching for a black artist. Ellison was immune to the destructive effects of black nationalism, perhaps because in *Invisible Man* he had already shown his mastery over every facet of black life, from folklore and dialect to urban hustling and pan-Africanism. This was why he reacted so strongly to Howe's well-argued but prescriptive essay. It seemed to confine the black writer to a path of anger, protest, and victimization. To a man who had aspired to write the Great *American* Novel, this was a much narrower role than the one he wished to play.

Ellison's response to Howe and Baldwin anticipated all the attacks that younger black writers would level against him in the late sixties and seventies. With considerable empathy, his novel had already sent up just such ideological currents in black life, from the Marxism of the thirties to Black Power notions that would flourish only more than a decade later. Born in Oklahoma in 1914, not long after its transition from Indian territory to statehood, Ellison had studied music at Tuskegee Institute between 1933 and 1936 before migrating to Harlem, where he began to write under Richard Wright's insistent prodding. Thus, he not only knew black life in the West, in the South, and in the largest northern ghetto, but at Tuskegee was exposed to the accommodationist ideas of Booker T. Washington ("the Founder"), which he would wickedly satirize throughout *Invisible Man.* All these, including his close links with the Harlem branch of the Communist party, are among the autobiographical strands out of which his novel is loosely woven. But these experiences appear even more directly in the essays that, as we now can see, form a major part of Ellison's literary legacy.

When Ellison first brought together his essays, reviews, lectures, and interviews in *Shadow and Act* (1964), they were reviewed respectfully as revealing adjuncts to his novel and as a promissory note for the fiction yet to come. A second collection, *Going to the Territory,* which appeared with no fanfare in 1986, seemed even more an act of propitiation. Well before the posthumous *Collected Essays* of 1995, however, it was becoming clear that this impressive prose was not simply an assortment of personal opinions but a major body of cultural criticism that had already inspired other black intellectuals and had begun to influence the national outlook on race, as Du Bois's critique of Booker T. Washington had done at the beginning of the century, as Wright had done for the 1940s, and as Baldwin had done for the fifties and early sixties. The key to Ellison's approach is his distinct way of exploring his double consciousness, his sense of identity as a Negro and as an American. His answer to Baldwin's question about being integrated into a burning house would surely have been "Yes, because it's *my* house" – and because not all of it is burning, not all the time: the property is still rich with undeveloped possibilities.

Of all African American writers and intellectuals, Ellison stakes the greatest claims – not for a separate black culture or literary tradition, but for an inestimably great role within *American* culture. He acknowledges a debt to Jewish American writers but insists that they did not escape provinciality until they saw their experience in American terms – not simply in ethnic or personal terms but as a characteristic feature of a larger world. Instead of simply exploring his own memories, the Jewish writer first "had to see himself as American and project his Jewish experience as an experience unfolding within this pluralistic society. When this was done, it was possible to project this variant of the American experience as a metaphor for the whole."

Where others pay lip service to "diversity," Ellison shows in fascinating detail how different currents have merged into the mainstream of our culture – not simply how Anglo-Saxon culture was altered by the folkways and speech of outsiders but how the children of immigrants and slaves adapted remote customs to their own usage. Cultural appropriation is the great theme of Ellison's essays, which explore the mixed origins and improvisational forms of both black and American identity. Through half a century of lecturing and writing, Ellison never tired of describing how different cultural forms, high and low, classical and vernacular, Eastern and Western, Northern and Southern, were braided together into an authentic American creativity. In the varied tradition of the early W. E. B. Du Bois, John Dewey, Horace Kallen, Randolph Bourne, and Alain Locke, Ellison's is a classically pluralist defense of cultural diversity. In a revealing tribute to Locke, Ellison stressed the danger of becoming "unconciously racist by simply stressing one part of our heritage," the genetic, racial part:

You cannot have an American experience without having a black experience. Nor can you have the technology of jazz, as original as many of those techniques are, without having had long centuries of European musical technology, not to mention the technologies of various African musical traditions. . . .
What I am suggesting is that when you go back you do not find a pure stream; after all, Louis Armstrong, growing up in New Orleans, was taught to play a rather strict type of military music before he found his jazz and blues voice. Talk about cultural pluralism! It's the air we breathe; it's the ground we stand on.

Part of Ellison's story was how a culture could be created by people who were neither free nor equal, by despised immigrants or oppressed slaves. In one example, he describes how slaves adapted European dance fashions brought over by their masters:

First the slaves mocked them, and then decided, coming from dancing cultures, that they could do them better — so they went on to define what is surely the beginnings of an American choreography.

He goes on to show that what began in rags in the slave yards eventually found its way into Negro dance halls and juke joints until it finally reached the stage. In Ellison's picture, popular and vernacular culture, located at the fringes of the social hierarchy, provides the pores through which the main body of culture breathes and renews itself. Blacks had "the freedom of experimentation, of trying out new things no matter how ridiculous they might seem," because "there was no one to take them too seriously." Oppression and dislocation had imposed "a great formlessness" on Negro life. They needed to experiment, to develop a new language, because they were forced into corners where they *had* to improvise, to re-create themselves, and because the cultural mainstream reflected no honest images of their own lives — or mirrored them only in distorted or one-dimensional forms, as in minstrel culture or in Hollywood movies.

To Ellison, white Americans have always "suffered from a deep uncertainty as to who they really are." On one hand this has forced them to seek a unified identity by scapegoating "outsiders," But the same national uncertainty gives these outsiders exceptional leverage – politically, to recall the majority to its professed ideals; culturally, to work within the many popular forms of expression that make America different from an ancient and traditional culture. "On this level," says Ellison, "the melting pot did indeed melt, creating such deceptive metamorphoses and blending of identities, values, and life-styles that most American whites are culturally part Negro American without even realizing it." He shows how, beginning at least as far back as *Huckleberry Finn,* the black presence led to "certain creative tensions" that had a decisive effect on the high culture as well.

In the opening piece of his second collection, "The Little Man at Chehaw Station," Ellison wrote a definitive (if idealized) meditation on the American audience, which he saw embodied in the little man behind the stove at a small railroad station near Tuskegee – the random individual whose judgment matters, who sees through the bogus performance, whose culture is at once eclectic and classical, popular yet demanding. If *Invisible Man* had a single ideal reader, it would be this man, completely ordinary yet protean and adventurous. "Possessing an American-vernacular receptivity to change, a healthy delight in creative attempts at formalizing irreverence, and a Yankee trader's respect for the experimental, he is repelled by works of art that would strip human experience – especially American experience – of its wonder and stubborn complexity." Whether or not such a man actually exists, for Ellison he is a paradigm of democratic life, in which culture and education have flowed through mysterious channels and "certain assertions of personality, formerly the prerogative of high social rank, have become the privilege of the anonymous and the lowly."

Such a figure, as Ellison sees it, can also become the agent, not simply the recipient of culture; in this guise he reappears later in the essay as a classic "American joker," a cool ghetto customer who performs some astonishing bits of personal theater before delighted onlookers outside Ellison's home on Riverside Drive. After describing this street-smart character's antics, including his flamboyant dress and body language, Ellison calls him "a home-boy bent on projecting and recording with native verve something of his complex sense of cultural identity." This man – or Ellison's projection of him – represents culture as pragmatic improvisation, for he is putting together his own personality out of bits and pieces of different traditions. Making himself up as he goes along, he demonstrates "an American compulsion to improvise upon the given." He "was a product of the melting pot and the conscious or unconscious comedy it brews." To Ellison, Americans have "improvised their culture as they did their politics and institutions: touch and go, by ear and by eye; fitting new form to new function, new function to old form."

In this kind of cultural analysis, focusing on eclectic American forms of self-invention, Ellison is at once expounding the technique of *Invisible Man,* situating it within American culture, and perhaps explaining why it was so hard for him to complete his second novel. Two years later he developed these ideas in an autobiographical lecture, "Going to the Territory," the title piece of the same collection. Here Ellison gave one of the most forceful descriptions of how our culture and identity have been shaped by creative tensions and a constant process of cultural assimilation. The very title alludes to Huck Finn's metaphor for reclaiming his freedom. Recalling his own school days in Oklahoma, not long after the territory had become a state, Ellison describes young black kids learning European folk dances, a sight that some might find "absurd" but to him was part of a necessary process of appropriating the Other, making creative use of what seems alien. Rather than expressing "a desire to become white," we were narrowing "the psychological distance between them and ourselves," as well as "learning their dances as an *artistic* challenge." This skill, this discipline, would be the black children's secret weapon as well as their key to an unnoticed freedom – "our freedom to broaden our personal culture by absorbing the culture of others," something that could develop and grow even "within our state of social and political unfreedom."

This might be seen as special pleading out of the writer's own autobiography, but to Ellison what he received was a gift, for it introduced him "to the basic discipline required of the artist." His music education also enabled him "to grasp the basic compatibility of the classical and vernacular styles which were part of our musical culture." This in turn would eventually shape his vision of American literature as the cultural correlative of democracy, an ongoing process of transformation mediated by the vernacular. The vernacular is not simply "popular or indigenous language" but a "dynamic *process* in which the most refined styles of the past are continually merged with the play-it-by-eye-and-by-ear improvisations which we invent in our efforts to control our environment and entertain ourselves." On one level this is a demotic version of Eliot's "Tradition and the Individual Talent," with its account of how the tradition is constantly being transmuted by new voices and creative departures. On another level, it is a beautifully articulated example of a fluid and functional pragmatist aesthetic within a democratic culture, an aesthetic of improvisation, spontaneity, and continuous transformation.

Far from seeing the vernacular as a dumbing-down of high culture, a view common among critics of popular culture in the 1950s, Ellison sees it as part of an ongoing process of cultural self-renewal. Arguing that "there is no necessary contradiction between our vernacular style and the pursuit of excellence," Ellison describes the vernacular as the medium in which we experiment with the languages and forms that will best express us. "While the vernacular is shy of abstract standards, it still seeks perfection in the form of functional felicity. This is why considerations of function and performance figure so prominently in the scale of vernacular aesthetics." This, of course, is nothing less than a description of jazz, for Ellison the very epitome of how vernacular artists refine and transform traditional materials. But it applies equally well to a writer like Twain, who showed how to turn regional speech into art "and thus taught us how to capture that which is essentially American in our folkways and manners."

Ellison's accounts of Twain, of jazz and the blues, and of his early musical education are also accounts of the creative process that shaped *Invisible Man* and made it an archetypal American novel. In his 1953 speech accepting the National Book Award, Ellison gives prime importance to the book's "experimental attitude," a phrase out of the pragmatist lexicon that would apply equally well to a modernist or a jazz aesthetic. Explaining why he turned away from the language of naturalism (including the hard-boiled manner of Hemingway and the proletarian writers), he notes that "despite the notion that its rhythms were those of everyday speech, I found that when compared with the rich babel of idiomatic expression around me, a language full of imagery and gesture and rhetorical canniness, it was embarrassingly austere." In its place he sought a language and form that were richer, more varied, and more mysterious, full of wordplay and allusion, metaphoric in plot as well as verbal style, so as to convey the fluidity and complexity of the world as he had experienced it. In its form as well as narrative line, *Invisible Man* would exemplify the vernacular process through which American culture had explored its contradictions, including its racial conflicts.

One of Ellison's most strongly held views was that race itself is little more than a mystification, that skin color and blood kinship are trivial markers – of little help in explaining the complexity of human culture. Ellison's aim was to put aside "the insidious confusion between race and culture which haunts this society." Whether seen as a source of pride (by nationalists), of shame (by racists), or of solidarity (by communal boosters), race alone determines little about what human beings can achieve. It is not a fate to which individuals have been ineluctably condemned, or an essence that defines or delimits them. In his response to Irving Howe, he complains that "Howe makes of 'Negroness' a metaphysical condition, one that is a state of irremediable agony which all but engulfs the mind." Ellison's pragmatic response – to Howe, to Baldwin, to white supremacists and black nationalists alike – is that identity is forged rather than given, created rather than determined by biology or social statistics. "It is not skin color which makes a Negro American but cultural heritage as shaped by the American experience."

For Ellison the construction of identity is analogous to the hard work of making art, involving a mixture of personal discipline and subtle cultural influences. In *Invisible Man,* he gives us an anonymous protagonist with no identity except what others are continually trying to impose on him, no strategy except his eagerness to please. In the whole spectrum of postwar fiction he is the ultimate outsider, telling his story from his underground lair. But through most of the novel he is also the character who most wanted to be an insider, to fit in and be accepted. The novel's episodic structure, prismatic language, and fluid technique reflect the process through which he tests and gradually sheds these imposed definitions, with all the illusions that came with them.

Like Voltaire's Candide, whose experience continually belies his teacher's insistence that this is "the best of all possible worlds," Ellison's protagonist is an unshakeable innocent, immature, eager to get ahead, trained in the habits of deference and humility through which blacks in America had traditionally gotten by. But life itself, full of surprises, repeatedly tells him otherwise, beginning with the death of his grandfather, who, after a long, quiet, humble existence, calls himself a spy and a traitor in the enemy's country, and urges him to "overcome 'em with yeses, undermine 'em with grins, agree 'em to death and destruction." Near the end of the book, the hero decides bitterly to do the same: "I'd let them swoller me until they vomited or burst wide open. . . . I'd yes them until they puked and rolled in it. All they wanted of me was one belch of affirmation and I'd bellow it out loud. Yes! Yes! YES! That was all anyone wanted of us, that we should be heard and not seen, and then heard in one big optimistic chorus of yassuh, yassuh, yassuh!"

The whole novel is a testing of his grandfather's double message of humility and enmity, of seeming accommodation and inner resistance, the first of many such messages he takes in without fully understanding them. The scene with his grandfather is also the prototype of Ellison's semiallegorical method. Like the heroes of other picaresque novels, the young man is less a full-blooded character than a convenience of an often symbolic, occasionally surreal plot. As in the riff just quoted, Ellison uses narrative as a freewheeling vehicle for ideas, wordplay, wild satire, ideological burlesque, and striking realistic detail. His description of the characters passing through the Men's House in Harlem, for example, is an acidly etched inventory of people living out their dreams and illusions; it is a miniature human comedy of the whole Harlem scene. His grandfather's death scene, however, is not realistic but stylized and emblematic — a piece of comic and tragic argument, that gives us a gritty version of a general view of life. His grandfather's words serve as a chorus or leitmotif recurring from episode to episode. The novel is tied together by many other such texts that reappear musically, a theme and variations marking the stages of the narrator's progress. Another text like this is "To Whom It May Concern – Keep This Nigger-Boy Running," which the boy understands as the implicit message he carries with him as he tries to make his way in the world. In so many other words, that is exactly what it is. At every step, he is given the illusion of progress but is actually meant to keep running in place, to get nowhere. Only by breaking with received messages, socially ascribed roles, conventional restraints, and respectable ambitions does he begin to come into his own.

The typical bildungsroman explores the passage from innocence to experience, a process by which the naïve or callow protagonist becomes the substantial person who narrates the book. The hero of *Invisible Man,* however, ends up nowhere, in a state of articulate hibernation, in a well-lit Dostoyevskyan hole in the ground, not in Harlem but in some "border area" where he can see without being seen. The novel is not about the shaping of a life but the unshaping of illusions, about achieving a new awareness of who and what you are. When the hero eventually puts his innocence behind him – the naïveté he had resumed in nearly every episode – it is not to make a life but to shed all the false lives for which he had been pointlessly striving. Along with the "running" metaphor, this suggests *Invisible Man*'s kinship to other picaresque fiction discussed in the previous chapter, such as *The Catcher in the Rye, On the Road, Lolita,* and *Rabbit, Run.* In these novels, the protagonist's deepest need is not to become a success, to settle into an ordered life, but to escape the one he already has – not to take on responsibility but to slough it off. Like Holden Caulfield, Ellison's hero eventually sees through the phoniness of nearly everyone around him, the fakery inherent in social role playing. He rejects the 1950s mantra of maturity, the demand for affirmation, and reaches for something that makes him an outsider, even a pariah. He wants to live his discontent, even if it is only half understood.

One thread of *Invisible Man* is Ellison's lively mockery of every kind of respectability, black or white, corporate or communist, middle class or working class. The good white citizens who organize the "battle royal" are lechers and sadists, treating the black boys like gladiators in a Roman arena. At college the young man tries but fails to live by the visionary ideals of the Founder and Dr. Bledsoe. Expelled, he learns what they really add up to – a way of manipulating whites into thinking that you serve and respect them. Up north, the trustee Emerson's son opens his eyes (for the moment) to how he is being jerked around. But the young Emerson is a parody of a well-meaning white liberal – patronizing, neurotic, and self-absorbed; the man urges him to study the earlier Emerson's ideas about self-reliance and seeks plaintively to be his friend – but ends up asking him to serve as his valet.

Each episode is dominated by just such a false god exacting tribute, a would-be mentor trying to determine his path. "Everyone seemed to have some plan for me, and beneath that some more secret plan." At the paint factory he is under the authority of an old Uncle Tom, Lucius Brockway, underpaid, overqualified, submissive to whites, and vicious to other blacks, especially those connected with the union. After an explosion out of Fritz Lang's science-fiction masterpiece *Metropolis,* he enters a surgical "white" world and is treated by men who subject him to surreal experiments, probing his sense of reality. "I fell to plotting ways of short-circuiting the machine." By trying to deprive him of his identity, to lobotomize him, they unwittingly open him up to a new, more fluid sense of identity that will flourish in the big city.

At the other extreme are the few characters who nurture him without an agenda of their own, or simply help open his eyes. Trueblood's tragicomic tale of incest introduces him to the earthy world of the shacks and sharecropper cabins that lie outside the field of vision of the respectable college. When he shows this world to one of the white trustees, he is cast out – for introducing a touch of reality onto a painted set. Another helpful figure is the vet who echoed his grandfather's advice as he headed north: "Play the game, but don't believe in it – that much you owe yourself." In Harlem he boards with Mary, whose maternal concern is as anchored and authentic as Trueblood's ribald comedy of love and lust. She is a warmhearted specimen of the common people, the substratum of personal reality that social theories tend to ignore or suppress. Each of the hero's false mentors claims to be putting him in touch with history, but it is only a conveyor belt toward an unwanted future, an abstract process that takes no account of his wishes or needs. "Look at me! Look at *me!*" he finally shouts, in what could be the motto for the whole novel. "Everywhere I've turned somebody has wanted to sacrifice me for my good – only *they* were the ones who benefited."

In one of the novel's richest scenes, he buys baked yams from a Harlem street vendor and is flooded with nostalgia for the home he left behind, a distant pastoral world he has been taught to rise above. Yet going back to this early world is no answer. He *must* see its value – must accept the common life, the sensory plenitude from which he sprang – but also must put it behind him. Just as the college is the false Eden from which he must fall in order to become himself, Mary's home is only a temporary shelter from the swirl of the city streets. Eating the yams makes him not only homesick but reflective. "What a group of people we were, I thought. Why, you could cause us the greatest humiliation simply by confronting us with something we liked." This leads him to a delicious fantasy in which he accuses Bledsoe of being "a shameless chitterling eater! . . . of relishing hog bowels!"

Bledsoe would disintegrate, disinflate! With a profound sigh he'd drop his head in shame. He'd lose caste. The weekly newspapers would attack him. The captions over his picture: *Prominent Educator Reverts to Field-Niggerism!* . . . In the South his white folks would desert him. . . . He'd end up an exile washing dishes at the Automat.

This goes on much longer — it is the kind of wild riff that marks the hero's moments of recognition — and it leads to a moral: "to hell with being ashamed of what you liked." But the mind keeps turning, and within a page or two he begins to see the limits of the yam view of life. "Continue on the yam level and life would be sweet — though somewhat yellowish. Yet the freedom to eat yams on the street was far less than I had expected upon coming to the city. An unpleasant taste bloomed in my mouth now as I bit the end of the yam and threw it into the street; it had been frost-bitten." In the end, he typically resolves his conflict with an outrageous pun: "I yam what I yam."

This yam scene is one of several turning points at the center of the book. It is preachy — Ellison is always making his points — yet full of the sensory exuberance that gives this novel its gusto. Much of the commentary on the novel has focused on the brilliant set pieces of the first half, which can be seen a dark comic American equivalent of *The Pilgrim's Progress*. But readers have sometimes stumbled over the seemingly over-long Brotherhood sections that follow, which are clearly based on Ellison's (and Wright's) experiences with the Communist party. Yet it is only here — and in the Harlem riots that follow — that Ellison begins to pull the many threads together, bringing the novel to an exhilarating conclusion. Just as the hero must leave Mary behind, he must give up the sanctuary of the Men's House, a temple of hollow propriety and foolish dreams and ambitions. (The Men's House is Ellison's version of the Harlem Y, where he first stayed when he came to the city in 1936.) By dumping the foul contents of a cuspidor over the head of a Baptist reverend whom he takes for Bledsoe, the hero throws away the crutch that protected him from a world "without boundaries" — from Harlem and the city. If in earlier episodes he is slowly shedding illusions, only to deal with new ones immediately afterward, in this part of the novel he gradually yields to the flux as he comes to recognize and relish his own invisibility. In his own way he enacts the process of self-making described in Ellison's (and Emerson's) essays.

The narrator's growth of awareness, his willingness to go with the urban flow, is played out through metaphors, such as the images of blindness and vision that run through the whole novel: the blindfolded boys at the battle royal, the college sermon about the Founder by the blind preacher Barbee, the torn photograph of a boxer who had been blinded in the ring, and finally the glass eye of Jack, the Brotherhood leader, which pops out at an unfortunate moment and reminds us of the limits of *his* vision. In the Brotherhood, the young man learns to see beyond race, as Richard Wright did among the Communists, but he is mocked and chastized when what he sees does not fit the current line. The Brotherhood liberates him at first, introducing him to a wider world, giving him both work to do and a fully developed set of ideas, along with a sense of hope, a solidarity with others. But finally it tries, like every other institution he gets entangled with, to impose its outlook on him. The Brotherhood pretends to have a scientific grasp of history; it claims to know what Harlem needs better than Harlem itself. But this is ultimately shown up as another example of whites patronizing blacks – and of inflexible organizations stifling spontaneity and individuality.

As the novel's Epilogue makes clear, Ellison is giving us a black-accented version of the anticonformist discourse of the 1950s, the social critique of the lonely crowd and the organization man. But because he is black, the narrator is faceless in a special and vivid way. He is invisible because no one really *sees* him; the Brotherhood recruits him but does not want him to think. "You made an effective speech," they tell him. "But you mustn't waste your emotion on individuals, they don't count. . . . History has passed them by." Though they object when he makes any appeal to color, he wonders whether he is being used simply because he is black. "What was I, a man or a natural resource?"

The second half of *Invisible Man* is also closely linked to midcentury novels and memoirs about the disillusionment with Communism, including Koestler's *Darkness at Noon,* Wright's *American Hunger* (the suppressed second half of *Black Boy*), and the collective volume *The God That Failed,* which included both Koestler and Wright along with Ignazio Silone and others. Since Ellison was young and marginal to the Harlem branch of the party and Wright was famous and central to the party's work among blacks, it is fair to assume that this part of *Invisible Man* is heavily indebted to Wright's experiences, as described in both *American Hunger* and Ellison's "Remembering Richard Wright." There Ellison expresses gratitude to

Wright for his willingness to confide in him about his problems with the party, "especially his difficulty in pursuing independent thought." When the narrator is brought up on trial, the charges echo those that had been directed against Wright – that he trusts his own judgment over the party's, that he speaks *for* blacks rather than *to* them, that he is too concerned with race. *Invisible Man* goes far beyond the anti-Communist genre, however, for the narrator's disillusionment is part of a larger process of casting off misconceptions and closely exploring his own identity.

When the narrator decides that his political mentors are simply white men with yet another plan for him, he realizes that even in the Brotherhood he needs to live a double life. He learns to live within a shifting sense of who he actually is. Standing before an audience on his party assignment, decked out in a new suit and a new name, he experiences a sense of vertigo, as if caught with his identity down. He fears that he might forget his name or be recognized by someone in the audience. "I bent forward, suddenly conscious of my legs in new blue trousers. But how do you know they're your legs? . . . For it was as though I were looking at my own legs for the first time – independent objects that could of their own volition lead me to safety or danger." He feels that he is standing simultaneously at opposite ends of a tunnel, both in the old life he has left behind and in a new world that is still disturbingly vague and unformed.

This was a new phase, I realized, a new beginning, and I would have to take that part of myself that looked on with remote eyes and keep it always at the distance of the campus, the hospital machine, the battle royal – all now far behind. Perhaps the part of me that observed listlessly but saw all, missing nothing, was still the malicious, arguing part; the dissenting voice, my grandfather part; the cynical, disbelieving part – the traitor self that always threatened internal discord. Whatever it was, I knew that I'd have to keep it pressed down.

Like so much else in the novel, this at once exemplifies and parodies Emersonian notions of self-transformation. As a spokesman for the Brotherhood, the narrator is shedding his old skin, exercising his power over language and people. Yet he is also simply playing another assigned role, keeping the dissenting parts of himself "pressed down." With a flash of panic he sees that "the moment I walked out upon the platform and opened my mouth I'd be someone else." But he also senses that he would become simply a party hack with an assumed name, someone arbitrarily forced to deny his past.

Only when he puts on dark green glasses and is everywhere taken for Rinehart, the hustler and trickster, the man of many faces and roles, is he willing to step outside history, acknowledge his invisibility, and yield to the fluidity of the world around him. Both the Brotherhood and the nationalists – personified by Ras the Exhorter, with his impassioned Marcus Garveyite rhetoric of racial pride – are locked into the hard lines of history as they see it. Only Rinehart, who is everywhere and nowhere at once, can negotiate the chaos of the ghetto, the boundary-free world of modern urban identity.

Could he be all of them: Rine the runner and Rine the gambler and Rine the briber and Rine the lover and Rinehart the Reverend? Could he himself be both rind and heart? What is real anyway? . . . His world was possibility and he knew it. He was years ahead of me and I was a fool. The world in which we lived was without boundaries. A vast seething, hot world of fluidity, and Rine the rascal was at home. Perhaps *only* Rine the rascal was at home in it.

This is the novel's version of the malleable, self-fashioned identity that Ellison invokes in his essays, a way of stepping out of imposed roles or shaping them to your needs. His friend Tod Clifton, the poster boy for the Harlem Brotherhood, has turned his back on the organization and plunged out of history. In Midtown he hawks Sambo dolls, whose fine strings symbolize how he himself felt manipulated. When Tod is shot down by a policeman, the narrator must find another, less suicidal way of reclaiming his individuality. Rinehart, the man of the city, provides him with a clue. "My entire body started to itch, as though I had been removed from a plaster cast and was unused to the new freedom of movement." He sees that compared to the South, where everyone knew him, the urban world can offer him freedom. "How many days could you walk the street without encountering anyone you knew, and how many nights? You could actually make yourself anew. The notion was frightening, for now the world seemed to flow before my eyes. All boundaries down, freedom was not only the recognition of necessity, it was the recognition of possibility."

Many of the midcentury works of deradicalization convey a wounded quality, a sense of apocalyptic combat, as in Whittaker Chambers's *Witness* (1952), or a mournful sense of loss, as in much of *The God That Failed*. Many former radicals portrayed Communism as a lost or spoiled idealism, something precious they would never be able to recover. But a heady exhilaration spills over in the last hundred pages of *Invisible Man,* the thrill of a man reclaiming his own life – the food that embarrassed him, the experiences that formed him, the music "that touched upon something deeper than protest, or religion." What does the Brotherhood know of "the gin mills and the barber shops and the juke joints and the churches. . . . and the beauty parlors on Saturdays when they're frying hair. A whole unrecorded history is spoken there." For these people it was not the

Brotherhood but Rinehart, with his dodges and disguises, his endlessly resourceful maneuvers, that represented "a principle of hope, for which they gladly paid. Otherwise there was nothing but betrayal."

The narrator reasserts his solidarity with those who lie outside history, the "transitory ones": "birds of passage who were too obscure for learned classification, too silent for the most sensitive recorders of sound." As in his recognition of a world "without boundaries," Ellison, through his character, is expressing his commitment to becoming an artist, at once shaping his own identity and keeping in touch with common experience. The Brotherhood's line, like other white views of Negro life, is enjoined from above, not experienced from below. "It was all a swindle, an obscene swindle. They had set themselves up to describe the world. What did they know of us, except that we numbered so many, worked on certain jobs, offered so many votes, and provided so many marchers for some protest parade of theirs." As he recognizes how he has been used, his Dostoyevskyan sense of humiliation helps him reclaim his own experience:

I began to accept my past and, as I accepted it, I felt memories welling up within me. It was as though I'd learned suddenly to look around corners; images of past humiliations flickered through my head and I saw they were more than separate experiences. They were me; they defined me. I was my experiences and my experiences were me, and no blind men, no matter how powerful they became, even if they conquered the world, could take that, or change one single itch, taunt, laugh, cry, scar, ache, rage or pain of it.

Through images of sight and insight, he gives us what seems like the novel's actual point of origin, the writer's own germinal moment of recognition that catapults him from the blindness of politics, ideology, and sociological abstraction to a grasp of the complexity of his own experience. Suddenly, all his old mentors merge into a single figure trying to bend him to their will — an external force that must be overthrown. "I looked around a corner of my mind and saw Jack and Norton and Emerson merge into one single white figure. They were very much the same, each attempting to force his picture of reality upon me and neither giving a hoot in hell for how things looked to me. I was simply a material, a natural resource to be used." This is Ellison's declaration of independence, his personal emancipation proclamation. The thrill he feels in writing it we also feel in reading it, not least because it provides the novel with such a strong formal resolution.

Did Ellison imagine that ordinary people, especially black people, could find freedom in the same way, by recognizing that reality and identity are malleable, that they were free to create themselves? Yes, for he believed that blacks have a culture in which they already have done so. He disliked deterministic visions of entrapment like the portrait of Bigger Thomas in *Native Son* and insisted that Richard Wright, in creating Bigger, had not done justice to his own wide experience. But Ellison's emphasis was always on *imaginative* freedom within political and social *un*freedom, within limits that could be only partly transcended. Writing about *The Great Gatsby* he describes "the frustrating and illusory social mobility which forms the core of Gatsby's anguish," yet he argues that the novel's black readers could not make Gatsby's mistakes. Accepting the National Book Award for *Invisible Man,* Ellison appealed instead to the shape-changing figure of Proteus as his paradigm for coping with America's "rich diversity and its almost magical fluidity and freedom." In his essays he tells us repeatedly that the effort that creates art — that requires craft, discipline, and a mastery over reality — is the same as the process that shapes individual identity and ultimately culture itself.

In one of many discursive texts set into *Invisible Man,* the narrator remembers a literature teacher's comments on Stephen Dedalus in Joyce's *Portrait of the Artist as a Young Man*:

Stephen's problem, like ours, was not actually one of creating the uncreated conscience of his race, but of creating the *uncreated features of his face.* Our task is that of making ourselves individuals. The conscience of a race is the gift of its individuals who see, evaluate, record. . . . We create the race by creating ourselves and then to our great astonishment we will have created something far more important: We will have created a culture.

Since *Invisible Man* is in many ways modeled on Joyce, and since Joyce himself highlights the word *race,* this is an especially momentous statement of purpose. *Invisible Man* is linked not only to the postwar discourse of anti-Communism but to the closely related defense of liberal individualism and cultural pluralism in the work of such social critics as Lionel Trilling, Reinhold Niebuhr, and Arthur Schlesinger, Jr. The case Trilling makes for the complexity and inwardness of art over the simplifications of ideology is echoed by both Baldwin and Ellison, yet Ellison gives it a radical — not a conservative — edge. His arguments for the diversity of both black and American life, for a cultural rather than a strictly political approach, for discipline and self-mastery, and for an acceptance of complexity and contradiction have in recent years provided such black artists and intellectuals as Albert Murray, Toni Morrison, Michael Harper, Wynton Marsalis, James Alan McPherson, Stanley Crouch, Gerald Early, and Henry Louis Gates, Jr. with a vigorous alternative to both black nationalism and Marxism.

Powerful as Ellison's essays are, his novel is even more impressive, a veritable *Ulysses* of the black experience, rich with folklore, verbal improvisation, mythic resonance, and personal history, in his words "a raft of hope, perception and entertainment" that does justice to the variety of African American life. Though it is a novel of the civil rights years, its perspective is neither integrationist nor rights-oriented but cultural. As angry as any text of black nationalists, it charts an odyssey through a whole way of life, a study of attitudes rather than abuses, deliberately written, as he recalled much later, in a voice of "taunting laughter," in a tone "less angry than ironic." The effort to go beyond anger and ideology to discover a common core of black experience is itself ideological, for there were many fifties attempts to pass beyond ideology that also appealed to "experience." Ellison does not simply proclaim an end to ideology, however; he enacts it. He was trying to avoid writing "another novel of racial protest instead of the dramatic study in comparative humanity which I felt any worthwhile novel should be."

The novel is rich with moments that are neither wholly realistic nor wholly allegorical but an emblematic mixture of both, such as the yam-eating scene or the hero's one-man uprising at the Men's House or the splendid vision of Ras on a great black horse, dressed in the garb of an Abyssinian chieftain, with fur cap, shield, and cape ("a figure more out of dream than out of Harlem"). Ras makes great speeches, but when the narrator, defending himself, throws a spear that locks his jaws together, Ellison is doing something that few other postwar novelists could get away with — creating a charged image that is at once an event, a metaphor, and a statement. Baldwin, in "Notes of a Native Son," had looked at the Harlem riots of 1943 through the lens of his own family history; Ellison, no less effectively, makes it emblematic of all the cross-currents of African American life. In *Invisible Man,* Marcus Garvey foreshadows the Black Panthers, thirties Marxism anticipates postsixties Marxism, and a midcentury conception of America's cultural diversity proves remarkably germane to an end-of-century debate over pluralism and multiculturalism. Summing up every ideology roiling the turbulent waters of black life, Ellison wrote a great ideological novel, perhaps the single best novel of the whole postwar era, at once his own inner history and the complex paradigm of a diverse and braided culture.

PHILIP ROTH: THE PRODIGAL SON OF THE JEWS

Philip Roth is by far the youngest writer discussed in this chapter, the only one whose mind was formed by the aftermath of World War II — by patriotism, prosperity, and social mobility – not by the Depression. Born in Newark in 1933, he was a generation younger than the writers invariably linked with him, Malamud and Bellow. He grew up without their memories of poverty, without immigrant Yiddish echoing in his ears. Yet he lived in a kind of ghetto nonetheless, a lower-middle-class Jewish neighborhood, where he attended nearly all-Jewish schools. Immigration had been sharply curtailed in the 1920s, but the children of immigrants, even as they assimilated, lived in largely homogeneous neighborhoods. In short, Roth grew up in an ethnically segregated yet pervasively American world, almost a textbook example of the kind of rich subculture that Ralph Ellison celebrates in his essays. It was a hybrid culture, in which American civics lessons, sports, dating rituals, radio programs, celebrity cults, and Hollywood myths were grafted onto ethnic roots. This was a world Roth would satirize but also idealize throughout his career.

Like Ellison, Roth developed an intimate knowledge of this culture – the speech, the mores, the cast of mind of those formed by it; like Ellison, too, he makes a great point of the *"Americanness"* of his identity. "My larger boyhood society cohered around the most inherently American phenomenon at hand – the game of baseball," he writes in his memoir, *The Facts: A Novelist's Autobiography* (1988), and goes on to compare the reassuring leathery smell of his mitt to his orthodox grandfather's well-worn phylacteries. Later in the book, after years of living in a mostly gentile world, he falls in with a group of educated Jewish friends who encourage his taste for farcical improvisations out of the background they all share. They were

an audience knowledgeable enough to discern, even in the minutest detail, where reportage ended and Dada began and to enjoy the ambiguous overlap. Unembarrassed by unrefined Jewish origins, matter-of-factly confident of equal American status, they felt American *through* their families' immigrant experiences rather than in spite of them and delighted in the shameless airing of extravagant routines concocted from the life we had all grown up with.

This is Roth himself, twenty years afterward, describing how he came to write *Portnoy's Complaint* (1969), still fending off charges of vulgarity and Jewish self-hatred that had been lodged against him ever since his first stories. Roth's literary debut came with a book that was almost as controversial, *Goodbye, Columbus* (1959), a novella and five stories acclaimed in reviews by Saul Bellow, Irving Howe, and Alfred Kazin but attacked by self-anointed spokesmen for the Jewish community.

Goodbye, Columbus had few of the Dada extravagances of *Portnoy's Complaint,* but it showed a superb ear for Jewish American speech and a wicked eye for satiric detail. This Roth was a realist, a student of Henry

James, not a fabulist like Bernard Malamud and I. B. Singer or a ruminative intellectual living mostly in his own mind, like Bellow. Outside the comedians of the borscht belt, no one could convey the full flavor of a garish Jewish wedding like Roth. The title novella relies on James's technique of building a scene obliquely through dialogue and seemingly neutral description. But Roth had also learned from Mary McCarthy's sexual frankness and well-developed sense of the ridiculous, her way of accumulating lethal details to cast a cold eye on the lives of her characters. For Roth, the Patimkins are not simply a family but social specimens, suburban Jews who have not yet lost their rough edges or their roots in the ghetto. Their lives are at once comically Jewish and stereotypically American.

Because the Patimkins made a great deal of money during the war, when "no new barracks was complete until it had a squad of Patimkin sinks lined up in its latrine," they were able to move from Newark to Short Hills, though their business remains in the old Jewish neighborhood, now largely black. Roth's protagonist, Neil Klugman, is seeing their daughter Brenda, a student at Radcliffe. They also have a jock son, just graduated from Ohio State, for whom they are planning the ultimate wedding, as well as a younger daughter who is spoiled and petulant. They have tennis lessons; a country-club membership; a second refrigerator (their old one from Newark) in the finished basement, reserved for fruit; and a cornucopia of sporting goods that seems to grow on trees:

Outside, through the wide picture window, I could see the back lawn with its twin oak trees. I say oaks, though fancifully, one might call them sporting-goods trees. Beneath their branches, like fruit dropped from their limbs, were two irons, a golf ball, a tennis can, a baseball bat, basketball, a first-baseman's glove, and what was apparently a riding crop.

Seen with this kind of coldly amused precision, suburbia is the promised land of the Jews, the postwar marker of wealth, success, and acceptance. Yet the Patimkins have stored all their old furniture in the attic, either as a reminder of their origins or as something to fall back on. Neil looks at them through a poor boy's eyes, with mixed feelings of cultural superiority and class anger. He works at the Newark Public Library and lives modestly with his Aunt Gladys in the old Jewish section of Newark. As his name suggests, Neil is also something of an intellectual, a "clever man," a bit too facile in his condescension. When he mentions Buber to Mrs. Patimkin, she wants to know whether he is orthodox or conservative. He is put off by the Patimkins' materialism, for he has a social conscience, which shows in his solicitude toward a young black boy who keeps coming to the library to look at a book about Gauguin.

Still, bringing culture to the black ghetto is not exactly Neil's prime motivation. Neil wants Brenda, but a Brenda detached from the values and middle-class inhibitions of her family. When he pushes her to go to the Margaret Sanger Clinic for a diaphragm, he makes his reasons clear:

"Brenda, I want you to own one for . . . for the sake of pleasure."
"Pleasure? Whose? The doctor's?"
"Mine," I said.

When Brenda leaves the diaphragm at home, where her mother discovers it, Neil suggests that she is unconsciously siding with her parents, looking for a way to thwart him or end the affair.

"It's you who's confusing things," Brenda said. "You act as though I wanted her to find it."
I didn't answer.

"Goodbye, Columbus" is not particularly bold or frank by later standards, but for the 1950s it was a daring story; it handles sex with a combination of self-will and self-righteousness that would become central to Roth's writing. Greater sexual freedom, the growing acceptance of sex as personal gratification rather than conjugal bliss, was an integral yet controversial part of postwar culture, brought into the open by the Kinsey reports of 1948 and 1953. In *Grand Expectations,* the historian James T. Patterson attaches it to the expanding culture of consumption. Neil's condemnation of Brenda for thwarting him is a mild one, but he attacks her with unshakeable self-assurance, a sense of entitlement. When the book first appeared, it seemed surprising that anyone could indict and dismiss someone on a presumption of her *unconscious* motives. Surely this was an appalling way of using Freudian logic – to assign blame, to feel misused. This would not be the first time one would need to take a reverse angle on Roth's heroes, to look at them from the viewpoint of the accused woman. Roth's great literary gifts were always matched by glaring blind spots, especially in his treatment of women. His protagonists were prone to paranoia, self-righteousness, a mixture of overweening need and intense suspicion, and a fear of being deceived, overwhelmed, or devoured. From *Goodbye, Columbus* and *My Life as a Man* (1974) to *I Married a Communist* (1998), Roth's heros are prone to feel victimized or betrayed by the women in their lives. The same aggrieved feelings would come into play in Roth's response to his critics, especially the Jewish critics – from the rabbis and other professional Jews who, perhaps obtusely, criticized his early stories to Irving Howe, who recanted his early praise and derided Roth in a 1972 essay. More than a decade later, Roth struck back by lampooning Howe as a sleazy, fast-talking pornographer in *The Anatomy Lesson.*

Compared to the works of Malamud and Bellow, nearly twenty years his senior, Roth's fiction speaks for the second generation. For Roth and his contemporaries, the pressure to rebel against the parents, including his literary parents, is matched by an urgent need for their approval; a loving immersion in ethnic Jewishness is balanced by a boundless contempt for the ghetto's provinciality, its limited horizons. Roth's work is not all of a piece, and it passes through several different phases, but the protagonists – from Neil Klugman and Alexander Portnoy to Peter Tarnopol (in *My Life as a Man,* Nathan Zuckerman (in *The Anatomy Lesson,* 1983, and other works of the Zuckerman saga), and Mickey Sabbath (in *Sabbath's Theater,* 1995) – tend to be variations on the same figure, roughly the same age and from the same background as the author. Like so many other second-generation males working out conflicts of identity, the Rothian figure needs to escape *and* to return home, needs to transgress yet also to be recognized as the most upright man who ever lived. Portnoy himself, preaching on a text from Freud ("The Most Prevalent Form of Degradation in Erotic Life," 1912), is caught between his mother and his lovers, his memories of tenderness and his raging libido, his not very convincing work on human rights and his convincing yet tormented assertion of his own rights. He tells his analyst, Dr. Spielvogel, that he is "torn by desires that are repugnant to my conscience, and a conscience repugnant to my desires," thus reminding us how verbal he is, how prepared to overwhelm everything, including his own pain, in a torrent of words.

The Rothian hero is a man defending himself, beset and put upon, but also someone in conflict with himself, exposed and vulnerable. Roth's work arrived at a confessional moment in American literature, when the barriers of privacy and discretion had been breached, when Robert Lowell was publishing *Life Studies* and Allen Ginsberg was completing *Kaddish,* but also when sex and the body were coming out into the open, not only with the publication of banned classics by D. H. Lawrence and Henry Miller but in learned but utopian works of cultural theory such as Herbert Marcuse's *Eros and Civilization* (1955) and Norman O. Brown's *Life Against Death* (1959), with its dithyrambic coda on "The Resurrection of the Body." Well-mannered young writers like Updike and Roth were slow to pick up on this explicit treatment of sex as personal salvation, certainly slower than Norman Mailer or James Baldwin. But by the late sixties, with Updike's *Couples* and Roth's *Portnoy,* they had marched to the head of the class.

Roth was not the only one to describe his generation as prematurely mature, burdened by too great a sense of moral responsibility. Roth and

Updike wrote on the cusp between two generations in a world whose values were rapidly changing. The writers' own conflicted feelings infuse Roth's early stories and Updike's *Rabbit, Run* with an edgy creative tension. For Rabbit this takes shape as a contrast between the luminous past and the humdrum present, between duty and the need for freedom, between settling into the rut of marriage and fatherhood and intimations of something beyond, something transcendent that sex might enable him to recapture. For Portnoy this is expressed through the Freudian clash between civilization and its discontents, between the mores of the tribe and the stubborn resistance of the individual will. This conflict was what brought Roth so much grief from his Jewish critics.

Neil Klugman is equally repelled by the vulgarity of the newly rich (the Patimkins and their country-club set) and the small-mindedness of the poor (his nagging, moralistic Aunt Gladys). He looks down at everyone indiscriminately: Old World Jews have no more appeal to him than grasping suburbanites. Even his co-workers at the library are shown up as narrow, rigid pedants with no imagination and no future. But at the end he is glad to leave Brenda and return to work on the Jewish New Year, as if to show that the library is his true synagogue. Only the black boy, who elicits his sentimental sympathy for the Other, is exempt from judgment: with his wide-eyed affection for Gauguin, the boy is an island of simplicity in a sea of decadence and compromise. Like the Columbus of the title, he stands for an earlier, more innocent America, Fitzgerald's "fresh, green breast of the new world."

The other stories in *Goodbye, Columbus,* though well crafted, depend even more schematically on the author's own quarrel with the Jews. "Epstein," the most sexually explicit story, foreshadows the less buttoned-up writer Roth would eventually become. In the end, however, it is little more than a farcical anecdote about an aging Jewish businessman who develops an embarrassing rash on his private parts. Roth cruelly mocks Epstein's unappetizing wife, with her blue-veined thighs and drooping breasts. Poor Epstein reaches out for a new life by sleeping with a widowed neighbor, but this autumnal love affair is cut off by his outraged spouse, who spies what she thinks is venereal disease; by an unfeeling family that believes that sex is only for the young; and finally by an ill-timed heart attack that pulls Epstein back to the living death of his stale marriage. This is a young man's view of middle age.

Roth is as harsh on the nonconforming young of his own generation as he is mocking of the sexuality of their elders. Epstein's leftist daughter reads Howard Fast and specializes in social protest; her folksinger boyfriend shows no inclination to find a real job. Along with a visiting

nephew, they are all disgusted by the old man's behavior and become witnesses to his shame. "Epstein" is written with a touch of pathos and empathy compared to the other stories. "The Conversion of the Jews" gives us
Roth's quarrel with the Jews in a purer form. Ozzie, a boy in Hebrew
school with a name right out of the pop culture of the fifties, gets into frequent trouble by questioning his teachers. Finally, when he is inadver-
tently hit, he races up onto the roof and threatens to jump, to become a
"martyr," unless the offending party, the intolerant Rabbi Binder, and
everyone around him acknowledge that "God can make a child without
intercourse."

Ozzie is confused and amused by what is soon happening around him,
but the story itself is more deliberate. By "catechizing" the rabbi, his class-
mates, his own mother, and even the old custodian who belongs to another
generation, by forcing them to get down on their knees as they repeat after
him, Ozzie is making comedy out of some very dark moments of Jewish
history, when Jews were forced to choose between death and mass conversion. Roth identifies with the young rebel turning the tables on his sanctimonious teachers. Assimilated Jewish writers often recalled their flimsy
religious education as bigoted and narrow-minded. The *melamed* or
Hebrew teacher in Michael Gold's *Jews Without Money* (1930) was a prototype of filth, ignorance, and corporal punishment, and Rabbi Binder is his
distant, more respectable successor. Ozzie takes special pleasure in seeing
Yakov Blotnik, the mumbling custodian, "for the first time in his life
upon his knees in the Gentile posture of prayer," for he suspects the old
man "had memorized the prayers and forgotten all about God." The story
claims to speak for tolerance and nonviolence ("You should never hit anybody about God," says Ozzie), but its transparent purpose is to rub the
noses of the assembled Jews in their *in*tolerance, their lack of enlightenment within a modern, enlightened nation.

By far the most controversial story in *Goodbye, Columbus* was "Defender of
the Faith," a finely textured piece of writing that embarrassed some Jews
when it found a wide audience in the genteel pages of *The New Yorker.* It
reaches impressively outside Roth's own Newark, focusing on a Jewish
sergeant, Nathan Marx, a hero of the European war, who is repeatedly
played upon by a Jewish recruit for special privileges. When he realizes that
this man, Sheldon Grossbart, has pulled strings to keep from being shipped
off to the Pacific, Marx pulls strings of his own to make sure he *is* sent out.
The story ends with a twist of moral ambiguity as Marx realizes the enormity of what he has done. As the other recruits think nervously about their
fate, he hears Grossbart behind him, swallowing hard, accepting his. "And
then, resisting with all my will an impulse to turn and seek pardon for my

vindictiveness, I accepted my own." But this twist provides little more than protective coloration for the main theme of Roth's narrative.

The story tells how an assimilated Jew, said to be a war hero but also someone with a Jewish conscience, a man who is vulnerable to an appeal to Jewish solidarity, casts off the tribal claims made by a more stereotypical Jew – an operator, a malingerer, probably a coward. Malamud typically used such an ethnic Jew – the marriage broker, Salzman, in "The Magic Barrel," Susskind in "The Last Mohican" – to show up the limitations of the more deracinated Jew: the confusions of identity, the pallid intellectuality. Roth does exactly the opposite: to him the challenge for the assimilated Jew is to fend off any appeal to ethnic kinship, even at some cost to his conscience.

Despite his name ("big beard"), there is nothing spiritual about Grossbart, nothing but manipulation and grubby self-interest. "Stop whining," Marx keeps telling him, "stand on your own two feet, Sheldon," as the man draws him into an intimacy he resists and dislikes. Nathan Marx, whose name combines the universalism of Lessing's Nathan the Wise and Karl Marx, is the real defender of the faith, not the faith of the Jews but of the Enlightenment, as embodied in the colorblind meritocracy of America and its citizen army. "The young man had managed to confuse himself as to what my faith really was," he says of one of Grossbart's friends, a soldier whose glasses give him "the appearance of an old peddler who would gladly have sold you the rifle and cartridges that were slung all over him." (In such later novels as *The Counterlife* [1987] and *Operation Shylock* [1993], Roth would become even more explicit in defending "diasporism" against the tribal claims of Zionists.)

American isolationists in the 1940s contended that the war was being fought for the Jews, was incited by the Jews, yet Jewish boys would somehow manage to avoid fighting it. Nathan Marx, of course, belies this canard, but we must take it on faith – his heroic combat days are over before the story begins. But the devious Sheldon Grossbart seems to confirm the libel, just as Portnoy fleshes out the caricature of the lustful Jew defiling WASP womanhood. Indeed, *Portnoy's Complaint* picks up Roth's quarrel with his people where *Goodbye, Columbus* leaves off. Roth's response to his Jewish critics in such essays as "Writing About Jews" (1963) and "Imagining Jews" (1974) – both collected in *Reading Myself and Others* (1975) – is that these types really exist, that Jews are unduly sensitive to criticism, and, finally, that previous Jewish writers, especially Malamud and Bellow, had erred in the opposite direction, portraying Jews as *too* spiritual, too asexual, too moral – always as victims rather than agents, never as the victimizers they can also become.

Implying that America has essentially solved the problem of anti-Semitism, Roth insists that since Jews are no longer threatened, they can be less sensitive about their image and give up their "timidity – and paranoia" (a curious argument from someone who would later grow so sensitive to criticism). He maintains that Jews must unlearn ghetto habits of fear, deference, and self-restraint that made sense only when their lives and welfare were in danger. This is very close to the theme of *Invisible Man,* as Roth himself acknowledges. Ellison's book shows us how the protagonist gradually emancipates himself from deference, from an eagerness to ingratiate himself, which is another version of the ghetto mentality. Yet by the late sixties, Roth's hero had as much Grossbart as Marx in him: his fiction turned more vulgar and ethnic, and "Imagining Jews" shifts this defense in a subtler direction. Malamud and Bellow, he says, consistently identify their Jewish characters, such as those in *The Assistant, The Magic Barrel,* and *The Victim,* with renunciation and self-abnegation, while saving appetite and self-will for non-Jewish characters like Henderson or Frank Alpine or more Americanized Jews, like the Chicago-born Augie March. Put more succinctly in *Portnoy's Complaint,* Roth's goal is to "put the Id back in Yid," to create the willful, transgressive Jewish protagonist of a new generation, transcending old fears and moral scruples of the ghetto.

Despite a remarkable continuity in Roth's work through four decades, the 1960s reshaped his fiction in decisive ways. It brought out the figure of the sexual outlaw already implied by the desperate Epstein and the sanctimonious Neil Klugman. His first two novels, *Letting Go* (1962) and *When She Was Good* (1967), still written under the sign of Henry James, were perfectly readable but unspeakably grim. The entanglements of their characters made the books seem aimless and shapeless. Their textured realism could do but scant justice to the spectacle Roth was seeing all around him, the carnival Tom Wolfe describes in his early journalism, the political confrontations Mailer describes in *his* journalism, the sight of a whole culture actually letting go. Though *Portnoy* became one of the literary milestones of the sexual revolution, Roth repeatedly cited other sources: the inspired mimicry of stand-up routines that took him back to his Jewish childhood, the heated atmosphere and satiric rage stirred up by the Vietnam War, and even his first wife's wild fabrications and "lunatic imagination," which

rendered absolutely ridiculous my conventional university conceptions of fictional probability and all those elegant Jamesian formulations I'd imbibed about proportion and indirection and tact. . . . Without doubt she was my worst enemy ever, but, alas, she was nothing less than the greatest creative-writing teacher of them all, specialist par excellence in the aesthetics of extremist fiction.

This last point may be little more than a piece of creative invention, a small appendage to *My Life as a Man,* with its frantic account of his unhappy marriage; the links to *Portnoy* seem questionable. Superficially, *Portnoy* seems to reflect the new sexual freedom that really took off with the licensing of the first contraceptive pill in 1960. But despite its confessional frankness and wild, unihibited vaudevillean tone, it is less about transgression than about Portnoy's inability to transgress. At war with the Jewish superego, the old incubus of morality, *Portnoy* is as much about guilt as about sex. If Malamud made a specialty of Jewish suffering, Roth's characters suffer from their failure to live, to be spontaneous; from their conflict between conscience and desire. "This is my life, my only life," Portnoy tells his analyst, "and I'm living it in the middle of a Jewish joke. . . . Is this the Jewish suffering I used to hear so much about?" He complains that he cannot smoke, drink, do drugs, borrow money, or even play cards. "Sure I say *fuck* a lot, but I assure you, that's about the sum of my success with transgressing." Even at fourteen Portnoy recalls being sick to death of the "saga of *his people* . . . sucking and sucking on that sour grape of a religion! Jew Jew Jew Jew Jew Jew!" He is fed up with the pompous rabbi who enunciates every syllable. "It is coming out of my ears already, the saga of the suffering Jews. Do me a favor, my people, and stick your suffering heritage up your suffering ass." Yet what is Portnoy but a suffering Jew, whining up a verbal storm, feeling the pangs of liberation as his forebears suffered the traumas of repression?

The uninhibited freedom that Portnoy cannot quite realize in his behavior he achieves in his language, ranting against Jews and gentiles alike, caricaturing his parents, railing against women, and giving an epic account of his youthful feats of masturbation. *Portnoy's Complaint* is a series of set pieces that remain wonderfully funny when they deal with family, childhood, and masturbation but turn dark and self-lacerating in the portrayal of his adult life. Few readers recall the last third of the novel, which grows quite ugly in Portnoy's frantic vituperation against *goyim* and women, anticipating the sense of grievance and bitter disappointment that dominates later books like *My Life as a Man, The Anatomy Lesson,* and *Sabbath's Theater.*

Irving Howe suggested in 1972 that "the cruelest thing anyone can do with *Portnoy's Complaint* is to read it twice," but the funny parts of the book, with their wonderful range of voices – the parents, their ass-licking son, the pompous rabbi, the horny teenagers – hold up very well, like great radio sketches. As an analytic patient, Portnoy does his stand-up routines lying down, but his rolling riffs and wild exaggerations never lose touch with reality. Ten years earlier, Roth had interrupted the wedding

220

LEOPARDS IN THE TEMPLE

scene in "Goodbye, Columbus" with a long monologue by Mr. Patimkin's less successful brother, Leo, the kind of sad sack other Jewish writers might have put at the center of the story. Roth uses him only as a momentary foil to his brother's family, to the Jews who have made it, but his voice, his muted self-pity, his coarseness and wistfulness, seem absolutely authentic, certainly more authentic than Neil's own narration, which reaches us through a filter of irony and literary decorum. Though Portnoy may be Neil ten years later, his voice is enlivened by the mimicry and pathos, the shifting kaleidoscope of emotions, that we heard from poor Leo but never from Neil himself.

Sometimes Portnoy's mimicry can seem like virtuosity for its own sake, more Woody Allen than Céline, as in his send-up of his parents, the same mother and father he used to keep in stitches with his "imitations." ("I used to leave them in the aisles at mealtime — my mother once actually wet her pants, Doctor, and had to go running in hysterical laughter to the bathroom from my imitation of Mister Kitzel on 'The Jack Benny Show'.") His voice can sound whiny and crude, out of a perverse need to shock and disturb us, but it can also be rich and complex in its shifting emotional tones, especially in his warm memories of a childhood that remained the real anchor of his life, though also perhaps the source of his later despair. (Later, in *American Pastoral*, it was precisely Roth's idealization of the postwar world of 1949 that led him to give so grim a picture of 1969, the same year *Portnoy* appeared.)

Portnoy is grounded not in kinky sex but in Proustian recollections of childhood and youth, as in this description of the *shvitz* or steam bath to which his father would take him:

The moment he pushes open the door the place speaks to me of prehistoric times, earlier even than the era of the cavemen and lake dwellers that I have studied in school, a time when above the oozing bog that was the earth, swirling white gasses choked out the sunlight, and aeons passed while the planet was drained for Man. I lose touch instantaneously with that ass-licking little boy who runs home after school with A's in his hand, the little over-earnest innocent endlessly in search of the key to that unfathomable mystery, his mother's approbation, and am back in some sloppy watery time, before there were families such as we know them, before there were toilets and tragedies such as we know them, a time of amphibious creatures, plunging brainless hulking things, with wet meaty flanks and steaming torsos.

This prose is the kind of rich supple instrument that, starting with *The Ghost Writer,* would transform Roth's later work from vivid caricature to subtle sensory evocation. When he was not working up routines about his histrionic mother, about fucking the family's dinner, about his Jewish nose, or about his penis falling off, Roth, like Norman Mailer during the same period, was beginning to explore how a language closer to speech could accommodate new resources of metaphor and syntax. Yet it is a literary language, not Ellison's vernacular, with complex sentences that grow musical and fluent when they deal with the remembered past. Though Roth's writing never became as baroque as Mailer's new style, it developed shades and resonances that paved the way for his experiments in metafiction and autobiography in the 1980s and 1990s. In a sense this complex style, with its self-conscious metaphors and its concern with perspective, grew out of Roth's old apprenticeship to Henry James.

It is significant that this long passage evokes the primeval world of the fathers against the cultural aspirations, the "good" behavior, the need for approval, which he associates with the mother. A matching passage near the end of the book recalls the baseball games of his childhood, in which the men of the neighborhood seemed to be showing him the only life he would ever need to know, the sweat-filled, rough-hewn world of ordinary Jewish males, muscular, gamy, and profane with insult and ridicule. What a contrast to the narcissism of his adult life, he thinks, "*Oh,* so alone! Nothing but *self!* Locked up in *me!*" It is not only free of punishing self-consciousness but it is a world without gentiles, a world without women, especially the gentile women he pursues so urgently, with such disastrous results. At the Turkish bath, pounding and punishing their flesh, purging themselves of the cares of their daily lives, "they appear, at long last, my father and his fellow sufferers, to have returned to the habitat in which they can be natural. A place without *goyim* and women."

These are Portnoy's fantasies as well as his memories, especially his fantasy of not becoming the person he is, not having the problems with women he has always had. Roth's tone is too subtle to allow for any simple reading. But these passages add to one's feeling that the key figure in the book is the stoical, eternally constipated father rather than the cartoonish, overbearing mother. This helps explain why, in sharp contrast to the mocking fury of Roth's early books, his later works would devote their most evocative prose to father figures (in *The Ghost Writer* and *I Married a Communist*) or to his actual father, by then old and dying (in *The Facts* and *Patrimony,* 1991). A blistering hostility toward both women and *goyim* disfigures the second half of *Portnoy's Complaint.* He lampoons the *shikses* and their families for their holiday customs, their repressed emotions, their physical beauty, their dignity. Yet to him "these people are the *Americans,* Doctor. . . . these blond-haired Christians are the legitimate residents and owners of this place." They represent the infinitely desirable, infinitely detestable Other, and Portnoy pines for their acceptance even as he longs to exact his vengeance.

The young Portnoy's mute attraction to the gentile girls across the lake, whom he sees ice-skating, is his attraction to America, the world of Henry Aldrich and Oogie Pringle that he knows from the movies and the radio. This is his desire simply to be ordinary, to belong. At thirteen, "skating behind the puffy red earmuffs and the fluttering yellow ringlets of a strange *shikse* teaches me the meaning of the word *longing*. . . . I learn the meaning of the word *pang*." Despite the irony and self-mockery that mingle with this longing, the overall effect is poignant. But Portnoy sniffing around the home of his first college girlfriend is a less attractive sight, for the scene is distorted by the venom and craving of the outsider. Later, he dumps her without warning. His affair with a blond New England WASP whom he dubs "The Pilgrim" is even less edifying. Getting her to suck his cock becomes the mission of his life, his way of bringing down the whole Social Register. In a more genial moment, he confesses to his doctor that "I don't seem to stick my dick up these girls, as much as I stick it up their backgrounds – as though through fucking I will discover America. *Conquer* America – maybe that's more like it."

In contrast to the ambiguous lure of such women, which is sensual yet also social, the world of the father is the solid, reassuring world of the Jewish family. "I naively believed as a child that I would always have a father present," Roth writes in *The Facts*, "and the truth seems to be that I always will." To be reconciled at last with the father, to play the role of the loving and successful Jewish son, is also "to become the hero one's father failed to be." Part of Roth still recoils from this belated return to the fold. Getting the last word in *The Facts*, Roth's transgressive alter ego, Nathan Zuckerman, denounces him for taking "a tone of reconciliation that strikes me as suspiciously unsubstantiated," and for trying to show "that your parents had a good son who loved them." He blames this not simply on the impulse to seem good, to look moral, but on Roth's "separating the facts from the imagination and emptying them of their potential dramatic energy." As devil's advocate he urges him not even to publish this memoir, which Roth is said to have written for therapeutic reasons while recovering from a breakdown. In this internal dialogue, Zuckerman refuses to see that the good-boy side of Roth – the man as devoted to his parents as he is to the Jews – is as vital to him as the side that Zuckerman usually embodies. The moral outlaw in Roth always longs for acceptance, even as he wants to shock and outrage.

Zuckerman's intervention is part of Roth's long campaign against reading his fiction as a transcription of his life, a campaign that began with *My Life as a Man* and went into high gear with the alternate narratives of *The Counterlife* and the interplay of memoir and commentary in *The Facts*.

Having been accused of the sin of confessional writing, of simply *being* his characters, unable to invent anything, he was determined to show how he embroidered his memories with dramatic projections and richly imagined alternatives. This led him belatedly into the company of such postmodernists as John Barth, Donald Barthelme, Robert Coover, and Thomas Pynchon, who were examining the premises of fiction while wondering how it could ever get written. If the chapters of *The Counterlife* read like alternate versions of the same story, the full title of his memoir, *The Facts: A Novelist's Autobiography*, plays on the ambiguous relationship between memory and imagination. Although Roth can be accused of being obsessed by his critics – his books are full of characters who tell him, quite sensibly, to let it go – his need to defend himself eventually led him onto new fictional terrain, risky, probing, and analytical, with subtle and ingenious variations that are also deeply felt. Like other postmodernists, his best imaginative flights were fueled by paranoia. His books turned insecurity into art.

Portnoy's Complaint made Roth rich and famous even as it summarized one side of the extremist fiction of the fifties and sixties. The civil rights movement, the growing youth culture, the campus uprisings and urban riots, the stealthy escalation of the Vietnam War, the new sexual freedom both among the young and in the suburbs, the spread of feel-good drugs like marijuana and hallucinogens like LSD, the growing impact of rock music, and the new ethos of the counterculture divided Americans along new lines and altered their private as well as their public life. Television amplified everything, from the look of the counterculture and the high jinks of the young to the racial conflicts of the South and the horrors of the Vietnam War. The official accounts of the war were far different from what people already knew. Americans felt lied to and manipulated, and this undermined their traditional respect for authority, even their sense of reality. All this was reflected in American fiction as obliquely as the Holocaust and the bomb had been assimilated a generation earlier. Already in 1961 Roth had complained that fiction as he knew it could hardly equal the American reality, which was more bizarre and extreme than anything a writer could credibly invent. As the decade went on, writers increasingly lost confidence that conventional fiction could do justice to what was unfolding before them. In this frustration at having to compete with the daily news, they turned from fiction to journalism, or from fifties realism to black humor. American fiction grew paranoid and apocalyptic, finding new combinations for outrageous comedy and unmitigated horror.

Reflecting the new challenge to authority yet seeking new ground from which to write, journalists, novelists, and poets found an anchor in the first person, as Salinger and the Beats had done before them, as Whitman,

Thoreau, and Emily Dickinson had done before them. Life imitated art as the countercultural young took on the spirit of the books they admired, such as *The Catcher in the Rye, Catch-22, On the Road,* and *One Flew Over the Cuckoo's Nest.* The antinomian mood of American letters revived as part of the new culture of carnival, youthful rebellion, political protest, and anxious moral witness. Roth's work, which had begun in the rebellion of American sons against immigrant fathers, found its place as part of the larger uproar in American life, which became a new conflict of generations.

Roth had found a new voice in *Portnoy's Complaint,* but he was not sure how to use it. The book "determined every important choice I made during the next decade," he says in *The Facts.* It rekindled the hostility of his Jewish critics, fueling Roth's own sense of grievance, which would later become central to the trilogy of novels he called *Zuckerman Bound* (1979–85), where Nathan Zuckerman, the author of some controversial stories and one scandalous novel, muses endlessly on the injuries that women, critics, and other insensitive readers have inflicted on him. In the decade between *Portnoy* and the first of these books, *The Ghost Writer,* Roth seemed genuinely lost. His satire on Nixon, *Our Gang* (1971), ran out of steam after the first chapter. *The Breast* (1972) and *The Great American Novel* (1973) were completely misconceived. *The Professor of Desire* (1977) was simply a feeble retread of *Portnoy,* with some swipes at his critics. His self-absorption lost its comic edge.

Only *My Life as a Man,* his almost incredible account of his first marriage, has some of the great confessional energy of *Portnoy,* besides being his first venture into telling a story analytically, through multiple perspectives. Unfortunately, these do not include any credible effort to explore the viewpoint of the outrageous wife, as the irrepressible Zuckerman points out after Roth retells the same story in *The Facts.* "If you want to reminisce productively," says Roth's alter ego, "maybe what you should be writing, instead of autobiography, are thirty thousand words from Josie's point of view. *My Life as a Woman. My Life as a Woman with That Man.*"

Roth had never been the kind of writer who could project himself imaginatively into another point of view, especially that of his "worst enemy ever." Roth's conflicts come to a head in the frantic pages of *The Anatomy Lesson,* where he even makes a plausible case for giving up writing. The confessional mode, he feels, has run out of steam for him, turned into navel gazing – his bad back, his reviewers, what next? "Fiction about losing my hair? I can't face it. Anybody's hair but mine." "Either there was no existence left to decipher or he was without sufficient imaginative power to convert into his fiction of seeming self-exposure what existence had now become. . . . He could no longer pretend to be anyone else." From this clumsy beginning, however, Roth makes his problem his subject. By the mid-1980s he developed a dialogue around it, which contributed to the intellectual density, the sheer intelligence of his late work. Such books as *The Counterlife, The Facts, Operation Shylock,* and *Sabbath's Theater* bring the critical debate about his work into the work itself. In an ingenious moment at the end of *The Counterlife,* the protagonist's wife withdraws from the novel, tired of being reduced to one of the "fictive propositions" in his "argumentative books." Roth's motive for this play on fact and fiction may be defensive, but he seems genuinely puzzled by the man he was, the writer he became, the way he was seen. He brought the spirit of the essay, the spirit of intellectual dialogue, into his fiction. As a novelist of ideas, he came to rival Bellow himself.

Belying Fitzgerald's dictum that there are no second acts in American lives, Roth managed to reinvent himself in every decade. *The Ghost Writer* freed him from the need to be outrageous, just as *Portnoy,* ten years earlier, had freed him from the need to be decorous. *The Counterlife,* in turn, liberated Nathan Zuckerman from his exclusive concern with himself, giving him both a wider historical purview (in the sections set in England and Israel) and a set of alternative lives. With the idea of the "counterlife" – the life you imagine rather than the life you live – the book became a meditation on fiction that assuaged both the voices of his critics and his own need for vindication. Soon literary honors flowed his way, his first since *Goodbye, Columbus,* and Jewish honors as well, as Roth was welcomed back like the prodigal son who had finally returned to the fold. *The Ghost Writer* was an especially important breakthrough. Roth's sense of injury still burned in the book, but Zuckerman also manages to look back benignly at the mentors of his early years, including Malamud and Bellow, and even at the Jewish iconography represented by Anne Frank and the Holocaust. This side of the book is not only mellow, it is magically evocative. The richly detailed treatment of the older writers eventually became the warm filial tone of *Patrimony,* and soon Roth was almost a beloved elder statesman of Jewish and American letters. As if unsettled by all this acceptance, Roth turned around in *Sabbath's Theater* (1995) and published the ugliest, most deliberately offensive book he had ever written.

Perhaps a product of the health problems and emotional crises that Roth passed through in the late eighties and early nineties, *Sabbath's Theater* reads like a work of profound self-loathing. After the mellow books that preceded it, Roth returns with a vengeance to the Theater of Cruelty, the need to shock. The book is a bitter retrospective on a career as a transgressive artist, and it smells of panic and hatred in the face of aging and dying. Roth had written in *The Facts* of helping his father as he is "trying to die. . . . [T]hat's his job now and, fight as he will to survive, he understands, as he always has, what the real work is." *Patrimony* was a quietly authentic account of how that work was done, almost an act of restitution on Roth's part. Mickey Sabbath's "real work" is also to die; he fails, but along the way he manages to make everyone in his life as miserable as he is.

Sabbath's life is an inspired metaphor for the dark side of Roth's career, as well as a belated eulogy for the transgressive moment in American art in the 1960s. This was when Sabbath had his brief moment of glory, doing street theater with finger puppets that tested the boundaries of both art and propriety. At Sabbath's theater, "the atmosphere was insinuatingly anti-moral, vaguely menacing, and at the same time, rascally fun." Sabbath had also worked with live actors, especially his first wife, but felt that their real personalities created an intrusive human presence that diminished the purity of his art. The puppets, on the other hand, offer him perfect control, the kind a novelist has, as compared to a dramatist.

Part of the metaphor is Sabbath's lewd use of his fingers, which not only control the puppets but give their own little performance to entice members of the audience. Sabbath's story is one long bout of sexual excess and compulsion, beginning with the whores who initiate him as a teenage sailor in South American ports and finally grinding down, some fifty years later, as he jerks off into the panties of an old friend's daughter. Sabbath's married but insatiable Croatian mistress is a female version of himself, with a "great taste for the impermissible," and she talks compulsively about the performance of her other lovers. But she dies early in the novel, and this begins to close the book on the frenzied sexuality that long ago took the place of his art. Sabbath's agile fingers are now crippled by arthritis. Fired years earlier from a teaching job for seducing a student, dependent for money on a wife he despises, he vents his grief and fury in the cemetery after dark, keening for his mistress and pissing on her grave.

Fearing revenge from her policeman son, Sabbath flees their small New England town and returns to New York, the scene of his short-lived fame thirty years earlier. Sabbath's days in New York, living on the kindness of friends, are one long attempt to hit bottom. He does all he can to degrade himself yet to remain somehow unbowed, to live the last of his days as defiantly, as outrageously, as he had lived in his prime. His friend tells him that he is a relic of an earlier era, someone who is "kept fresh by means of anarchic provocation": "Isn't it tiresome in 1994, this role of rebel-hero? What an odd time to be thinking of sex as rebellion. . . . [Y]ou persist in quarreling with society as though Eisenhower is president!" Now the street performers of Sabbath's day have been replaced by homeless bums and beggars, the puppets of his Indecent Theater by warm, childlike Muppets. Briefly,

Sabbath too turns panhandler, begging on the subway, searching for another way to degrade himself and thus to savor a new experience.

Looking back over his life, Sabbath regrets not his provocations but his timidity, his meekness. Roth gives Sabbath's memories a testamentary quality, a tone of ultimate defiance. "To everyone he had ever horrified, to the appalled who'd considered him a dangerous man, loathsome, degenerate, and gross, he cried, 'Not at all! My failure is failing to have gone far *enough!* My failure is not having gone *further!*'" Sabbath had lived the life of the artist-hero but had actually produced little. "He'd paid the full price for art, only he hadn't made any. He'd suffered all the old-fashioned artistic sufferings – isolation, poverty, despair, mental and physical obstruction – and nobody knew or cared. . . . He was just someone who had grown ugly, old, and embittered, one of billions." But Sabbath's disappointment, his debasement, his very anonymity are meant to give his plight a more universal quality. He hears his late mother saying to him, "This is human life. There is a great hurt that everyone has to endure." Clearly this is the key line of the book, which is a work of great pain but also immense self-pity.

The novel's epigraph is from *The Tempest* – Prospero's valediction, "Every third thought shall be my grave" – but its atmosphere comes straight out of *King Lear*; it is the story of an old man raving and raging against life. The last pages are close to unbearable as Sabbath, wearing both a yarmulke and an American flag, returns to his mistress's grave in the hope that her son will kill him, for he has been repeatedly defiling it. All passion spent, he will stage his suicide as a final joke, his last piece of entertainment. "He had not realized how very long he'd been longing to be put to death. He hadn't committed suicide, because he was waiting to be murdered." But the policeman-son refuses to play the role assigned to him, and simply dumps him on the road, the figure of the Wandering Jew who cannot die, an Ancient Mariner living under the sign of Cain. "How could he leave? How could he go? Everything he hated was here." This is how the book ends.

In its fierce antinomian energy yet its sense of devolution and disintegration, *Sabbath's Theater* may or may not have been Roth's momentary retrospective on his career. It raised his battles with his critics to a level of cosmic principle. It resurrected the romantic image of the scorned and embattled artist while highlighting its futility. In the end Sabbath wonders,

What had happened to his entire conception of life? It had cost him dearly to clear a space where he could exist in the world as antagonistically as he liked. Where was the contempt with which he had overridden their hatred; where were the laws, the code of conduct, by which he had labored to be free from their stupidly harmonious expectations?

It would be absurd to identify Sabbath with Roth but equally absurd not to see him as a projection of Roth. *Sabbath's Theater* is an ugly, brilliant book, a dark, paranoid book, an execration in the face of critics who had long since stopped criticizing, a gauntlet thrown down to feminists who had long since stopped caring. If Ellison's work, after taking us through every kind of emotional and ideological excess, represents the ultimate victory of moderation, the triumph of the center, *Sabbath's Theater* brings us back to the old apocalyptic fury. With its deliberate evocation of a fragile moment of transgressive art, now thirty years passed, it can also be seen as the last novel of the 1960s, combining the frantically beleaguered hero of *Herzog* with the surreal fantasies of *An American Dream* and the sexual and verbal excess of *Portnoy*. It is hard to say why Jewish writers were led to produce such works of masculine megalomania and self-pity, but it is easy to see how they answered to the intoxicated spirit of the moment. For "the new mutants" of the counterculture, as Leslie Fiedler called them in 1965, gender differences were beginning to break down, but not for Bellow, Mailer, and Roth, who were writers at the barricades of the gender wars as well as the culture wars. Their novels of the 1960s obliquely refracted the anxieties and confrontations of the era, to which *Sabbath's Theater* would come as an immense, angry footnote.

BIBLIOGRAPHY

INDEX

BIBLIOGRAPHY

Note: This select bibliography does not list primary texts, separate articles, or critical studies of individual writers. It does include broad historical accounts of the period, general studies of postwar fiction, useful collections of reviews by individual critics, essay collections by the writers themselves, especially those in which they comment on themselves or their contemporaries, and biographies that have added substantially to what we know about these writers' careers, including a few that arrived too late for me to use in this book.

Aldridge, John W. *After the Lost Generation: A Critical Study of the Writers of Two Wars.* New York: McGraw-Hill, 1951.

Allen, Frederick Lewis. *The Big Change: America Transforms Itself, 1900–1950.* New York: Harper and Brothers, 1952.

Atlas, James. *Bellow: A Biography.* New York: Random House, 2000.

Bates, Milton J. *The Wars We Took to Vietnam: Cultural Conflict and Storytelling.* Berkeley: University of California Press, 1996.

Baumbach, Jonathan. *The Landscape of Nightmare.* New York: New York University Press, 1965.

Bawer, Bruce. *Diminishing Fictions: Essays on the Modern American Novel and Its Critics.* Saint Paul, Minn.: Graywolf Press, 1988.

Barone, Michael. *Our Country: The Shaping of America from Roosevelt to Reagan.* New York: The Free Press, 1990.

Barth, John. *The Friday Book: Essays and Other Nonfiction.* New York: G. P. Putnam's Sons, 1984.

Belgrad, Daniel. *The Culture of Spontaneity: Improvisation and the Arts in Postwar America.* Chicago: University of Chicago Press, 1998.

Biskind, Peter. *Seeing Is Believing: How Hollywood Taught Us to Stop Worrying and Love the Fifties.* New York: Pantheon, 1983.

Bone, Robert A. *The Negro Novel in America.* New Haven: Yale University Press, 1965.

Boyd, Brian. *Vladimir Nabokov: The American Years.* Princeton, N.J.: Princeton University Press: 1991.

Boyer, Paul. *By the Bomb's Early Light: American Thought and Culture at the Dawn of the Atomic Age.* New York: Pantheon, 1985.

Campbell, James. *Talking at the Gates: A Life of James Baldwin.* New York: Viking, 1991.

Caute, David. *The Great Fear: The Anti-Communist Purge under Truman and Eisenhower.* New York: Simon and Schuster, 1978.

Chafe, William H. *The Unfinished Journey: America since World War II.* New York: Oxford University Press, 1986.

Charters, Ann. *Kerouac: A Biography.* San Francisco: Straight Arrow, 1973.

Cheever, Susan. *Home before Dark.* Boston: Houghton Mifflin, 1984.

Clarke, Gerald. *Capote: A Biography.* New York: Simon and Schuster, 1988.

Cowley, Malcolm. *The Flower and the Leaf: A Contemporary Record of American Writing since 1941.* Ed. Donald W. Faulkner. New York: Viking, 1985.

———. *The Literary Situation.* New York: Viking, 1954.

Crossman, Richard, ed. *The God That Failed.* New York: Harper, 1950.

Dearborn, Mary V. *Mailer: A Biography.* Boston: Houghton Mifflin, 1999.

Deveaux, Scott. *The Birth of Bebop: A Social and Musical History.* Berkeley: University of California Press, 1997.

Dickstein, Morris. *Gates of Eden: American Culture in the Sixties.* Cambridge, Mass.: Harvard University Press, 1997.

Diggins, John Patrick. *The Proud Decades: America in War and Peace, 1941–1960.* New York: W. W. Norton, 1988.

Donaldson, Scott. *John Cheever: A Biography.* New York: Random House, 1988.

Eisinger, Chester E. *Fiction of the Forties.* Chicago: University of Chicago Press, 1963.

Ellison, Ralph. *The Collected Essays of Ralph Ellison.* Ed. John F. Callahan. New York: The Modern Library, 1995.

Fiedler, Leslie. *Collected Essays,* 2 vols. New York: Stein and Day, 1971.

———. *Love and Death in the American Novel.* New York: Stein and Day, 1966.

Fishman, Robert. *Bourgeois Utopias: The Rise and Fall of Suburbia.* New York: Basic Books, 1987.

Foreman, Joel, ed. *The Other Fifties: Interrogating Midcentury American Icons.* Urbana: University of Illinois Press, 1997.

Friedan, Betty. *The Feminine Mystique.* New York: Dell, 1975.

Giddins, Gary. *Visions of Jazz: The First Century.* New York: Oxford University Press, 1998.

Gilbert, James B. *Another Chance: Postwar America, 1945–1968.* Philadelphia: Temple University Press, 1981.

———. *A Cycle of Outrage: America's Reaction to the Juvenile Delinquent in the 1950s.* New York: Oxford University Press, 1986.

Goldman, Eric F. *The Crucial Decade—and After: America, 1945–1960.* New York: Vintage Books, 1960.

Goodman, Paul. *Growing Up Absurd: Problems of Youth in the Organized Society.* New York: Random House, 1960.

Goulden, Joseph C. *The Best Years, 1945–1950.* New York: Atheneum, 1976.

Graebner, William. *The Age of Doubt: American Thought and Culture in the 1940s.* Boston: Twayne Publishers, 1991.

Green, Michelle. *The Dream at the End of the World: Paul Bowles and the Literary Renegades in Tangier.* New York: HarperCollins, 1991.

Guilbaut, Serge. *How New York Stole the Idea of Modern Art: Abstract Expressionism, Freedom, and the Cold War.* Trans. Arthur Goldhammer. Chicago: University of Chicago Press, 1983.

Guttmann, Allen. *The Jewish Writer in America: Assimilation and the Crisis of Identity.* New York: Oxford University Press, 1971.

Hamilton, Ian. *In Search of J. D. Salinger.* New York: Random House, 1988.

Hassan, Ihab. *Radical Innocence: The Contemporary American Novel.* Princeton, N.J.: Princeton University Press, 1961.

Hendin, Josephine. *Vulnerable People: A View of American Fiction since 1945.* New York: Oxford University Press, 1978.

Hodgson, Godfrey. *America in Our Time.* Garden City, N.Y.: Doubleday, 1976.

Howe, Irving. *Celebrations and Attacks: Thirty Years of Literary and Cultural Commentary.* New York: Harcourt Brace Jovanovich, 1980.

———. *The Critical Point: On Literature and Culture.* New York: Horizon Press, 1973.

———. *Decline of the New.* New York: Horizon Press, 1970.

Hoffman, Daniel, ed. *Harvard Guide to Contemporary American Writing.* Cambridge, Mass.: Harvard University Press, 1979.

Hughes, Robert. *American Visions: The Epic History of Art in America.* New York: Alfred A. Knopf, 1997.

Hyman, Stanley Edgar. *Standards: A Chronicle of Books for Our Time.* New York: Horizon Press, 1966.

Jackson, Kenneth T. *Crabgrass Frontier: The Suburbanization of the United States.* New York: Oxford University Press, 1985.

Jezer, Marty. *The Dark Ages: Life in the United States, 1945–1960.* Boston: South End Press, 1982.

Jones, James. *WWII.* New York: Ballantine Books, 1975.

Jones, Peter G. *War and the Novelist: Appraising the American War Novel.* Columbia, Mo.: University of Missouri Press, 1976.

Kaplan, Fred. *Gore Vidal: A Biography.* New York: Doubleday, 1999.

Karl, Frederick R. *American Fictions, 1940–1980: A Comprehensive History and Critical Evaluation.* New York: Harper and Row, 1983.

Kazin, Alfred. *Contemporaries.* Boston: Atlantic-Little, Brown, 1962.

———. *Bright Book of Life: American Novelists and Storytellers from Hemingway to Mailer.* Boston: Atlantic-Little, Brown, 1973.

Kerouac, Jack. *Selected Letters, 1940–1956.* Ed. Ann Charters. New York: Viking, 1995.

Klein, Marcus. *After Alienation: American Novels in Mid-Century.* Chicago: University of Chicago Press, 1978.

———. ed. *The American Novel since World War II.* New York: Fawcett, 1969.

Koppes, Clayton R., and Gregory D. Black. *Hollywood Goes to War: How Politics, Profits, and Propaganda Shaped World War II Movies.* Berkeley: University of California Press, 1990.

Leeming, David. *James Baldwin: A Biography*. New York: Alfred A. Knopf, 1994.

Leuchtenburg, William E. *A Troubled Feast: American Society since 1945*. Boston: Little, Brown, 1973.

Leverich, Lyle. *Tom: The Unknown Tennessee Williams*. New York: Crown, 1995.

Lhamon, W. T., Jr. *Deliberate Speed: The Origins of a Cultural Style in the American 1950s*. Washington: Smithsonian Institution Press, 1990.

Limon, John. *Writing after War: American War Fiction from Realism to Postmodernism*. New York: Oxford University Press, 1994.

Lingeman, Richard. *Don't You Know There's a War On?: The American Home Front, 1941–1945*. New York: G. P. Putnam's Sons, 1970.

MacShane, Frank. *Into Eternity: The Life of James Jones, American Writer*. Boston: Houghton Mifflin, 1985.

Mailer, Norman. *Advertisements for Myself*. New York: G. P. Putnam's Sons, 1959.

Manso, Peter. *Mailer: His Life and Times*. New York: Simon and Schuster, 1985.

Margolies, Edward. *Native Sons: A Critical Study of Twentieth Century Negro American Authors*. Philadelphia: J. B. Lippincott, 1968.

May, Elaine Tyler. *Homeward Bound: American Families in the Cold War Era*. New York: Basic Books, 1999.

May, Lary, ed. *Recasting America: Culture and Politics in the Age of Cold War*. Chicago: University of Chicago Press, 1989.

Miller, Douglas T. and Marion Nowak. *The Fifties: The Way We Really Were*. Garden City, N.Y.: Doubleday, 1977.

Miller, Ruth. *Saul Bellow: A Biography of the Imagination*. New York: St. Martin's Press, 1991.

Mills, Hilary. *Mailer: A Biography*. New York: Empire Books, 1982.

Morris, Jan. *Manhattan '45*. New York: Oxford University Press, 1987.

Nadel, Alan. *Containment Culture: American Narratives, Postmodernism, and the Atomic Age*. Durham, N.C.: Duke University Press, 1995.

Navasky, Victor S. *Naming Names*. New York: Viking Press, 1980.

Nicosia, Gerald. *Memory Babe: A Critical Biography of Jack Kerouac*. New York: Grove Press, 1983.

O'Neill, William L. *American High: The Years of Confidence, 1945–1960*. New York: The Free Press, 1986.

Patterson, James T. *Grand Expectations: The United States, 1945–1974*. New York: Oxford University Press, 1996.

Pells, Richard. *The Liberal Mind in a Conservative Age: American Intellectuals in the 1940s and 1950s*. New York: Harper and Row, 1985.

Peretti, Burton W. *Jazz in American Culture*. Chicago: Ivan R. Dee, 1997.

Podhoretz, Norman. *Doings and Undoings: The Fifties and After in American Writing*. New York: Farrar, Straus and Giroux, 1964.

Riesman, David, with Nathan Glazer and Reuel Denney. *The Lonely Crowd: A Study of the Changing American Character*. New Haven: Yale University Press, 1961.

Rosenberg, Bernard, and David Manning White, eds. *Mass Culture: The Popular Arts in America.* New York: The Free Press, 1964.

Ross, Andrew. *No Respect: Intellectuals and Popular Culture.* New York: Routledge, 1989.

Roth, Philip. *Reading Myself and Others.* New York: Farrar, Straus and Giroux, 1975.

Saunders, Frances Stonor. *The Cultural Cold War: The CIA and the World of Arts and Letters.* New York: The New Press, 2000.

Sawyer-Lauçanno, Christopher. *An Invisible Spectator: A Biography of Paul Bowles.* New York: Weidenfeld and Nicolson, 1989.

Schapiro, Meyer. *Modern Art, 19th and 20th Centuries: Selected Papers.* New York: George Braziller, 1978.

Schaub, Thomas Hill. *American Fiction in the Cold War.* Madison: University of Wisconsin Press, 1991.

Shechner, Mark. *After the Revolution: Studies in the Contemporary Jewish-American Imagination.* Bloomington: Indiana University Press, 1987.

Schlesinger, Arthur M., Jr. *The Vital Center: The Politics of Freedom.* Boston: Houghton Mifflin, 1962.

Schorer, Mark. *The World We Imagine: Selected Essays.* New York, Farrar, Straus and Giroux, 1968.

Scruggs, Charles. *Sweet Home: Invisible Cities in the Afro-American Novel.* Baltimore: Johns Hopkins University Press, 1993.

Sheed, Wilfrid. *The Morning After: Selected Essays and Reviews.* New York: Farrar, Straus and Giroux, 1971.

Snowman, Daniel. *America since 1920.* New York: Harper and Row, 1970.

Sollors, Werner. *Beyond Ethnicity: Consent and Descent in American Culture.* New York: Oxford University Press, 1986.

Solotaroff, Theodore. *The Red Hot Vacuum and Other Pieces on the Writing of the Sixties.* New York: Atheneum, 1970.

Tanner, Tony. *City of Words: American Fiction, 1950–1970.* New York: Harper and Row, 1971.

Truman, Harry S. *Memoirs,* 2 vols. Garden City, N.Y.: Doubleday, 1956.

Tytell, John. *Naked Angels: The Lives and Literature of the Beat Generation.* New York: McGraw-Hill, 1976.

Vidal, Gore. *United States: Essays, 1952–1992.* New York: Random House, 1993.

Warshow, Robert. *The Immediate Experience: Movies, Comics, Theatre and Other Aspects of Popular Culture.* Garden City, N.Y.: Doubleday, 1962.

Whitfield, Stephen J. *The Culture of the Cold War.* Baltimore: John Hopkins University Press, 1996.

Whyte, William H., Jr. *The Organization Man.* New York: Simon and Schuster, 1956.

Williams, Dakin, and Shepherd Mead. *Tennessee Williams: An Intimate Biography.* New York: Crown, 1983.

Wood, Michael. *America in the Movies.* New York: Basic Books, 1975.

INDEX